Storytelling in World Cinemas

Volume Two: Contexts

Edited by Lina Khatib

WALLFLOWER PRESS
LONDON & NEW YORK

A Wallflower Press Book
Published by
Columbia University Press
Publishers Since 1893
New York • Chichester, West Sussex
cup.columbia.edu

A complete CIP record is available from the Library of Congress

ISBN 978-0-231-16336-1 (cloth : alk. paper)
ISBN 978-0-231-16337-8 (pbk. : alk. paper)
ISBN 978-0-231-85025-4 (e-book)

Design by Elsa Mathern

Columbia University Press books are printed on permanent
and durable acid-free paper.
This book is printed on paper with recycled content.
Printed in the United States of America

c 10 9 8 7 6 5 4 3 2 1
p 10 9 8 7 6 5 4 3 2 1

Contents

Telling Women's Stories

Storytelling and Religio-Cultural Encounters

Acknowledgements

The idea behind this book was inspired by an essay written by my former student Celia Sommerstein on the influence that traditional storytelling strategies in Korean theatre had on those in Korean cinema. This led me to organisie a symposium entitled 'The Form and Context of Storytelling in World Cinemas' in March 2006, supported by the University of London's Screen Studies Group. I would like to thank Mandy Merck and Laura Mulvey for their encouragement and help with making the symposium happen, and for paving the way for this book to be born. I would also like to thank Yoram Allon for being a wonderful editor and the contributors to the book for their hard work and patience.

This book is dedicated to the late Robert Dash whose legacy continues through this work.

Contributors

Isabel Arredondo is Professor of Spanish at SUNY Plattsburgh. She is the author of *De brujos y naguales: La Guatemala imaginaria de Miguel Ángel Asturias* (1997), '*Palabra de Mujer': Historia oral de las directoras de cine mexicanas 1988–1994* (2001) and *Motherhood in Mexican Cinema 1941–1991: The Transformation of Femininity on Screen* (2013). She specializes in Latin American women's film and silent film and her current research also includes Latin American Super 8 films.

Yifen T. Beus received her PhD in comparative literature from Indiana University, Bloomington, and is currently Professor of International Cultural Studies at Brigham Young University–Hawaii. Her interests include de-Westernising storytelling, self-reflexivity and deterritorialisation in cinema. Her works have appeared in such journals as *Nineteenth-Century French Studies*, *Quarterly Review of Film and Video* and *African Cultural Studies*.

Shohini Chaudhuri is Senior Lecturer in Contemporary Writing and Film at the University of Essex. She has published two books – *Contemporary World Cinema: Europe, the Middle East, East Asia and South Asia* (2005) and *Feminist Film Theorists* (2006) – and articles on contemporary cinema in journals such as *Screen*, *Camera Obscura* and *South Asian Popular Culture*. Her most recent work deals with atrocity and the ethics of spectatorship in twenty-first-century cinema.

Sue Clayton is Programme Director of MASTFiR, an MA in Screenwriting for Film and Television (Retreat Programme) at Royal Holloway, University of London, and has published in a number of books and journals including *New Writing, New Cinemas* and the *Journal of Media Practice*. She has written and directed over twenty award-winning feature films, television documentaries and campaign films, including *The Disappearance of Finbar* (1996) starring Jonathan Rhys Meyers. Most recently she made the award-winning *Hamedullah: The Road Home* (2011) about a young refugee deported back to Afghanistan, which won Best Documentary at the London Independent Film Festival. She has collaborated on a play, *Mazloom* (2012), on this theme, and is in development on *Nowhere to Hide*, a feature film on the same topic.

Robert C. Dash was a professor in politics at Willamette University and an associate editor of the journal *Latin American Perspectives*. He published in the areas of Latin American and Latino politics and culture.

Anna Dempsey is Associate Professor of Art History at the University of Massachusetts, Dartmouth. She has published articles on cinematic public space, architecture and gender in several journals. An essay on contemporary Islamic cinema is included in 'Images of Children and Childhood in the Middle East', a special issue of *Comparative Studies of South Asia, Africa and the Middle East* (2012). She is currently writing a book titled *Working Women Artists: Images of Domesticity and the Construction of American Modernism, 1880–1930*.

Dijana Jelača is a doctoral candidate in Communication at the University of Massachusetts, Amherst. She holds an MA in Feminist Theory and Film from New York University. Her recent publications include works that appeared in *Communication Studies* and *Universals and Contrasts*. Dijana's current research interests revolve around the convergence of affect and trauma theories, especially as they pertain to cinema and its insight into the workings of post-traumatic memory.

Hester Joyce is a Senior Lecturer in Media Arts at La Trobe University, Melbourne. She is co-author of *New Zealand Film and Television: Institution, Industry and Cultural Change* (2011) and a contributor to the edited anthology *Making Film and Television Histories* (2011). Her research interests include arts policy, creative arts practice and screenwriting. She is also a credited stage and screen actor.

Lina Khatib heads the Program on Arab Reform and Democracy at Stanford University's Center on Democracy, Development, and the Rule of Law. She is the author of *Filming the Modern Middle East: Politics in the Cinemas of Hollywood and the Arab World* (2006), *Lebanese Cinema: Imagining the Civil War and Beyond* (2008), and *Image Politics in the Middle East: The Role of the Visual in Political Struggle* (2012). She is a founding co-editor of the *Middle East Journal of Culture and Communication*.

Nam Lee is Assistant Professor in Film Studies, Dodge College of Film and Media Arts at Chapman University in Orange, California. She has published book reviews and articles in *Film Quarterly*, *Quarterly Review of Film and Video*, *Asian Cinema* and *Film International*. She also organises and programs the annual Busan West Asian Film Festival at Chapman University.

Willow G. Mullins is an adjunct professor at Washington University in St. Louis. She is the author of *Felt* (2009). Her research interests are centred on material culture, commodification between global cultures and the effects of colonialism and postcolonialism on narrative. She is currently working on a book on Western narratives of consumption in the global craft marketplace.

Konrad Ng is Director of the Smithsonian Institution's Asian Pacific American Center and an assistant professor in the Academy for Creative Media at the University of Hawai'i-Mānoa. His professional and scholarly work explores the cultural politics of Asian and Asian American cinema and digital media.

Anjali Gera Roy is a Professor in the Department of Humanities and Social Sciences at the Indian Institute of Technology Kharagpur. She has published more than eighty essays on literary, film and cultural studies. Her recent publications include *Bhangra Moves: From Ludhiana to London and Beyond* (2010), *Partitioned Lives: Narratives of Home, Displacement and Resettlement* (with Nandi Bhatia, 2008), *Magic of Bollywood: At Home and Abroad* (2012) and *Travels of Bollywood Cinema: From Bombay to LA* (with Chua Beng Huat, 2012).

Zahia Smail Salhi is Professor of Modern Arabic Studies at the University of Manchester. She is author of *Politics and Poetics in the Algerian Novel* (1999), co-editor with I. R. Netton of *The Arab Diaspora: Voices of an Anguished Scream* (2011; second edn.), and editor of *Gender and Diversity in the Middle East and North Africa* (2010). She has published several articles and book chapters on Maghrebi literature and cinema with a focus on women's writing and the representation of women in literature and film.

Saša Vojković is Professor of film and media at the Academy of Drama Arts, University of Zagreb. She is author of three books , *Subjectivity in the New Hollywood Cinema: Fathers, Sons and Other Ghosts* (2001), *Filmic Medium as (Trans) Cultural Spectacle: Hollywood, Europe, Asia* (2008) and *Yuen Woo Ping's Wing Chun* (2009). She is the guest editor and contributor of the Special Edition of *New Review of Film and Television Studies* on South Eastern European Cinema (2008).

Patricia Varas is Professor of Spanish and Latin American studies at Willamette University. She is the author of *Las máscaras de Delmira Agustini* (2003) and

Narrativa y cultura nacional (1993), and co-editor of *Identidades americanas más allá de las fronteras nacionales: Ensayos en homenaje a Keith Ellis* (2012). She has contributed various essays on Latin American cinema, modernity, literature and culture to different journals and edited volumes.

Darrell Varga is Canada Research Chair in Contemporary Film and Media Studies at Nova Scotia College of Art and Design in Halifax, Canada. He is the editor of *Rain/Drizzle/Fog: Film and Television in Atlantic Canada* (2008); co-editor of *Working on Screen: Representations of the Working Class in Canadian Cinema* (2006); author of *John Walker's Passage* (2012); and author of the forthcoming book *Shooting From the East: Filmmaking in Atlantic Canada*. Darrell's current research includes the aesthetics and politics of documentary media; he is also a documentary filmmaker.

Introduction to Volume Two

Lina Khatib

This second volume of *Storytelling in World Cinemas* continues the journey of film stories around the world to answer the questions of *what* stories are told in films and *why*, both in terms of the forms of storytelling used – following on from volume one of this collection – and of the political, religious, historical and social contexts informing cinematic storytelling. As with the first volume, this book approaches storytelling from a cultural/historical multidisciplinary perspective.

The premise of this book is that cinematic stories come from somewhere – religious belief systems, historical developments, cultural encounters, social relations, folklore, developments in the film industry... the list is virtually limitless. Those elements play a role in determining what stories are told, how and why. Thus, this volume overlaps with volume one in its allusion to cinematic storytelling form, but supplements that with an analysis of context through grouping influences on storytelling under four main headings: cultural politics, postcolonialism, women, and religio-cultural encounters.

Part one of the book deals with the way cultural politics has an impact on cinematic storytelling. Konrad Ng's and Hester Joyce's chapters examine the effect of social transformations in China and New Zealand on cinemas from each country. Ng's chapter explores the troubling portrayals of contemporary Chinese life in Sixth Generation filmmaker Jia Zhangke's films. Jia's unique film language, a form that mixes fiction and documentary, and his focus on marginal lives, reveal how China's current context of large-scale and rapid development has impacted on cinematic storytelling and given rise to a form of critical realism. While China's current social context is characterised by growing affluence and cultural globalisation, Jia's films suggest that Chinese 'progress' is, at best, an ambivalent achievement; alienation and disjuncture now haunt the Chinese experience. Ng shows how Jia plots his narratives of Chineseness through global popular culture, practices of consumption and large-scale urbanisation to reflect how China's pursuit of modernity and reform has dissolved cultural tradition and the nation as anchors of experience. Jia's use of long-takes, realist and ironic *mise-en-scène*, crowded and colloquial sound design and casting of non-professional actors alongside professional actors affectively convey and capture the disorienting experiences of contemporary China. For Jia, cinematic storytelling is a way to intervene in the context from which it emerges.

Hester Joyce's chapter focuses on the development of a 'Maori way' in New Zealand cinema brokered by negotiations and transformations in the status of Maori in New Zealand based on the requirements of the Treaty of Waitangi (a treaty between Maori and the Crown agreed in 1840, ratified from 1980 onwards) demanding equity in all areas for indigenous Maori. Joyce shows how as the first Maori films were being made, the notion of partnership between Maori and Pakeha (white settlers) was just being established within Treaty negotiations. Maori cultural and political action has impacted ANZ cinema as a whole, not only in terms of industrial practices (which became infused with Maori traditions), but also in terms of cinematic storytelling strategies (such as the use of cameras) driven by Maori cultural mores. Maori cinema can thus be seen as an example of 'fourth cinema', a cinema 'that engages with the lived experience of its filmmakers and its subjects, ignoring the parameters of development, production and distribution of the first cinema, and privileging its own' (Joyce, p. 29).

Nam Lee's and Robert Dash and Patricia Varas's chapters deal with how cinema can offer social critique in the absence of freedom to do so. As such, both chapters deal with the use of allegory and folklore as a storytelling technique driven by the constraints of the political contexts in which films are made and which they choose to comment on. Lee's chapter focuses on Korean cinema during the time of the military government in the 1980s. While Korean cinema is well known for its stylised thrillers and horror films, Lee goes back to examine the work of the most experimental and innovative filmmaker of 1980s Korean cinema, Lee Jang-ho, whose early 1980s films have been an inspiration for Korean New Wave directors. What distinguishes Lee's films is that their socially-conscious realist stories which comment on the social issues of the time – such as class divisions and the lack of freedom of expression – incorporate various traits of and metaphors from *minjung* (people's) art, from literature to theatre to dance. Nam Lee shows how traditional folk art forms were rediscovered as powerful tools to transform audiences' social consciousness during the 1970s, and *minjung* culture activists adapted these forms to dramatise contemporary social and political problems – a strategy then adopted by the cinema of Lee Jang-ho in the struggle against military dictatorship. Lee's films can be read as a national metaphor 'in which the stories of protagonists' destinies are often allegories of the oppressive situation of Korean society in the early 1980s' (Lee, p. 37).

Another protagonist whose destiny is a metaphor of that of the nation is Alsino in the film *Alsino y el cóndor* (1982) by Miguel Littín, which was the first feature film produced in Nicaragua during a period of intense US pressure to diplomatically isolate, economically strangle, and militarily undercut the Sandinista National Liberation Front (FSLN) regime, which came to power in 1979. The FSLN was, in turn, determined to exert control over their national destiny in the face of the concerted US effort to reassert its hegemony. In their chapter about this film, Robert Dash and Patricia Varas discuss Littín's dual aesthetic and ideological task as he confronts two very different kinds of audiences: He must tell a story of the revolution in an appealing manner to a public engaged with the Nicaraguan struggle, and he must reach out to a larger and less knowledgeable public that has to be moved to international solidarity. Dash and Varas show how Littín achieves this through using a narrative structure that applies a child's point of view; oral elements that recall the traditional Latin American fable of Alsino who dreamt of flying like a bird; and a lyrical language and sound that support fragmented images unusual in political propaganda. With its mixture of realism and mythology, the film's representation of Alsino's dream of flying becomes a metaphor for Latin America's aspiration to be free of US intervention and imperialism.

In the chapter that follows, Isabel Arredondo goes back to cinema history to comment on the way the US represented Latin America in late 1920s and 1930s travelogues about Mexico, leading part two of the book which deals with storytelling and postcolonialism. Arredondo offers a postcolonial reading of those travelogues, particularly their 'use of a scientific observer's commentary to legitimise their colonisation of other cultures' (Arredondo, p. 73). In the first three decades of the twentieth century, travelogues were the prevalent way of representing foreign countries to US audiences. Arredondo examines the narrative strategies in those travelogues, particularly their use of a first-person narrative or an omniscient narrator who appropriates a far-away country. Arredondo's chapter pinpoints the context which has driven colonised (whether in the literal or figurative sense) peoples to strive to assert control over their own representation, as seen in Hester Joyce's chapter and as Willow Mullins's and Yifen T. Beus's chapters also illustrate.

As Mullins argues, a 'central theme in postcolonial discourse is the attempt to actively remember and record histories as a way to mediate the rupture in historical and cultural continuity caused by colonialism' (p. 77). She addresses this through an analysis of Aktan Abdykalykov's films from Kyrgyzstan. Filmed in the first decade after independence from the Soviet Union, Abdykalykov's films are invested in a process of telling and re-telling histories to both mediate the ruptures caused by Russian imperialism and Soviet collapse and to construct national identity on a global as well as a personal scale. His work complicates and questions a Western binary that opposes the traditional and modern by modelling his films on the pattern of a traditional Kyrgyz quilt, which is pieced together from fabrics given out as part of funeral proceedings. Thus Abdykalykov replicates in film the process of making the quilt and creating identity – through remembering, reworking and piecing together histories. This use of folklore mirrors that in the films of Lee Jang-ho and Miguel Littín and also those of Assia Djebar discussed in Zahia Smail Salhi's chapter, and has parallels with the use of Maori cultural mores in New Zealand cinema, and thus illustrates how cinema can negotiate tradition and modernity in the process of identity production and cultural commentary, turning 'to the traditional for source material precisely because of the ability of stories to define and reaffirm cultural standards and norms' (Mullins, p. 85).

However, it would be misleading to assume that going back to tradition is the only way in which postcolonial cinema resists marginalisation and reclaims national narratives. Yifen T. Beus's chapter argues that one of the most effective strategies of resisting the Western centre is through the 'writing of Otherness', namely using adaptation of Western texts as a method of writing back. She focuses on African cinematic adaptations of the Romantic novella and opera, *Carmen* (1845), to show how those films utilise the motif of Carmen and intertextuality as rhetorical tropes, navigating between the colonial and postcolonial story spaces in an act of returning the gaze while displaying a self-reflexivity about the politics of storytelling and representation.

Part three of the volume starts with a further discussion of postcolonial politics but draws attention to the crucial gender dimension involved. In Zahia Smail Salhi's chapter, a critique of the masculinisation in postcolonial discourse and remembering is offered through an analysis of the work of Assia Djebar. Salhi focuses on Djebar's film *The Nouba of the Women of Mont Chenoua* (1978), which pays tribute to the heroism of Algerian women during the struggle against French colonialism – omitted from the numerous war films made in post-independent Algeria – and challenges the image of women as mute objects and renders them active subjects. She shows how the film's storytelling structure, linking four narrative threads, follows the form of a *nouba*, a classical Maghrebian/Andalusian musical suite, in which women play active parts either as the main singers of the *nouba*, or as part of the chorus and orchestra. The *nouba* becomes a stylistic technique and a metaphor for restoring the voice of women. Through this, Salhi illustrates how women, both in front of and behind the camera, become commentators on the progression of history who challenge oblivion and marginalisation.

A similar trajectory is followed by Anna Dempsey in her chapter on women in Iranian cinema. Dempsey offers an analysis of the representation of women in public space in Iranian New Wave films to comment on the marginalisation of women after the Islamic Revolution of 1979. By looking at visual tropes in the films, particularly the spatial movements of the women, Dempsey shows how women's stories become indicators of historical shifts. The Islamic Revolution is presented as having robbed women of much of their liberties; restrictions on women's mobility in public space are used as a metaphor for this oppression. However, the films are more remarkable for their representations of women's negotiations in this public space and their efforts at resistance. Dempsey argues that this visual representation, coupled with the open-ended nature of the narratives offered in those films, means that the stories of the women in the films are to be continued.

In Dijana Jelača's chapter that follows, women are presented as metaphors for the land, both objects of patriarchal control. The life trajectories of women in the films of former Yugoslavia discussed in the chapter mirror that of the country itself, their plight aligning with that of the Balkan territory they inhabit. Jelača explores questions of national identity and territoriality by linking the female body to the national body before the country's violent break-up. By re-examining the historical context in which the films were made, Jelača reveals the films' implicitly feminist critique of masculinist violence, even before that violence completely overtook the territory of former Yugoslavia. The films couple patriarchy with nationalism, and through their stories argue 'that in order for further violence to be avoided, patriarchy must be put to rest' (Jelača, p. 141). As such, the chapter argues that the storytelling in those films is explicitly framed by the tense political climate of the country in which they were made, and demonstrates how they critically unpack some of the most problematic nationalist narratives circulating at the time.

But women's representations in the national context differ between different cinemas. Despite the general dominance of patriarchy, cultural imaginings are not devoid of stories of females who are 'knowing subjects' as opposed to objects. Such women are found in the Chinese cultural imaginary informing Hong Kong martial arts films. Saša Vojković argues in her chapter that women-warriors in those films have their origins in Beijing opera, martial arts novels and traditional Chinese stories of the fantastic and the supernatural. Their presence in Hong Kong cinema is testimony to how narrative representation is not only governed by genre norms, 'but also by a certain mode of cultural expression that informs the film's fabula. The actions these women are able to perform have to do with the connection between the narrative and the rules and norms that regulate what kind of female character is imaginable and conceivable' (Vojković, p. 146) in cultural heritage in general. Vojković relates this representation to the Buddhist and Taoist elements of Chinese cultural heritage, where, unlike in Confucianism, the way towards transcendence is equally applicable to both men and women (in Buddhism), and the body of Tao prioritises the human body over cultural and social systems.

As such, it is important to examine the role that religion and belief systems play in inspiring cinematic storytelling. Part four of the book is dedicated to such an examination. Religion here is not approached as a system of belief *per se*, but as a cultural system too. In other words, when discussing Buddhism, shamanism and Islam in the last three chapters of the book – all of which deal with films about people encountering those from different cultures and with different religious beliefs than themselves – the focus is not so much on religious beliefs, but on the social and cultural dimensions that religions carry. Shohini Chaudhuri and Sue Clayton illustrate in their chapter on Bhutanese cinema how Buddhism's holistic perspective on what constitutes a dream and what constitutes reality impacts the way characters in Bhutanese film are presented. So instead of a hero with individual human subjectivity being the controlling force of the narrative, the 'hero's' journey is decentred as multiple realities are considered. Clayton's own cultural encounter – as a screenwriter and director from the 'West' working on a collaborative film project with Bhutanese partners – illustrates the way those Buddhist principles shape the trajectory in which a film story can go.

Like the way Bhutanese films call for a different perspective on what is reality and what both the characters and the audience are seeing, so does Inuit cinema in Canada. Darrell Varga's chapter focuses on *The Journals of Knud Rasmussen* (2006), a film about the contact between shamanism and Christianity voiced through a native Inuit point of view. The film's story is about the near-eradication of traditional spiritual practices and the process of recovery, but Varga shows how this process goes beyond the story of the film and can also be engendered by the process of making the film itself and its relationship with previous Inuit films, namely *Atanarjuat: The Fast Runner* (2001). Through representing this religio-cultural encounter, the film comments on the concept of story as a vehicle of history that calls for an examination of representation and value (cultural, but also social and economic). As Varga puts it: 'This is a film about seeing the spirits, and about the loss of sight that accompanies cultural and spiritual change, but it is also providing us with a lesson in how to see' (p. 180).

The final chapter in the book by Anjali Gera Roy continues the commentary on religio-cultural encounters and imaginations but this time does so by examining the presence of the Persio-Arabic *qissa* (story) of *Majun Laila* in Hindi cinema. Roy starts by acknowledging the influence of Hindu religious narratives on Bollywood cinema, but argues for going beyond that into examining the role that stories from the Islamic and Arab worlds play in Indian cinematic narratives. Roy argues that with much of Hindu tradition not being focused on stories of romantic love, or presenting 'a template for the idealised marital union through the figures of the duty-abiding Rama and his loyal wife Sita' (p. 190) in the epic *Ramayana*, the Persio-Arabic *qissa* has come to provide a template for the hero in Hindi films in the form of the infatuated Majnun, and the object of his desire in the garb of Laila, creating a sensual image of the Muslim female as a site of forbidden desire. As such, the *qissa* of *Majnun Laila* is used to disrupt the *dharmic* principle, with the lovers meeting a tragic end because of this, but the story has been reincarnated so many times in Hindi cinema that it 'shows the deep implication of the Islamic in the Hindu' (Roy, p. 191).

And thus the storytelling in this book ends, but one must acknowledge that cinema is a living being, constantly evolving, and a cultural being that cannot be fully understood in isolation from other arts and forms of cultural expression. It is also a product of history as well as a historical commentator. The chapters in this volume illustrate the diversity of storytelling contexts in world cinemas, and, as in the previous volume, also bring to the surface the various synergies that exist between those different contexts. They aim, as those presented in volume one, to arrive at a well-rounded examination of the cultural context in which storytelling in cinema exists and which it is shaped by.

Storytelling and Cultural Politics

Stories as Social Critique: The Vision of China in the Films of Jia Zhangke

Konrad Ng

The selection of acclaimed film director Zhang Yimou to orchestrate the opening and closing ceremonies of the Beijing 2008 Summer Olympics gestures to the important role that cinema has played in depicting Chinese cultural life. Zhang's spectacle at the Olympics reflected how China was depicted in his films – lush, historical and sweeping – and portrayed the country as a grand and booming civilisation. Yet, if cinema expresses the dynamics of the context from which it emerges and if this context influences what and why stories are told, then what social insights are revealed by the emergence of China's so-called Sixth Generation, a film movement characterised by 'amateur' aesthetics, contemporaneity, independence and disaffection? This chapter explores how the body of work of Sixth Generation filmmaker Jia Zhangke can be seen as a comment on China's contemporary social and economic ethos.

Few other filmmakers have come to symbolise the Sixth Generation and its troubling portrayals of contemporary Chinese life. Jia's films have earned praise from film critics and festival programmers as well as multiple awards from prestigious international film festivals, including the top prize at the Venice Film Festival. Jia is praised for his unique film language, a form that mixes fiction and documentary, and for the thematic focus of his work. His films highlight the profound transformations taking place in Chinese society and the experiences of people left behind in the pursuit of modernisation and reform. Although China's current social context is characterised by growing affluence and cultural globalisation, Jia's films suggest that Chinese 'progress' is, at best, an ambivalent achievement; alienation, disjuncture and disorientation now haunt the Chinese experience. His stories reveal how contemporary

Chinese life is not characterised by a grand national history, as is symbolised by the selection of Zhang Yimou to stage the Olympic ceremonies. Rather, the narrative of Chineseness is plotted through global popular culture, practices of consumption and large-scale urbanisation. To study Jia's stories, it is instructive to discuss the social context of the Sixth Generation and how it gave rise to 'amateur' filmmaking.

A context of transformation

In the field of Chinese film, the term 'generations' encompasses the historical context and aesthetic and narrative style of different periods of cinema in Chinese history. The Sixth Generation is a group of filmmakers who attended the Beijing Film Academy during the 1990s and acquired a film education that considered high production values as being synonymous with the tradition of Chinese cinema. Their experience of Chinese life was shaped by the reform and modernisation movement initiated by Deng Xiaoping during the early 1980s and the Tiananmen Square protests of 1989. Deng's reforms would start an era of profound social and economic development and Tiananmen Square would breed a sense of cynicism about government authority. China's economy transitioned into a global socialist market, a system far from its communist roots as a closed, centrally planned system, and experienced an economic boom characterised by rapid and sweeping development and an uneven rise in the standard of living.

Chinese society also saw the introduction and increased availability of new information technologies that began to change social practices. Computers, CDs, VCDs, DVDs, pagers, cell phones and the internet slowly became part of everyday life. As such, the confluence of an open market, development and new technologies 'globalised' the Chinese experience. That is, the narrative and aesthetic material for Chinese stories could come from global flows, what Arjun Appadurai calls ethnoscapes, mediascapes, technoscapes, financescapes and ideoscapes, such that the Chinese imaginary could be 'a space of contestation in which individuals and groups seek to annex the global into their own practices of the modern' (1996: 4). In this sense, the experience of Chineseness is inter-articulated with global flows and no longer fully defined nor contained by national borders. Put differently, Chinese contact with new forms of popular culture, consumption, sociality and identity have entangled the global in Chinese society. As Zhang Zhen notes in her study of contemporary Chinese urban cinema, Sixth Generation filmmakers were witness to a large-scale, post-socialist and global transformation in Chinese mentality, ideology and infrastructure. For Zhen, it is a shift experienced acutely in China's growing urban spaces. She claims that the context of the Sixth Generation is characterised by

widespread privatization and a blatant form of capitalism that voraciously mixes the rawness of industrial capitalism and the slickness of the computer-age postindustrial capitalism thriving alongside the residues of socialism. The cities are the most visible and concentrated sites of this drastic and at times violent economic, social, and cultural transformation. (2007: 5)

This context of reform, modernisation and globalisation influenced the cinematic storytelling of the Sixth Generation in a number of ways and is fully expressed in Jia's cinematic storytelling form.

The filmmakers of the Sixth Generation sought independence from the Chinese state film system and the elitist and historical cinematic storytelling style preferred by the Chinese government to make films and tell stories that reflected daily life. They channelled their experience of China's pursuit of reform and the effects of a market-driven society and economy into raw, urban, documentary-like films that were critical of government and society. They rejected the call for cinematic story-telling to be a medium of high art and culture and favoured the immediacy and populist attitude that film could provide. Sixth Generation documentary-influenced aesthetics included favouring the use of video over 16mm or 35mm film, hand-held camera, long takes and unfiltered sound. Their films treated traditional Chinese life and nation as fractured and disposable commodities, abstract concepts that are eclipsed by the allure of global popular culture, new communications technologies and an emerging consumerist mentality. As such, Sixth Generation stories tend to be peppered with references to popular culture with action situated in spaces of leisure and consumption such as *karaoke* bars. Characters are preoccupied with the exchange of goods and entertainment as opposed to work and government service.

To preserve the integrity and critical spirit of their cinematic stories, many of the Sixth Generation filmmakers worked 'underground'; that is, they were open to pro-ducing, exhibiting and distributing their films without the approval or support of Chinese government agencies. China's new open economy provided forms of interna-tional financing and distribution that could circumvent the state studio system, and the advent of DVDs, VCDs and independent film clubs helped promulgate and sup-port the Sixth Generation film culture. Similarly, the emergence of video technologies enabled film productions to be more nimble. Analogue and digital video cameras and computer-based film editing allowed Sixth Generation directors to make films independent of institutional support and capture the experience of events as they unfold.

Enabled by innovations in technology, market reforms and cultural openness and shaped by the disorienting rhythms of their time, the Sixth Generation filmmakers have created a unique film language that draws attention to the artifice of cinema as a way to return to real-life experiences. Sixth Generation cinematic storytelling adopts the gritty textures of realist, documentary and independent film traditions to tell stories about declining familial traditions, the commoditisation of nation and society, and restless lives struggling for relevance in a rapidly developing urban world. As Zhang Zhen contends, the Sixth Generation is characterised by a sense of urgency; they feel compelled to document the present as it is. She contends that the Sixth Generation attempts to record and interpret their

> relationship to the ordinary people around them – friends, family members, neighbors, colleagues, as well as strangers, who inhabit or come to inhabit the ever-expanding social and material space of the cities … a space that is at once enchanting and oppressive, liberating and violent. (2007: 18)

'Amateur' style and storytelling

Jia is recognised by the international film community as one of the leading figures in the Sixth Generation film culture. Prompted by the disorienting rhythms of his films' social context, Jia's storytelling form is known for its critical realist aesthetic and the contemporaneity of its stories. Indeed, Jia's film language treats daily life in China as an aesthetic unto itself. Perhaps one of the clearest articulations of Jia's storytelling vision can be found in his 1999 essay, 'The Age of Amateur Cinema Will Return'. Valerie Jaffee offers an instructive analysis of Jia's essay in relation to China's independent documentary film movement. She argues that Jia's call for amateur cinema was a reaction to what he saw as the cinematic excess of the Fifth Generation, a film culture in which Zhang Yimou is a leading director. For Jia, the Fifth Generation and its gilded sense of professionalism, pretentious historical stories and emphasis on high production values presents a form of cinematic storytelling that is disconnected from the dispiriting textures of daily Chinese life. Jaffee contends that while amateur cinema is partly a technical art form of 'low budgets and technical minimalism, on-site shooting, and a focus on daily life in contemporary society' (2006: 79), ultimately, Jia's notion of amateur cinema is not about untrained individuals making films for leisure. Rather, amateur cinema is 'primarily an attitude, not a lifestyle condition – an attitude composed of self-deprecation and disinterest in convention… [It is about] connecting this attitude to the possibility of the rise to the status of filmmaker of individuals lacking conventional credentials' (2006: 82). She further argues that Jia's attitude reflects 'a deconstructive impulse directed at institutions through which Chinese society circumscribes the zone of legitimate cultural production' (2006: 84). In other words, who controls the meaning of Chineseness?

To this end, Jia's cinematic aesthetic uses techniques associated with the neo-realist and documentary filmmaking traditions. In particular, Jia's films are composed of long takes, on-location shooting, picturesque depth-of-field, the inclusion of ambient sound, minimalist musical scores, long silences, stilted dialogue, non-professional actors and the use of thick local dialects. Most of his films are shot on high definition digital video, a medium that he uses to depict urban settings with an immediate and haunting resonance. Zhen describes this Sixth Generation aesthetic as the ability to capture the 'everyday and the immediacy of happenings' (2007: 18). For her, this 'on-the-scene' filmmaking blurs the boundaries between documentary and fiction filmmaking to transform cinematic storytelling into a form of critical examination. She contends that the Chinese digital video aesthetic is 'grounded in social space and experience – contingent, immanent, improvisational and open ended' (2007: 19). In his study of the relationship between Sixth Generation film culture and Euro-American conceptions of independent art-house film, Jason McGrath argues that the realism of Jia's films can be fully understood if his cinematic pedigree is traced to

> the broader indigenous movement of postsocialist realism that arose in both documentary and fiction filmmaking in China in the early 1990s [and] the tradition of international art cinema – in particular a type of aestheticized long-take realism that became prominent in the global film festival and art house circuit by the late 1990s. (2007: 82)

In this sense, Jia's cinema is rooted in the 'postsocialist' context from which he emerges; it is a film tradition that believes that 'just going out into public with a camera and capturing the unvarnished street life found there serves to unmask ideology while documenting the realities of contemporary China' (2007: 85). However, McGrath contends that Jia's film style is also shaped by the global character of his context; his films resemble the style of international art cinema 'with its aestheticized realism, with its durations and ellipses [and] presents an alternative to Hollywood-style storytelling' (2007: 103). These two cinematic traditions, McGrath suggests, form Jia's style of storytelling.

In terms of film narrative, Jia's characters and stories are drawn from his experience of the dramatic changes in Chinese society. His characters are not aristocratic or historical figures, but despondent characters in or from his hometown of Fenyang, a city in the province of Shanxi. Jia treats the experiences of Fenyang as a microcosm of China's pursuit of reform and modernisation in which former small towns experience rapid urban development and malaise as opposed to prosperity. Characters are often left behind or displaced by their changing environment and find themselves powerless or take flight to larger cities. While the standard of living has improved for these emerging large cities, Jia's characters tend to be lost in the newly transformed surrounding spaces of leisure and consumption. Characters find themselves invested in performance, music videos, television, music, bars and *karaoke*. Throughout his films, Jia's stories explore the waning influence of tradition and the role of the state as characters show the malleability and commodification of traditional and nationalist Chinese values.

A filmography of critique

Jia's first feature film, *Xiao Wu* (1997), follows the life of its eponymous anti-hero and reveals how Chinese values of brotherhood fail to anchor friendship or social relations in a world defined by unrestricted commerce and urban development. Xiao Wu is a thief who follows a flexible code of honour so as to match a world in which Confucian and Maoist values are twisted by free market capitalism; Xiao Wu's world is composed of exploitative entrepreneurialism. His childhood friend, Xiao Yong, is a successful businessman who has made his wealth from trafficking cigarettes and managing *karaoke* bars, both activities that are now seen as legitimate examples of 'free trade' and 'entertainment'. After Xiao Wu appears unexpectedly at Xiao Yong's wedding, the groom rejects Xiao Wu's wedding gift because it is stolen and thus, 'dirty', not having come from 'legitimate' sources of income. Spurned at the wedding, Xiao Wu also meets a *karaoke* girl named Mei Mei and the two share a fleeting and empty relationship.

Stylistically, *Xiao Wu* follows the naturalism of the neo-realist film tradition to provide a critical commentary on post-socialist China. The film is a manifestation of China's social and economic reforms and the demise of traditional cultural practices. New electronic goods, demolition, construction, unfettered trade, clubs, bars and prostitution flourish, while legality gives way to an increasingly abstract and flexible sense of Confucian custom. The editing favours long takes, allowing the scenes to unfold from a voyeur's point of view. Jia casts non-professional actors to allow for harsh, sometimes indiscernible, local dialects that distinguish the rural from the urban.

In 2001, Jia premiered his pop culture odyssey film, *Platform*. The film presents a pensive portrait of Chinese life during the 1980s, the decade when Deng Xiaoping initiated China's programmes of social and economic reform. The film illustrates how popular culture has become the paradigm for family values. It follows the lives of the Fenyang Peasant Culture Group, a travelling performance troupe of young people who start the decade in bellbottoms staging pro-Maoist cultural productions and end the decade as the West-inspired, 'All Star Rock and Breakdance Electronic Band', a punk rock electric act who invert Confucian and Maoist values. The Fenyang Peasant Culture Group represents the Confucian family and the group's transformation from patriarchal harmony to melodramatic fracture is an allegory for China's cultural transformation and the rising influence of popular culture on social life. Shot on 35mm, the film is a slow-paced cultural study of context and China's social and economic transformations. Jia uses long takes so that the viewer can reflect on the discernable changes from scene to scene. The narrative meanders, punctuated by changes to daily life such as the introduction of electricity, the emergence of new social trends and reactions to social reforms such as China's 'one child' policy. Jia traces the group members' metamorphosis from having a steadfast belief in China to a growing sense of alienation from the nation they once knew. The group invests itself in the world of music, entertainment and popular culture. *Platform* takes its title from a popular song from the 1980s; the song's lyrics and mood embody the decade's odd mixture of anxiety, detachment and departure from social values grounded in Chinese tradition and nation.

Jia's next film, *Unknown Pleasures* (2001), continues his cinema of real life and offers a self-referential and contemporaneous study of the Chinese experience through the lives of four disaffected urban young people living in Datong. Xiao Ji, a man without visible means, is obsessed with Qiao Qiao, a fierce but vulnerable young woman who makes her living promoting liquor and is the mistress of a local thug. Bin Bin and Yuan Yuan are stuck in a relationship of convenience, passing the time singing *karaoke*, watching Monkey King videos and avoiding decisions about the future. Bin Bin has lost her job, but has no motivation to find another one. Yuan Yuan remains an uninspired student. The film closes when Bin Bin and Xiao Ji, finding inspiration in Quentin Tarantino's *Pulp Fiction* (1994), decide to rob a bank but fail miserably. *Unknown Pleasures* reveals the influential role of popular culture and the malaise of the post-Deng era. The bonds of traditional Chinese society and nation are absent; the characters receive direction and connection not from each other but from the world of popular culture and activities of leisure and consumption. In one scene that emphasises the authority of film, Xiao Wu from *Xiao Wu* makes a brief appearance in the film to complain that it is impossible to find copies of important films like *Xiao Wu*. The film conveys the prevalent feeling of alienation and fracture through its crude dialects, improvised dialogue, natural sound and a detached cinematography consisting of lengthy takes, medium and long shots and natural lighting. As the title suggests, *Unknown Pleasures* comments on the contemporary Chinese experience as being rooted in popular culture and acts of leisurely consumption; in this world, Chinese cultural identity is disconnected from traditional sources of Chinese cultural production.

Jia's *The World* (2004) is considered one of his strongest films in terms of its aesthetic innovations and critical exploration of the cultural and economic effects of China's integration into a capitalist global community. The film suggests that the remnants of traditional Chinese society no longer exist. It follows the lives of young men and women who have come from China's rural communities and other post-communist countries such as Russia to live and work at Beijing's real-life World Park, a Las Vegas/Disney simulacra of world cultures and monuments. The film's characters come to the burgeoning tourist attraction in search of work and stardom only to find that World Park life falls short of its promises. They are hired to be dancers and security guards and become stuck in a place and time where the park's slogan, 'See the world without leaving Beijing!', conveys a cruel irony about their lives. Jia stages the action in such a way that the melodrama of their lives is perpetually overshadowed by the lavish, cross-cultural performances of world cultures played by Chinese dancers and miniatures of world icons such as the Taj Mahal, the Eiffel Tower, the Great Pyramid and the World Trade Center. Each member of the film's ensemble cast lacks a sustained narrative arc and the film avoids privileging the story of any particular character. Characters appear and disappear from the story without any strong narrative sense of cause and effect. Throughout *The World*, Jia employs natural lighting, long takes, long shots, an evocative musical score, playful animated sequences, overlapping dialogue and World Park sounds to ask viewers to consider the film's feelings of isolation, confusion and malaise. The film uses the artificial terrain of World Park to craft a reality that may be global in appearance, but is haunted by feelings of alienation and 'Disneyfication'. By highlighting the impoverished lives behind the spectacle of globalisation, *The World* presents Chinese modernity as an ambiguous achievement. It uses the artificial landscape of World Park to highlight the interconnected, but ultimately alienated and tradition-less, ethos of contemporary Chinese life.

Jia continues his dispiriting study of the Chinese experience and transformation in the evocative film, *Still Life* (2006). The film presents a portrait of human displacement caused by the Three Gorges Dam project through the journey of two characters. Shen Hong and Sanming are searching for family members in Fengjie, a small town on the Zhangtze River that is being flooded as a result of the project. Sanming has not seen his ex-wife, Missy, for over sixteen years. He is shocked by the demolition of Fengjie, lamenting the town's enormous changes and loss of history. Shen Hong searches for her husband, Guo Bin. She contacts a mutual friend who is vague about her husband's whereabouts. The search by both characters presents different worlds through which to understand Chinese life in Fengjie. Sanming lives among migrant labourers charged with demolishing structures that will be submerged by the flood. Sheng Hong resides among white-collar workers involved in recording and developing Fengjie life after the cessation of the flooding. Neither Sanming nor Sheng Hong is able to reunify with their family; they both remain individuals in search of a sense of family that no longer exists.

In *Still Life*, the world is in a process of disappearance; the scarred landscape of Fengjie and the stillness of the Zhangtze River express a ghostly malaise with thought-provoking resonance. The cinematography and gritty production design of the film treat Fengjie like a living mausoleum; the film is populated by semi-nude male workers, tourists, heavily-accented local dialects, grey weather, muddied water, green hills consumed by concrete buildings, slowly moving diesel-fuelled boats, motorcycles and cars, unruly street sounds and evocative musical interludes. *Still Life* is divided into loose chapters marked by titles of commodities such as 'Cigarettes', 'Liquor', 'Tea' and 'Toffee'. Similar to *The World*, the film features a brief animated sequence in which a sculpture representing the people of Fengjie launches into the sky like a rocket ship. The cinematic experience of *Still Life* leaves the notion of Chinese history and family as spectral concepts that haunt the modern Chinese experience.

Jia's subsequent film, *24 City* (2008), is an exercise in dissolving the differences between fiction filmmaking and documentary. The film explores the decommissioning and conversion of a fifty-year-old state-owned military factory into luxury apartments and the life experiences of the factory workers. Set in the city of Chengdu, Sichuan, the story is told through the testimony of four workers played by actors and interviews with actual factory workers. The common thread that runs throughout their oral history is how the identity of the workers is tied to the nationalist role of the factory and how they have found themselves now obsolete or forgotten parts of the modern Chinese economy and history. Their connection to the factory is a familial one and throughout the film, the workers express an ambivalent attitude towards the emergence of capitalist practices and the quickly forgotten familial relationships of new China. Like Jia's previous two films, *24 City* is a picturesque eulogy to a time of Chinese life that has been eclipsed by the market reforms pursued by the Chinese government. *24 City* demonstrates Jia's aesthetic style with on-location shooting, natural lighting and long takes and the film's musical score displays a greater range with its inclusion of pop music. As the story unfolds, the increasingly blurred boundary between fiction and non-fiction prompts the audience to be active viewers; they are asked to disentangle non-professional actors from 'real' actors and evaluate the veracity and emotional sincerity of their stories and experiences. This activity leads to a larger engagement with the meaning of Chinese identity in the wake of disposable traditions.

Conclusion

Jia Zhangke's body of work resists the visual ethnography of a singular China on the rise. His films emerge from a context of profound social and economic change to argue that contemporary Chinese life is a cacophonous existence that struggles with the demise of cultural traditions. Jia treats cinematic storytelling as a way to document the large transformations that define the present and depict the disaffected lives that are lost in the change or go unrecognised in official films. Jia's China is defined by popular culture and has internalised a capitalist mentality. As Paul Pickowicz notes in his study of underground filmmaking in China:

> The picture of China that emerges in many underground films is thus not merely 'diverse'; it is a view that reveals a China that is fractured into many parts and strikingly disconnected, a China in which people go about, without much guidance or knowledge, sorting out their own individual 'identities'. (2006: 15)

While the time of Jia and the Sixth Generation film culture has not yet passed, they have nonetheless made a major contribution to Chinese cinema. Reflective of the context from which it emerged, the Sixth Generation marked the moment when Chinese cinematic storytelling could be contemporaneous in its stories and aesthetics and openly critical toward government and society. That is, political criticism is now part of the cultural production of Chineseness.

What is unique about Sixth Generation stories in Chinese cinema is that the movement is capturing experiences of a nation without precedent. China is a massive, growing, communist world power with a longstanding history and sense of civilisation. Yet the country remains very much a cultural, economic and political experiment that has yielded mixed results. Sixth Generation films mine the forms of alienation, contradiction and tension that define this time so as to document the Chinese experiences that go unrecognised by popular films. If philosophers Gilles Deleuze and Felix Guattari contend that the instructiveness of film 'is not simply a question of film-content: it is cinematic-form ... which is capable of revealing [a] higher determination of thought, choice [and] link with the world' (1987: 178) then I argue that the critical cinematic storytelling of Jia Zhangke is the philosophy of contemporary Chinese existence. His films affectively materialise complex experiences and offer provocative thoughts about the role of cinematic storytelling in capturing its context.

Bibliography

Appadurai, A. (1996) *Modernity at Large: Cultural Dimensions of Globalization*. Minneapolis: University of Minnesota Press.

Deleuze, G. and F. Guattari (1987) *A Thousand Plateaus: Capitalism and Schizophrenia*. Trans. B. Massumi. Minneapolis: University of Minnesota Press.

Jaffee, V. (2006) ' "Every Man a Star": The Ambivalent Cult of Amateur Art in New Chinese Documentaries', in P. Pickowicz and Y. Zhang (eds) *From Underground to Independent: Alternative Film Culture in Contemporary China*. Lanham: Rowman & Littlefield Publishers, 77–108.

McGrath, J. (2007) 'The independent cinema of Jia Zhangke: From Postsocialist Realism to a Transnational Aesthetic', in Z. Zhen (ed.) *The Urban Generation: Chinese Cinema and Society at the Turn of the Twenty-first Century*. Dunham: Duke University Press, 81-114.

Pickowicz, P. (2006) 'Social and Political Dynamics of Underground Filmmaking in China', in P. Pickowicz and Y. Zhang, *From Underground to Independent: Alternative Film Culture in Contemporary China*. New York: Rowman & Littlefield, 1–22.

Zhen, Z. (2007) 'Introduction: Bearing Witness: Chinese Urban Cinema in the era of "Transformation" (zhuangxing)', in *The Urban Generation: Chinese Cinema and Society at the Turn of the Twenty-first Century*. Durham: Duke University Press, 1–48.

Taonga (cultural treasures): Reflections on Maori Storytelling in the Cinema of Aotearoa/New Zealand

Hester Joyce

> Maori filmmakers have to address several issues not of their choosing when they decide on a project of fiction. […] The Maori filmmaker carries the burden of having to correct the past and will therefore be concerned with demystifying and decolonizing the screen. (Mita 1992: 49)

> It is easy for the Maori to make films because we have things to say, we have stories to tell to make some dent in the way that people are looking at us. (Merata Mita, quoted in Martin 1989: 30)

> There is a category that can legitimately be called 'Fourth Cinema', by which I mean Indigenous Cinema – that's Indigenous with a capital 'I'. (Barclay 2003: 7)

To speak of Maori storytelling within New Zealand's national cinema is to call up the land's histories and its people's memories. To write, as I am, as *manuhiri* (visitor), as Pakeha (settler), about Maori film suggests engagement. So I begin with the words of two filmmakers, Barry Barclay and Merata Mita whose bodies of work reflect an ongoing articulation of issues central to the representation of their people on screen.[1] Barclay's work includes short films, television documentaries, documentary and narrative feature films as well as a body of writing about Maori and indigenous representation. Mita's body of work encompasses a similar range of genres and media. At the heart of their work is the imbedding of 'core values that govern life … *whanaungatanga, mana, manaakitanga, aroha, tapu, mana tupuna, wairua* and *aroha*' (kinship, spiritual power, hospitality, love, prohibited, descent, soul/spirit)

21

(Barclay 2003: 11). For both, filmmaking is a manifold political and cultural activity. In this it is impossible to talk about Maori film without acknowledging New Zealand's colonial legacy, racist past and present-day postcolonialism. What identifies Maori storytelling in the cinema is its cultural particularity and historical specificity. Maori are *tangata whenua* (the people of the place), the indigenous people living on a group of islands in the southernmost Pacific, now called Aotearoa/New Zealand (ANZ).[2] Maori and Moriori (another Pacific Island people) migrated to Aotearoa in the fourteenth century (Ministry for Culture and Heritage/*Te Manatu Taonga* 2008). During eighteenth-century European exploration, Abel Tasman and James Cook mapped the South Pacific including ANZ. The islands were colonised initially by whalers and traders in the late 1700s and then claimed by Britain in 1840, marked by the signing of the Treaty of Waitangi with Maori. The Treaty is the founding document between Maori and the British Crown, and was signed by representatives of the Crown, Lieutenant-Governor William Hobson and forty Maori *rangatira* (tribal leaders). There were Maori and English versions of the document and the two parties had different understandings about definitions of *kawanatanga* (governance) and sovereignty that had been agreed upon. Much of the social and political change in ANZ in the late twentieth century has been because of reconsideration of the spirit and principles of the Treaty of Waitangi (New Zealand History/*Nga Korero Aipurangi o Aotearoa* 2008). It is the legacy of the engagement, partnership and persistent relationship between Maori and Pakeha that informs the cinema of ANZ. Maori cinema exists both within and outside of the national cinema and the two cinemas' histories are coupled politically not least because the film industry developed, and became government supported, during a period of strong Maori political activism in the late 1970s and early 1980s.

Maori storytelling influences the national cinema in a complex weaving manner, giving rise to Pakeha films about Maori, films reflecting Maori/Pakeha interaction, and 'Maori films'. But although Maori have been the subject of cinematic representation since the inception of the industry, their control of Maori representation has been limited. The films of the early 1900s were ethnographical documentaries or European depictions of romanticised 'South Seas people'. Between 1939 and 1972 ANZ feature filmmaking was sporadic and pioneered by Rudall Hayward and John O'Shea. Their four feature films, *Rewi's last Stand* (Hayward, 1940), *Broken Barrier* (O'Shea, 1952), *Don't Let It Get You* (O'Shea, 1966) and *To Love a Maori* (Hayward, 1972), were either stories of Maori/Pakeha colonial wars or personal explorations of interracial relations. Hayward and O'Shea, Pakeha filmmakers, believed that these issues were at the heart of ANZ's national identity. Barclay argues that 'Maori films' are those written and directed by Maori and are set in a Maori world (1998: 10), and belong to an emerging 'fourth cinema' (2003: 9). In these terms, Barclay argues that there are five indigenous features: *Ngati* (Barclay, 1986), *Mauri* (Mita, 1988), *Te Rua* (Barclay, 1992), *Once Were Warriors* (Lee Tamahori 1994) and (the Maori *Merchant of Venice*) *Te Tangata Whai Rawa O Weneti* (Don Selwyn, 2001). Two of the most successful films in ANZ's cinema are Maori stories, *Once Were Warriors* and *Whale Rider* (Niki Caro 2002), the latter adapted and directed by a Pakeha from a Maori novel by Witi Ihimaera.

There are pivotal moments in ANZ cinema history that indicate turning points in the development of a Maori cinema. ANZ is unique in the partnership that has grown between Maori and Pakeha and this is reflected in that complex intersection of concerns in many of the nation's films. This chapter will focus on films for and by Maori and on how Maori cultural and political action has impacted on ANZ cinema as a whole. A key issue is representation – Barclay argues that Maori projects should be in Maori hands. While Maori continue to operate within Western and Pakeha-dominated cinemas, he sees Maori cinema as operating 'outside the national orthodoxy' (2003: 11).

Politics and policy

The establishment of the most recent phase of a national film industry in ANZ began with the formation of the New Zealand Film Commission (NZFC) in 1978. This was the result of persistent lobbying by filmmakers through the preceding decade. Although the NZFC was a non-governmental organisation, it relied on government funding, and was run by a government-appointed board who in turn appointed staff. *The New Zealand Film Commission Act* (1978) established governance of the NZFC and charged it with production of 'New Zealand films' and the development of a local film industry. The definition of a 'New Zealand film' is fluid and reflects the prevailing cultural assumptions associated with definitions of national identity at any one time. The *Act* requires that content, location and creative staff be considered in regards to the definition and financial support of projects (p. 695). Within the rhetoric of national identity associated with the formation of a film industry during the 1970s, there was little reference to ANZ's indigenous population or to other racial or ethnic minorities. There was no mention of the Treaty of Waitangi or of the NZFC's obligations with respect to Maori. There was no requirement in the *Act* for Maori representation on its board and no Maori were elected to it during the 1970s. A previous government had issued a paper on broadcasting that reflected prevailing cultural attitudes. *The Broadcasting Future for New Zealand 1973* called for a 'will to assist and foster the New Zealand consciousness' (p. 8). A section titled 'Interpreting New Zealand Society' expressed the contemporaneous halcyon sentiments that New Zealand was a racially united nation:

> The continued preponderance of imported material could bring uncertainty and instability to a society even when it is as homogeneous as New Zealand's, even when the social distances between its groups (Maori and Pakeha, farmer and city dweller, artist and artisan, the young and the old) are much less marked than in the majority of developed democracies. (Ibid.)

Despite increased political action from the 1960s, Maori participation in filmmaking was restricted, and it was not until the mid-1980s that the first Maori initiated documentaries, *Patu!* (Mita, 1983), *Neglected Miracle* (Barclay, 1985) and feature films, *Ngati* and *Mauri*, were produced. Maori production paralleled political activism and developments in Treaty of Waitangi negotiations. Both Mita and Barclay recognise that *Nga Tamatoa* (warrior children), an urban-based Maori activist group, informed their politics and filmmaking (see Mita 1992: 46 and Barclay 1992: 123). *Nga Tamatoa* (1970–79) fought institutional and systemic racism through protection of the Maori language, protesting against violations of the Treaty and fighting continued confiscation of land. Acknowledgement of Maori rights through legislative changes was in response to Maori resistance gaining strength with protests at Waitangi and Bastion Point and land marches through the 1970s. The *Race Relations Act* legislating against discrimination based on colour, race, ethnic or national origin was passed in 1971 (Human Rights Commission/*Te Kahui Tika Tangata* 2008). Formal recognition of the Treaty occurred with the *Treaty of Waitangi Act* in 1975 the Waitangi Tribunal was established. The *Act* was amended in 1985, allowing the Tribunal to hear grievances dating back to 1840. Further, in 1986 the Tribunal's report noted that *taonga* (cultural treasures) 'includes intangible as well as tangible things' (Orange 1990: 110) – for example, Maori stories and the right for Maori to access and control their own representations and filmmaking. Also in that year government departments were instructed to 'consult with appropriate Maori people on all significant matters affecting the application of the Treaty' (Orange 1990: 106). The *Maori Language Act*, making Maori an official language of ANZ, was passed in 1987. Both these pieces of legislation impacted on the NZFC which then engaged a *kaumatua* (elder), Rei Rakatau. The *kaumatua* was not considered a staff member but a resource to be accessed when required for spiritual guidance and wisdom, and to lift *tapu* (bless locations). Annual *hui* (meetings) with *Te Manu Aute* (the association of Maori filmmakers and broadcasters) were also instituted in the late 1980s.

By 1992 the NZFC was required to state its purpose more clearly. The NZFC had, since the late 1980s, funded production trainees and financed Barclay's filmmaking *wananga* (school) (*New Zealand Film Commission Board Minutes* 1985: Section 8.6). The NZFC published its own guidelines on Treaty of Waitangi obligations:

> The Film Commission is mindful of the special needs of Maori and of its obligations under the Treaty of Waitangi. This commitment underpins every aspect of the Film Commission's work and its assistance programmes (Programmes of Assistance and Policy Guideline Handbook 1995).

In June 1997 the NZFC's *Briefing Notes*, containing funding decisions and other industry news and information, was published in Maori as well as English. This action went some way to acknowledging changes in legislation in the preceding decade. In a paper submitted to the NZFC, Barclay alleged that despite what the Commission had said in print, the record of its support for Maori projects had deteriorated rather than improved in the 1990s. He supported his allegations with statistics of the low funding allocations to Maori-originated projects (1998: 4).

Influences on Maori cinematic storytelling

Maori storytelling in the cinema is strongly influenced by the complementary mediums of television drama and documentary. A seminal documentary work by Barclay was *Tangata Whenua* (1974), a six-part television series devoted to Maori political and cultural history. As well as representing previously unknown aspects of Maori life to Pakeha-dominated television audiences, the production 'allowed for Maori expression in its own terms' (Murray 2007: 88). *Tangata Whenua* was the beginning of the development of Barclay's aesthetic, a culturally informed way of both filming and representing Maori, 'a storytelling approach ... a *marae* [meeting ground] approach' (Barclay 1992: 116) that evolved in his later works and is elaborated in his writings in *Our Own Image* (1990). The series was a collaboration with Pakeha historian Michael King and the filming process emulated the cultural processes of a *marae*, where the camera is a non-intrusive 'friend', where the community is the actor, where voices are heard, and images are given and then returned (see Barclay 1990: 10–16). Mita says of the series: 'It broke new ground; it put Maori perspectives on the small screen, in most cases without Pakeha interpretation' (1992: 46). Like Barclay, Mita's work began in documentary. *Bastion Point – Day 507* (1980) is her record of events in the 1980s significant to Maori land claims and *Patu!* is her documentary record of the anti-apartheid movement protest action against the 1981 Springbok rugby tour of ANZ. Both films, she argues, express a Maori approach to filmmaking, 'driven by identity, resolution and survival' (1992: 47).

Mita describes the ANZ cinema of the 1980s as a 'white neurotic industry' that did not address the crucial issue, 'colonial dislocation' (ibid.). Arguably the industry was Pakeha and male dominated as suggested by the content of many of the films supported by the NZFC during this period. However, the political events of the 1980s are reflected in the wider industry in films that attempt, at least, to represent the reconfiguring of Maori/Pakeha relations, colonialism and national identity, albeit from a Pakeha perspective. Such films include *Pictures* (John O'Shea, 1981), *Utu* (Geoff Murphy, 1983), *Other Halves* (John Laing, 1984), *Came a Hot Friday* (Ian Mune, 1985), *Sylvia* (Michael Firth, 1985), *The Quiet Earth* (Geoff Murphy, 1985), *Queen City Rocker* (Bruce Morrison, 1986), *Mark II* (Mike Walker, 1987) and *Ruby & Rata* (Gaylene Preston, 1990). As well as films, mainstream television dramas and series set in local communities inevitably included Maori characters and stories. For example one of the earliest, *Pukemanu* (1971), a social realist series set in a timber town in the central North Island, necessarily involved Maori characters as Maori were forestry industry workers in the region. *The Governor* (1971), a historical drama depicting Maori land wars of the 1840s, and a soap serial, *Close to Home* (1975–83), had Maori characters and stories. *Shortland Street* (1991–2008), began with a main character, a Maori doctor, Dr Ropata (Temuera Morrison), whose cultural and political beliefs influenced character relationships and narrative trajectories within the series.

A significant example of the influence of Maori storytelling on the Pakeha dominated cinema of the 1980s is *Utu*. *Utu* (revenge) follows in the tradition of Rudall Hayward and John O'Shea's features in exploring Maori/Pakeha relations. It is a set in the colonial period of the Maori land wars and uses generic aspects of the western. American critic Pauline Kael reviewed the film's release in New York: 'Murphy uses the conventions of John Ford's cavalry – Indians, westerns, but he uses them as a form of international shorthand – to break the ice and get going, and for allusions and contrasts' (1985: 241). *Utu*'s story was written during the 1981 Springbok tour protests and reflected on the contemporary significance of the film's historical re-enactment. For example, the co-writer Keith Aberdein (2000) recalls that he would have liked to see a few thousand Maori warriors on Auckland streets in the present day, suggesting that, that way, the fight against apartheid in sport would have been easily won.

As well as bridging the past and the present, *Utu* is also an interesting example of a blend of international and local demands. The story could be described as baroque in its attempt to confine the anarchic turmoil of colonisation in ANZ. It is the story of Te Wheke who begins as a British conscript but accepts the mantle of a Maori warrior who seeks *utu* for the annihilation of his tribal home by English soldiers. Te Wheke is both the protagonist with whom the audience identifies and the disorder motivating the story. He is steeped in *Tikanga Maori* (customary values) and is British educated, exacting revenge while reading passages from *Macbeth*. His duality is reflected in subplots of two Pakeha characters that also explore revenge that is both personally and politically motivated. Williamson, a settler, seeks revenge on Te Wheke for the loss of his wife and home. Scott, an army lieutenant, pursues Te Wheke for the death of a young Maori woman he loves. The usual civilising function of the western narrative, to repatriate the man who has taken up violence through marriage to a 'white' woman or to banish him, is confounded. The film tries to reconcile Maori and Pakeha concerns, finally giving way to an ending that observes Maori protocol. In the last scene Te Wheke is captured and put on trial in a 'bush court'. Each of the players has reason to take revenge on him and the conventions of the western demand a return to order in the form of the reassertion of colonial power. His brother Wiremu, who is without *utu*, sacrificially shoots him, thus ending the conflict. Aberdein believes the ending showed that the Maori way of dealing with Te Wheke's death was 'vastly more sophisticated and culturally intelligent than any of the white characters had shown' (2000).

Bruce Babington argues that although cultural specificity exists in the content of Maori film, 'the idea that Maori film utilises formal modes different from mainstream

New Zealand filmmaking is hardly sustainable, confusing as it does content, and even in certain cases some discernibly different production and distribution elements, with aesthetic systems' (2007: 241). Yet there is a difference between Maori and Western notions of filmmaking. For Maori, filmmaking is process. A film is an artwork, *taonga*, and living. Just as a person speaks, so too does a film, and is thus accorded customary rites. Beyond a film's materiality is the experience of it within its community. For example, film images are returned to the people they are taken from in the first instance (see Barclay 2003: 11). Stuart Murray argues that

> Barclay is aware that Maori filmmaking is only an extension of being Maori within New Zealand. The complexities of film production – of funding, script development, crewing, promotion and more – enact the wider questions of prejudice and belonging that characterize participation in the national culture as a whole. (2007: 100)

As Barclay suggests, to consider a film's 'exteriority', the surface features, ignores its function outside the national orthodoxy. In his essay on 'fourth cinema' he advocates a utopian vision of a cinema in which the indigene controls the camera and turns the gaze back from within the indigenous world (2003: 10). Maori films speak a double discourse – a voice that will speak to and for Maori but one that might also be heard beyond. In his vision, fourth cinema embraces such a process. In light of the concept of the film as *taonga*, he regards distribution as part of the life of the film. He cites occasions where Maori have accompanied their film to different countries to introduce them with traditional ceremony. Vincent Ward's *Rain of the Children* (2008) is an example of the culture in practice. The film is a revisiting of an earlier film, *In Spring One Plants Alone* (1980), in which Ward documents living with a woman of the Tuhoe people, Puhi, and her son. *Rain of the Children* is Ward's view of his preoccupation with Puhi, who had been married to the son of Rua Kenana, a Tuhoe prophet of the late nineteenth century. Her earliest memories were of the Maori Land Wars of colonial ANZ. The later film contains footage of Puhi, archival images of the Tuhoe people, interviews with *kaumatua* and with Puhi's descendants. As an example of the film's status as *taonga* (even though it was directed by a Pakeha and is his vision), it was taken to the New Zealand International Film Festival 2008 by four hundred members of Tuhoe. The film was greeted with customary rites, a *powhiri* (welcome) there and at its first screenings in Sydney and Melbourne, Australia. In Barclay's ideal, films would always be treated in this traditional way (2003: 11).

Ngati: story and community

> It has been said that the work of film director Barry Barclay experiments with the actual process of filmmaking itself. Throughout his career Barclay's particular vision has been shaped by a long-term commitment to make films which serve the interests of Maori people first. (Parekowhai 1988: 75)

Ngati was released to critical acclaim at the Cannes 1987 film festival, being the first ANZ film to be selected for Critics' Week. Helen Martin points out that '*Ngati* was the first New Zealand feature to be made principally by Maori and the world's first feature by an indigenous culture living within a white majority culture' (Martin and Edwards 1997: 128). At the time of the film's completion and before its recognition at Cannes, Barclay described its process as 'politically deliberate – political in the way it was made, a serious attempt to have Maori attitudes control the film' (quoted in Lomas 1987: 2). Concerning representation Barclay asks the question: 'the Maori world has its own ways of talking and listening... How can we take that maverick yet fond friend of ours – the camera – into the Maori community and be confident it will act with dignity' (1990: 9). He develops a thesis that articulates a 'Maori way' that he incorporated into the film's shoot. Prior to *Ngati*'s production he ran a *wananga* (school) for training technicians so that most of his crew would be Maori. Each day's shooting started with a prayer. If elders were not ready at scheduled times the crew waited until they were and community members, including children, were welcomed on set to watch the production. He incorporated some of the techniques that he used in the *Tangata Whenua* series, such as long lenses, end-slating and long-distance sound rigs, to keep the mechanism of filming at a respectful distance from the participants. Barclay raises a similar question about a 'Maori way' in his development of the story for *Ngati*: 'Who are we scripting for? There was a time when we made films to open a window on our own culture. No longer. If you are writing for your own people, explaining everything is something you can leave to others' (1990: 53).

Mita observes that in the making of her two films *Mauri* and *Mana Waka* (1990), her communal approach to production caused some discomfort within the administrative structures of the NZFC (1992: 53). It is *tika* (appropriate) to consult orally with tribal groups about the process of filming and the management of images which is contrary to the hierarchical industry practices of organisations like the NZFC. In writing *Ngati*, Barclay and screenwriter Tama Poata[3] negotiated the structural difficulties of the NZFC development process. Analysis of the development of the script demonstrates the intersection, sometimes collision, of NZFC policy requirements and a 'Maori way'. Teshome Gabriel in his analysis of third world cinema suggests that 'third world filmic representation is open for an elaboration of the relation "viewer/film" on terms other than those founded on psychoanalysis', relying more 'on an appeal to social and political conflicts as a rhetorical strategy and less on the paradigm of oedipal conflict and resolution' (1989: 39). He further argues that third world filmmakers were producing films that restructured accepted film practices and establishes a comparison between indigenous oral and written traditions and Western filmmaking characteristics. Among those of the oral tradition he cites, 'artisan occasion for collective engagement', 'multiple centres and plot lines' and 'individual linked into social fabric' (1989: 42–6). Although *Ngati* predates Gabriel's analysis, some of these characteristics can be seen in Barclay's process and in the content of the *Ngati* story.

However, while Gabriel argues that indigenous filmmaking has processes specific to particular communities, Barclay's 'fourth cinema' arises from cultures outside the national orthodoxy, spiritually and often materially. Maori cinema is, he suggests, one of those that 'are ancient remnant cultures persisting in the modern nation state' (1993: 11). A fourth cinema, then, is one that engages with the lived experience of its filmmakers and its subjects, ignoring the parameters of development, production and distribution of the first cinema, and privileging its own.

Ngati is set in a coastal Maori village, Kapua, on the north-eastern coast of ANZ. The community is observed over a spring holiday weekend in 1949. The lives of Kapua's inhabitants are revealed through three interwoven story strands. Greg, a newly qualified doctor, at the behest of his father who had previously been the local practitioner, visits from Australia. The local abattoir, the community's principal source of income, is threatened with closure and a local boy, Ropata, is dying of the incurable 'Maori illness'. There is conflict in Ropata's family about the nature and treatment of his illness, which his sister Sally, along with the local Pakeha doctor, calls leukaemia. Greg is made the responsibility of Jenny, the schoolteacher, and one of the few Pakeha in Kapua. For Greg, the visit becomes a journey of discovery, as he learns that he is not an outsider but Maori by descent through his mother. The story strands are resolved as the community takes over the running of the meatworks as a collective. Ropata dies of his illness and as his passing is mourned Greg realises that Kapua is where he belongs.

The film documents daily goings-on within the Kapua community. It has an observational style through which the story unfolds passively rather than being driven by a heroic quest. The plot summary demonstrates the main themes explored by Poata and Barclay: the destructive effects of urbanisation on rural Maori values, the conflict between traditional approaches to individual and community well-being and modern medical practices, and the importance of the community network in protecting and nurturing its people. The themes of increasing urbanisation manifest in conflicts over Ropata's medical treatment and in the community's response to the new abattoir. The conflicts are balanced by Greg's growing acceptance of his traditional roots as he decides to return to Kapua to practice medicine. Although the film's setting is 1949 these issues were at the forefront of Maori activism in the 1980s.

Ngati's storylines were autobiographical, based on events in Poata's childhood on the east coast of the North Island in the late 1940s. What began as two boys' observations of Maori soldiers returning from World War II became the story of a community's response to the adverse effects of urban drift and their negotiations between tribal and Western medical approaches to the illness of a *mokopuna* (grandchild). Poata recalls,

When I was a child a boy died in our community … I saw the medical side of the boy's death in the film as witnessing the clash of cultures, new medicine as opposed to Maori *tohunga*-ism, [that is] fixing by spiritual means (Quoted in Cairns and Martin 1994: 123).

The first treatment of the story, submitted to the NZFC in 1985, was a fourteen-page document called '*Te Mate*. A Glimpse: Based on actual events in Tokomaru Bay after the last war' (*Ngati* papers 1985). This was an evocation of the community and characters, in note form, with some dialogue and scenes indicated. The submission challenged the NZFC's processes in a number of ways. A development document would usually be a story outline or scene breakdown in narrative prose, possibly including character descriptions. The story was expected to comply with the NZFC's developing emphasis on defined narrative structure in submissions. *Te Mate* upset the standard character hierarchy of feature films by having eight protagonists of equal importance, with a focus on the community, rather than the individual. Poata described his intention by suggesting a metaphor of a 'net' story structure following the three stories equally, with an accretion of information, in contrast to the prevailing classical action-based paradigm:

> I do believe though in telling the story as it is. A message (whichever way) will come through anyway, whether it is the fact that places like Kapua survive in spite of depressions, famine, wars or epidemics etc ... or that different races of people did live in harmony (and still do) does not really matter. The thing that matters most is that these are the realities in drama form of a living people. (*Ngati* papers 1985)

In contrast to foregrounding the community over a heroic protagonist, the film's chronology adheres formally to a Western timeframe, with the main events set over eight days – a weekend plus five days over Ropata's death and *tangi* (funeral). Gabriel argues that in third world cinema time is assumed to be subjective. The cult of ancestors links past to present suggesting that there is a deeper meaning of art in traditional communities and that one needs 'to belong and/or understand cultural or folk nuances' to interpret them (1989: 43). Although *Ngati* appears to conform to conventional notions of time and space, Cushla Parekowhai suggests the film's setting has other metaphorical functions:

> In *Ngati* the world which Barry Barclay creates offers the experience of entering into an imaginative relationship which transcends time and space. Where the small settlement of Kapua is physically locked into a known landscape bounded by an infinite sea, the real community of 'Cloud' is an every space. (1988: 76)

Parekowhai understands this complexity through her insight into a conversation between Old Eru and Tione towards the end of the film where the *kaumatua* speaks of timelessness in relation to the curability of Ropata's illness. The conversation is about valuing the past and the future, and trusting that Ropata's cure is beyond individuality and rests in the continuance of community. While *Ngati* represents a particular landscape for a Western audience, for non-Pakeha, the setting, Kapua (cloud), also exists outside historical and temporal definition in a 'nostalgic near-past' (ibid.). Thus, she argues, acts of *aroha* (love) resonate across time, representing communal intent.

During a search for locations Poata wrote a series of anecdotal vignettes which were used to flesh out the film's world and later became community events against which the story unfolds. They included picking fruit, fishing for flounder in the foreshore shallows and using horses to transport carcasses of meat along the beach. Poata's attention to cultural detail is demonstrated in the final draft dialogue. For example, Jenny's mother, Sam, says of Greg: 'That's what his father sent him back here for and all his relations are watching.' This is edited to read: 'That's what his father sent him back here for, to meet his other family.' Barclay comments that Poata believed the term 'watching' was a Pakeha term for what the *hapu* (sub tribe) were doing. He also noted that although Jenny and Sam are Pakehas, they 'see themselves as Kapua people' (*Ngati* papers 1985). Jenny is more aware of traditional ways than Greg who, although Maori by birth, is a stranger to his own culture. The film not only represents a Maori community from a Maori perspective, but also integrates Pakeha into that community on Maori terms. Poata's vision was inclusive, according to Barclay, allowing non-Maori a place: 'He brought our country (our two people of the Treaty) to the screen in an inclusive and thoroughly confident manner, perhaps for the first time' (Barclay 2006: 29). The finished film enacts a partnership in that the Pakeha characters allow non-Maori audiences intimate access to the community being depicted. This subtlety demonstrates Poata and Barclay's grace in bridging the divide between Maori culture and Pakeha and international audiences. The project stands as a beacon to remember and be mindful of indigenous cultural practices.

Te Reo Maori/Language

Maori cinema is inextricably linked to Maori television. If the project of Maori cinema is to present Maori stories on screen then television is equally suited to the task. The fight for representation is inextricably tied to a right to speak. Parallel to the passing of the *Maori Language Act* (1987), there was a continuing drive toward the protection of the language and its speakers. This included creation of *Te Kohunga Reo* (language nests for preschoolers), *Kura Kaupapa Maori* and *wananga* (Maori universities). When ANZ broadcasting was deregulated, New Zealand on Air (NZOA) was created as an independent funding agency for the promotion of local content on television and radio. *Te Manga Paho* (1993) was established to promote Maori language and culture in broadcasting and funding for a Maori television channel was granted in 1998. While there had been a limited number of television programmes dedicated to Maori content on existing television channels, opportunities for Maori language to be broadcast were fewer. The Maori television channel began broadcasting in March 2004 (Maori Language Commission/*Te Taura Whiri i te Reo Maori*). This potted history of the intersection of language and cultural rights over representation illustrates the cumulative effect of a range of political movements and the persistence of Maori in the face of systematic colonial and postcolonial neglect.

In his revision of film theory, *An Accented Cinema*, Hamid Naficy argues that cinemas of 'displacement and deterritorialisation' are structured by the filmmakers' histories and identified by orientation towards homeland (2001: 21). Although Maori stand on their land (*Tangata whenua*), aspects of Naficy's analysis can be applied to Maori representation. Maori cinema is created 'in the interstices of social formations and cinematic practices ... as simultaneously local and global, and [they] resonate against the prevailing cinematic production practices' (2001: 6). He suggests that accented cinemas are 'mulatta' texts, 'multilingual, multivocal, multiaccented', and are signified 'by narrative strategies which subvert that mode's realistic treatment of time, space and causality' (2001: 22).

Makatu (the quivering) (2001–02) is a significant Maori television series that functions within Naficy's definition of an accented cinema. Self-described as 'contemporary tales of the unexpected in which ordinary characters encounter mysterious phenomena from Maori mythology' (*Mataku* DVD Box set 2005), the series is set in present day ANZ and explores the interaction of the banality of daily life with phenomena of Maori spirituality. The 13-part half-hour drama series was funded jointly by NZOA, *Te Manga Paho* and NZFC and broadcast on a free-to-air commercial channel in ANZ and sold internationally. Produced, written and directed by Maori, it represents a strong example of the progress of indigenous screen storytelling since the 1980s. Its importance lies in its validation of Barclay's notion of a 'Maori way'. The series provided Maori practitioners who worked primarily in the dominant industry with an opportunity to engage with Maori material. In the simplest analysis the stories validate a Maori oral tradition, language and traditional beliefs. In the first instance the stories are bilingual with dialogue flowing freely between *Te Reo Maori* and English, with both subtitled. Each episode is a self-contained story in which a protagonist is taken out of their comfort zone by strange happenings. Each tests its characters' faith in religious precepts and otherworldliness.

The stories also have a global reach in that they are comparable in content to mainstream television series like *Buffy the Vampire Slayer* (1997–2003). The difference is that contemporary issues, for example drug abuse and urban dislocation, are resolved using Maori mythology, and not always happily. In *Nga Tuahine* (The Sisters), a dispossessed young woman uses alcohol to blank out being sexually abused by her (Pakeha) landlord. She is saved by her young sister, whom she believes died when they were both children. Her sister is a 'shape-shifter' and, taking the older sister's shape, seduces the landlord and kills him. The older sister then chooses to return to that 'other' life by jumping to her death from her apartment balcony. There are tales of cursed rocks that have witnessed deaths across time and therefore remain *tapu* (prohibited). The modern day domestic settings – kitchens, bedrooms, houses – are contrasted with sacred islands, enchanted forests and spiritually empowered artefacts. Western temporal constraints are confounded by characters who have passed away reappearing to warn, guide or harm the contemporary protagonists. In *Iwi Ngaro* (The Lost Tribe) an army unit on war games in remote bushland is ambushed by an ancient and violent lost warrior. The local Pakeha ranger, a Scotsman steeped in *Te Reo* and *Tikanga Maori*, guides the modern day Maori soldiers to the site where the warrior is passing from this world to his otherworld. There they witness his banishment from both worlds. In *Te Tipua* (The Godchild), a beautiful and talented young criminal is called to account for using her foresight talents immorally in gambling game. The gods eventually reincarnate her as an innocent child.

The *Mataku* series follows in the wake of Maori filmmakers who, like Barclay and Mita, take control of Maori storytelling and ownership of their images. *Tikanga Maori* informs their stories' narrative structures and the programmes' *mise-en-scène*. Barclay argues that *Ngati*'s release in 1987 was the beginning of a golden period of Maori production with three more 'Maori' films being released over the next seven years: *Mauri, Te Rua* (Barclay, 1991) and *Once Were Warriors*. The notion of partnership was just being established within Treaty negotiations as these films were being made – and this remains one of the most productive periods for Maori films. Since then Maori cinema has continued to be a complex array of strategies that brings Maori to screen. From depictions in colonialist films in the early twentieth century, to working within a Pakeha-dominated industry, to developing a 'Maori way', Maori cinema has meant political insistence, active engagement and persistent negotiation. Maori works on screen challenge the dominant cinemas, while speaking on their own terms, through community, through *Te Maori*. In this they are *taonga*.

Acknowledgement

Sections of this chapter appear in T. Dunleavy and H. Joyce (2011) *New Zealand Film & Television: Institution, Industry and Cultural Change*. Bristol: Intellect.

Notes

1   Barry Barclay's tribal affiliation is Ngati Apa, Merata Mita's tribal affiliations are Te Arawa and Ngati Pikiao.
2   Maori comprise approximately 16 per cent of the population of New Zealand.
3   Tam Poata's tribal affiliation is Ngati Porou.

Bibliography

Aberdein, K. (2000) Interview with author, 22 February.
Babington, B. (2007) *A History of New Zealand Fiction Feature Film*. Manchester:Manchester University Press.

Barclay, B. (1990) *Our Own Image*. Auckland: Longman.

_____ (1992) 'Amongst the Landscapes', in J. Dennis and J. Beiringa (eds) *Film in Aotearoa New Zealand*. Wellington: Victoria University Press, 116–29.

_____ (1998) 'The New Zealand Film Commission and Maori Filmmakers', Unpublished paper submitted to the New Zealand Film Commission, February 1998. Wellington: New Zealand Film Archive.

_____ (1999) 'The Vibrant Shimmer', *The Contemporary Pacific: A Journal of Island Affairs* (Fall): 390-413.

_____ (2003) 'Celebrating Fourth Cinema', *Illusions*, 35, 9-12.

_____ (2006) 'In Memoriam: Tama Poata 1936-2005', *Onfilm* February: 29.

Cairns, B. and H. Martin (1994) *Shadows on the Wall*. Auckland: Longman.

Human Rights Commission/*Te Kahui Tika Tangata* (2008). Official Website. On-line. Available: http://www.hrc.co.nz (accessed on 13 November 2008).

Gabriel, T. H. (1989) 'Towards a Critical theory of Third World Films', in J. Pines and P. Willemen (eds.) *Questions of Third Cinema*. London: British Film Institute, 30-52.

Kael, P. (1985) *State of the Art*. New York: Dutton.

Lomas, R. (1987) '*Ngati*: A First for the Maori', *Illusions*, 5: 2–3.

Makatu Box Set. 13-part television series. (South Pacific Pictures: Producers: Carey Carter, Rhonda Kite 2001–02).

Maori Language Commission/*Te Taura Whiri i te Reo Maori* (2008). Official Website. On-line. Available: http://www.tetaurawhiri.govt.nz/english (accessed on 21 November 2008).

Martin, H. and S. Edwards (1997) *New Zealand Film 1912–1996*. Auckland: Oxford University Press.

Martin, H. (1989) 'Through a Maori Lens', *NZ Listener*, October 14.

Ministry for Culture and Heritage/*Te Manatu Taonga* (2008). Official Website. Available: http://www.mch.govt.nz (accessed on 21 November 2008).

Mita, M. (1992) 'The Soul and the Image', in J. Dennis and J. Beiringa (eds) *Film in Aotearoa New Zealand*. Wellington: Victoria University Press, 36–56.

Murray, S. (2007) 'Images of Dignity: The films of Barry Barclay', in I. Conrich and S. Murray (eds) *New Zealand Filmmakers*. Detroit: Wayne State University Press, 88–102.

Naficy, H. (2001) *An Accented Cinema: Exilic and Diasporic Filmmaking*. New Jersey: Princeton University Press.

New Zealand Film Commission Act 1978. Reprinted 1 October 1995. Statutes of New Zealand, Vol 34. Wellington: Government Print.

New Zealand Film Commission Board Minutes (1985) 2 August. Wellington: NZFC.

New Zealand Film Commission *Ngati* project assessments (1985). Wellington: NZFC.

New Zealand History/*Nga Korero Aipurangi o Aoteaora* (2008) Official Website. Available: http://www.nzhistory.net.nz (accessed on 23 November 2008).

Ngati papers (1985) Pacific Films Collection. New Zealand Film Archive, Wellington.

Orange, C. (1990) *An Illustrated History of The Treaty of Waitangi*. Sydney: Allen & Unwin.

Parekowhai, C. (1988) '*Te Poho o Paikea*: Barry Barclay and Ngati', *Art New Zealand*, 45, 75–7.

Peters, G. (2007) 'Lives of Their Own: films by Merata Mita', in I. Conrich and S. Murray (eds.), *New Zealand Filmmakers*. Detroit: Wayne State University Press, 103-20.

Programmes of Assistance and Policy Guidelines Handbook (1995). Wellington: NZFC.

Reid, J. (1984) 'Shelton: A Delicate Balance', *Onfilm* April/May: 11.

The Broadcasting Future for New Zealand (1973) Wellington: Government Print.

The *Minjung* Cultural Movement and Korean Cinema of the 1980s: The Influence of *Minjung* Theatre and Art in Lee Jang-ho's Films

Nam Lee

Declaration of Fools (*Pabo sŏnŏn*,[1] Lee Jang-ho, 1983), one of Korea's most inventive and experimental films of the 1980s, begins with a sequence in which a movie director plunges to his death from the rooftop of a high-rise building in Seoul. First comes a close-up of the movie director's feet balancing precariously on the edge of the rooftop, and then the camera tilts upward to reveal his sombre face: it is Lee Jang-ho, the director of the film, himself. Clad only in his underwear, Lee engages in a brief but exaggerated warm-up exercise before looking down at the busy traffic below, firmly shutting his eyes, and jumping off the building. In the next shot, his falling body becomes a newspaper floating downward in slow motion; then the film cuts to a shot of his body lying on the ground surrounded by a crowd. Among the crowd is Ttong-ch'il, the crippled protagonist of the film, who unintentionally becomes the person to whom the director speaks his last words. After Lee's death, Ttong-ch'il goes up to the rooftop to collect the clothes and shoes the director had left there. Ttong-ch'il puts them on and heads into the streets of Seoul to begin his tragicomic journey. The entire sequence is shown without dialogue or diegetic sound; however, as we watch the newspaper fall down in slow motion, we hear the roar of cheering crowds at pro-baseball and pro-soccer games issuing from the soundtrack, followed by the director's hoarse voice uttering 'Motion picture on the verge of extinction.'

This suicide scene serves as an effective prelude to the main narrative of the film. By making Ttong-ch'il inherit his clothes and wallet, Lee implies that Ttong-ch'il's despondent journey through 1980s Korean society is a metaphor for his own. The film is Lee's declaration of the 'death of cinema' in Korea and his symbolic suicide as a filmmaker. During the scene in which Lee whispers his last words to Ttong-ch'il, we hear a voice-over narration from a child: 'One day, Ttong-ch'il met a movie director who jumped from a rooftop. In those days, people were not interested in movies at all. Everybody was into sports. The movie director died alone.'

In the context of Korean society in 1983, this narration is an (in)direct critique of the newly established military regime and its cultural policy, generally referred to as '3S Policy'.[2] Although the narration is read like a book by a child and the story is told from a future standpoint to avoid censorship, the film is nevertheless Lee's desperate outcry against the country's military dictatorship. In several interviews, Lee explained that he made the film at a moment of complete desolation and hopelessness:

> I submitted *Children of Darkness 2* (*Ŏdum ŭi chasiktŭl 2*) as the title of the film. However, they wouldn't allow it. It was a period when the cultural policy of Chun Doo-hwan's regime revealed its true character. I was in utter despair. I couldn't bear it anymore and I thought of giving up filmmaking altogether. Then I decided to make a film with complete self-abandonment. So I went back to the Ministry of Culture and Public Information, submitted ten titles and asked them to choose one. They chose *Declaration of Fools*. The title made me even more miserable, so I filmed it in just the opposite way to what I would normally do, because I decided not to take responsibility for the outcome. I also let the actors do whatever they wanted. Then, while looking at the rushes, it occurred to me that this could also be a way of making a film, and that's when I started to put the film together. So a mutant was born. Chun Doo-hwan's regime has greatly contributed to the making of the film. (Quoted in Yi and Yi 2006: 63–4)

Declaration of Fools is indeed a 'mutant', not only in Lee Jang-ho's *oeuvre* but also in the history of Korean mainstream filmmaking. Because of the severe censorship practices of the *Yusin* regime (1972–79), the tradition of social realist drama that had characterised the golden age of Korean cinema in the 1960s died out in the 1970s,[3] and escapist commercial films, such as bar hostess movies, light comedies and action films dominated the film scene instead. Most mainstream movies in the 1980s including melodramas, action films, light comedies and the newly emerging erotic movies, also followed the conventions of 1970s escapist cinema. There was hardly any attempt to challenge government censorship with socially conscious subject matter, let alone formal experimentation. However, with the brief slackening of censorship that occurred right after the assassination of Park Chung-hee in 1979, a number of filmmakers seized the opportunity to revive the tradition of social realist cinema in the early 1980s.

Among these filmmakers, Lee Jang-ho stands out as the leader of this newly revived trend of social realism or critical realism as it was sometimes dubbed by Korean film historians. Film historian Yi Hyo-in points out that the term social realism or critical realism was used to describe the Korean New Wave films of the 1980s and 1990s because 'they revealed the absurdities of Korean society or portrayed its inhuman conditions in a critical fashion' (2001: 310). Lee's film *A Fine, Windy Day* (*Param purŏ choŭn nal*, 1980) opened the way for films that dealt directly with contemporary social issues, and in the next three years, he turned out three more such films: *Children of Darkness* (*Ŏdum ŭi chasiktŭl*, 1981), *Widow's Dance* (*Kwabu ch'um*, 1983) and *Declaration of Fools*. In the last of these he took the indirect approach of an allegorical depiction of harsh reality in the face of newly enforced film censorship. It was exceptional in that it was more expressionistic, absurdist, metaphoric, exaggerated and surreal compared to the previous three films.

Frederic Jameson's notion of 'third world national allegory' is useful in understanding the often indirect approach Lee takes to raise and critique social issues in his films. Jameson argues that 'all third world texts are necessarily allegorical, and in a very specific way: they are to be read as national allegories' (1986: 69). Although Aijaz Ahmad makes a valid point when he criticises Jameson by pointing out that 'allegorisation is by no means specific to the so-called third world' (1987: 15), Jameson's idea becomes a reasonable tool in understanding the implicit meaning of certain third world texts that were written or filmed in a politically oppressive situation. When freedom of expression is restricted to such an extent that no hint of social critique is allowed, writers and filmmakers have to resort to allegory or metaphor to express their thoughts. National allegory has useful resonance in an examination of Lee's films in which the stories of protagonists' destinies are often allegories of the oppressive situation of Korean society in the early 1980s. In particular, *Declaration of Fools* was made under conditions of strict censorship that prohibited any direct social critique, which is why the film applies extreme symbolism.

The four films Lee Jang-ho made between 1980 and 1983 deserve particular attention in the history of Korean cinema in that they are arguably the first group of films that consciously incorporate the tenets of *minjung* (people) aesthetics, as well as the idea of a *minjung* historiography that challenges the official histories disseminated by the military government. By examining these films in relation to the political and cultural discourses of the time, this chapter will illustrate how Lee integrates socio-political realities and *minjung* aesthetics into his films' narrative and style, thus constructing what might be called 'mainstream *minjung* cinema'. These films not only adapted novels of *minjung* literature for the screen but also incorporated various traits of *minjung* art, especially *minjung* theatre.

Minjung as subjects of history

What is *minjung* and its significance in the history of South Korea and what impact did the *minjung* cultural movement of the 1970s and 1980s have on filmmaking? In order to place Lee Jang-ho's cinematic experiments within the larger context of the cultural movement of the 1980s, it is necessary to look at the modern history of Korea. The 1980s was a period of major transformation in the political, social and cultural environment, with a rise of *minjung* consciousness that began to build up during the 1970s *Yusin* regime. Literally, *minjung* means 'the people' (*min*) and 'the mass' (*jung*), however, the exact definition of the term is still debatable. In the South Korean political and cultural context, *minjung* are those who are oppressed, exploited and marginalised by the oppressive power. Political, social and cultural activists regarded *minjung* as subjects of history who could bring revolutionary changes to the political and economic system. Therefore, in the 1980s, *minjung* referred to a confederation of labourers, peasants, urban poor, students and intellectuals who comprised a major force in the struggle against the military dictatorship; and one of the main objectives of the 1980s South Korean political, social and cultural movement against military dictatorship was to raise historical and social consciousness of the *minjung*.[4]

Eighteen years of military dictatorship came to an abrupt end with the assassination of President Park Chung-hee on 26 October 1979 spreading hope of democracy. This hope was soon crushed by another military coup on 12 December 1979 by General Chun Doo-hwan. Massive demonstrations against his takeover spread nationwide, and the military sent troops to the southwestern city of Kwangju to suppress demonstrations, resulting in an unprecedented massacre in May 1980. Although it failed, the Kwangju Uprising made a great impact on the anti-government struggle of the 1980s, urging a change of gear from a movement led by students and intellectuals, to a *minjung* movement.[5] Students and intellectuals regarded South Korea's major political and social problems, including national division, as structural problems embedded in the country's socio-political system and/or in its neocolonialist relationship with the United States.

Because there was no way reform at the top could be achieved without popular agitation, the logical course was a revolution with the *minjung* as its major force. Emphasis was put on efforts to empower the oppressed and marginalised *minjung*. This rise of *minjung* consciousness rendered a new driving force for anti-government nationalist struggle, and the liberation of the *minjung* was added to democratisation (*minju*) and reunification of *minjok* (nation) to form the 'three "*min*"' ideology, the basis of South Korea's nationalist movement.[6] Therefore, at the risk of oversimplification, we could say that the main focus of the nationalist movement in twentieth century South Korea shifted from the *Minjok* (anti-colonialism) to the *Minju* (anti-dictatorship) and finally to the *Minjung* (anti-neocolonialism) movement.

Minjung cultural movement and *minjung* literature

Minjung also became the central idea in the cultural movements of the 1970s and 1980s because *minjung* historians and literary critics argued that national reunification would be achieved through expansion of the *minjung* culture. Franz Fanon's emphasis on the necessity of reconstructing national culture for postcolonial nations left a deep impression on the discourse of the *minjung* cultural movement, and it was literary critics and theorists who played the leading role in the discussion. The debates and discussions about *minjok* literature gradually developed into discussion about *minjung* literature. Whereas *minjung* literature was defined as 'for the *minjung*, of the *minjung*' in the 1970s, the definition gradually changed to 'for the *minjung*, by the *minjung* and of the *minjung*' by the 1980s, emphasising the literary works written by *minjung* themselves.

During the 1970s, literary critics such as Paik Nak-chung and Yŏm Moo-woong defined *minjok* literature as a literature based upon a thorough understanding of the nation as a whole, in terms of its historical conditions and its current realities. The focus of the discussions about *minjok* literature, on 'what to write and how to write', shifted to those of *minjung* literature in the 1980s. In 1975, Paik Nak-chung, the leader of the national literary theory, wrote in his article 'Minjok munhak ŭi hyŏn tangye (The Present Stage of National Literature)': 'Facing the crisis that threatens the dignity and survival of the nation (*minjok*), our national literature must, in order to exist as literature, have its roots in the recognition of this crisis. National crisis is the very real basis of, and the existing value of, the notion of national literature', and added that, 'the restoration of democracy is the goal of, and the immanent task, of national literature at this stage' (1985: 12). Five years later, in 1980, he wrote, 'nation is neither a metaphysical being nor a fixed entity. It is defined by the lives of the majority of the nation, the meaning of which changes with the unfolding of history. Thus, it is inevitable for the true national literature to have the quality of *minjung* literature' (1985: 54).

Madang kŭk as *minjung* theatre

This literary movement stimulated similar movements in other cultural spheres, such as fine art, theatre and music. In theatre, traditional folk art forms were rediscovered as powerful tools to transform audiences' social consciousness during the 1970s, and *minjung* culture activists adapted these forms to dramatise contemporary social and political problems. One of the important emerging forms of theatre was *madang kŭk*, meaning 'open court play', which drew inspiration from Korea's traditional culture and performing arts, such as mask-dance (*t'alch'um*), farmers' dances (*nong'ak*) and shaman rituals (*gut*). In *madang kŭk*, traditional performance styles were blended with contemporary social and political issues. *Madang kŭk* performance groups were formed in almost every university. In 1981 and again in 1984, Im Chin-t'aek, a leading figure of the *minjung* theatre and *madang kŭk* movements, adapted Hwang Suk-yŏng's short story *Dream of a Strong Man* (*Jangsa ŭi kkum*, 1974) for theatre performance and ran a successful local tour. The original story was set in the 1960s, however, Im changed it to the 1980s to comment on contemporary issues.

In the art scene, images of *minjung* art – woodblocks, student banners and murals and demonstration placards – glorified labourers, peasants and traditional performing arts. *Minjung* artists criticised the dominance of modernism and abstract art and stressed the importance of content rather than technique. Also, some artists paid particular attention to the strong tradition of portrait painting in Korea and tried to revive the genre by depicting portraits of ordinary people (*minjung*). *Norae Undong*, meaning 'Song Movement', also arose in the 1970s and early 1980s. Invented by pioneers like Kim Min-ki, the songs had politically and socially conscious lyrics. Many of the songs were sung during demonstrations.

Therefore, the 1980s can be characterised as the period in which the *minjung* cultural movement gained force and popularity in Korean cultural scene. The goal of the movement was to revive the lost art of the people because folk culture, with its latent subversive and transformative power, could lead the movement into a revolutionary era, where the *minjung* would become the subject of history. The methodology of the *minjung* cultural movement is essentially a re-reading of Korean history as the history of the *minjung*'s struggle. The movement represents that history as a paradigm of change and thus confronts the official history propagated by the military regime.[7]

Korean cinema of the 1980s also began to show the influence of the *minjung* cultural movement. A number of filmmakers made major works of *minjung* literature into films such as *A Fine, Windy Day* (Lee Jang-ho, 1980), *A Small Ball Launched by a Dwarf* (*Nanjangi ka ssoa ollin chagŭn kong*, Lee Won-se, 1981), *Children of Darkness* (Lee Jang-ho, 1981), *Kkobang Villagers* (*Kkobang tongne saramdŭl*, Bae Chang-ho, 1982), *Declaration of Fools* (Lee Jang-ho, 1983) and *Dreams of a Strong Man* (*Changsa ŭi kkum*, Shin Seung-su, 1985). The underground *minjung* cinema movement also developed into a documentary movement that recorded demonstrations and labour strikes. Documentary filmmakers, such as Kim Dong-won, encouraged labourers and the urban poor to become filmmakers in their own right from the late 1980s and onwards.

Minjung aesthetics in Lee Jang-ho's films

As previously stated, one of the central tenets of various *minjung* arts is that they are reviving traditional cultural forms such as folk art, mask-dance (*t'alch'um*) and shaman rituals (*gut*) which strongly reflect the effort to retrieve Korean identity in the face of increasing cultural imperialism. And these traditional art forms were modernised to create a cultural forum where contemporary social issues were raised and criticised, often in the form of satire. Lee Jang-ho is one of the first filmmakers who consciously adopted these art forms for mainstream cinema.

Many prominent artists of *minjung* theatre and dance, such as Im Chin-t'aek, Kim Myŏng-gon, and Kim Kyŏng-nan, collaborated with Lee's filmmaking, and the narrative structure of *Declaration of Fools* resembles that of *madang kŭk* (open-court play), a modernised version of the Korean traditional mask-dance or *t'alch'um*. *A Fine, Windy Day* also features elements of the mask-dance and other traditional dances in its narrative. However, it is *Declaration of Fools* that stands out as one of the most experimental features in Korean film history because it ventures into new territory not only in its subject matter but also in its self-conscious film style. *Declaration of Fools* is the only film of Lee's that attempted to create what might be called a *minjung* film language. As previously, mentioned, Lee Jang-ho was going against all dominant filmmaking conventions when shooting *Declaration of Fools*. However, ironically, it is this same self-abandonment which produced the most interesting film style in the Korean cinema of the 1980s.

Although short lived, Lee's cinematic experiments served as a major inspiration for the new generation of film directors, such as Park Kwang-su, Jang Sun-woo and Park Chong-won, who emerged as the Korean New Wave directors in the late 1980s and revived a long-forgotten but venerated tradition of Korean cinema: a social realist cinema that speaks to real social issues. They also incorporated elements of *minjung* aesthetics and *minjung* historiography.

A Fine, Windy Day and the symbolic function of *T'alch'um*

Lee Jang-ho opened the door for a new trend of social realism in 1980, with the release of *A Fine, Windy Day*.[9] It was his comeback film after four years of forced inactivity following his arrest on charges of possessing marijuana. Lee started his film career as a very successful commercial director. His first feature film, *Home of the Stars* (*Pyŏldŭl ŭi kohyang*, 1974), set a box office record at that time. In his memoir, he confesses that while in hiatus, he realised: 'I had been totally ignorant of the society I lived in and of Korea's history. I did not realise that Korean cinema was not depicting Korean realities until I was forced to leave the film scene' (1999). When he was allowed to work again after Park Chung-hee's assassination, he vowed he would 'revive the realism that had vanished from Korean cinema'. In his idle days, he had read Yŏm Mu-wung's book, *Minjung munhak ŭi sidae* (*The Age of Minjung Literature*, 1979), which inspired him to make *A Fine, Windy Day* based on a novella written by a prominent writer of national literature, Choi Ilnam, *Our Vine* (*Uridŭl ŭi nŏngk'ul*, 1979). He also socialised with prominent novelists of *minjung* literature such as Lee Mun-gu and Song Ki-won, both of whom moved to a village and wrote stories about their lives in a rural area.

A Fine, Windy Day begins with close-up images of a farmer and a boy, which remind one of Korean traditional portrait paintings. Traditional portrait painting was indeed on the verge of extinction when the *minjok* and *minjung* art movement rediscovered and revived it. These portrait scenes also imply that the roots of the film's protagonists are in the agricultural village. In fact, Lee inserts these portrayals of ordinary people throughout the film. The film is an adaptation of Choi's novella, but Lee made one important change to the narrative. To highlight the differences between the rich and the poor and to present a confrontation between Westernised and traditional values, he added a rich young college girl who flirts with one of the three protagonists. The film concerns three young men in their twenties – Tŏk-pae, Ch'unsik and Kil-nam – who move to Seoul from the rural countryside and struggle to make it in the big city. The film realistically depicts the actual situation of those who migrated to the capital city to find jobs. The background of the film is the aggressive economic development and land development boom of that period, which intensified the suffering of the urban poor.

Tŏk-pae, one of the protagonists and a stutterer who works as a delivery man in a small Chinese restaurant, falls in love with Myŏng-hŭi, a rich college girl. His love is not fulfilled, however, because she is just flirting with him out of boredom and a desire to irritate her rich boyfriend. Her rejection of Tŏk-pae's love symbolises the irreconcilable gap between the two classes as well as Tŏk-pae's broken 'Seoul Dreams', and Tŏk-pae becomes a boxer in order to fight the harsh reality of his situation. In the film, the rich are depicted as Westernised and immoral, and allegorised as collaborators with neocolonialism, and the poor are depicted as innocent victims, as evidenced in the relationship between Tŏk-pae and Myŏng-hŭi. Myŏng-hŭi is always accompanied by Western piano music. On her first and only date with Tŏk-pae, Myŏng-hŭi takes him to a discotheque where rich kids are enjoying themselves to Western disco music. At first, Tŏk-pae is quite lost on the dance floor because he has never been to a discotheque before. However, Tŏk-pae is reminded of the farmers' dance he used to observe in his rural village and begins to dance in the traditional mask-dance (*t'alch'um*) fashion. Everyone in the dance hall, including some foreigners, is impressed by his dance and he dominates the dance floor, becoming the hero of the night.

This use of the mask-dance can be read as symbolic resistance to the ruling class. According to literary scholar Cho Dong-il, the aesthetic principle of the mask-dance drama[10] offers a theoretical ground for symbolic inversion. He locates the power of mask-dance drama in its ribald humour and satire, which denotes the *minjung*'s energy in confronting the dominant and in subverting the hierarchical social order. He states that 'the most important aspect in discussing the history of mask-dance is the fact that it is *minjung*'s theatre. Among various forms of traditional arts, it is the mask-dance that expresses the *minjung* consciousness most truthfully, and boldly criticises the society from *minjung*'s viewpoint' (1979: 8). He locates this *minjung* consciousness in the conflicts between *yangban* (noble class) and servants, and also between *yangban* and the peasants in the play: 'Satire and criticism of *yangban* is expressed clearly in the "comedic trial" in which servants severely mock and denounce *yangban*' (1979: 46). In particular, the mask-dances performed in cities are daring in that 'they confront *yangban* without showing any fear and all the more, they show a firm belief in *yangban*'s fall' (1979: 97). This revolutionary aesthetic of folk theatre and the mask-dance, especially the Pongsan mask-dance drama that most boldly defames the very authority of the rulers, became an icon of the people's resistant spirit and a mark of *minjung* identity during the 1970s.

Declaration of Fools as a cinematic *madang kŭk*

Lee Jang-ho takes the revolutionary aesthetics of folk theatre one step further in *Declaration of Fools*, because the film itself is structured like a *madang kŭk*, a modernised version of a mask-dance drama. The open structure of the mask-dance theatre, as opposed to a linear narrative structure, and the incorporation of shamanic ritual are two of the crucial elements of the *madang kŭk*, and *Declaration of Fools* employs all of these elements. Im Chin-t'aek, the leader of the *madang kŭk* movement in the 1970s and 1980s, defined *madang kŭk* as 'the ideology and the art form of the *minjung* theatre of our time that inherited the legacy of our traditional folk theatre, especially the mask-dance' (1990: 43). The movement started as a reflection on the fact that the history of Korean theatre has been written as an implantation of Western theatre during the Japanese occupation, totally excluding the history of traditional *madang kŭk*.

Declaration of Fools provides an excellent example of a film in which the *minjung* aesthetic currents of the time, especially that of *madang kŭk*, are translated into a new cinematic language. Placed within the context of the political and cultural movements of the time, the film demonstrates the ways in which Lee tried to highlight class differences as the main problem of Korean society. It also depicts the manner in which he conveys his idea that the *minjung* is the main force that will set a new course for Korea's future – the core idea of *minjung* historiography.

Declaration of Fools is a story of Ttong-ch'il, a cripple, thief, pickpocket, beggar and later a pimp, who roams the country in his effort to make a living. It is loosely based on a novel, *Children of Darkness* (1980), written by Hwang Suk-Yŏng, one of the most prominent writers of national literature. It is a true story of the life of Lee Dong-ch'ŏl, who dictated his story to Hwang. The novel was a sensation at the time because it vividly depicted in raw language the lives of marginalised people living in slums. It was also considered to be an example of literature written *by* a *minjung* with help from a professional writer. In fact, after the success of *Children of Darkness* Lee Dong-ch'ŏl wrote his own novel, another novel written in a reportage style, titled *Kkobang Villagers* (*Kkobang tongne saramdŭl*, 1981), which was also adapted into a film (*The People of Kkobang Village*, 1982) by Bae Chang-ho in 1982.

Declaration of Fools takes the form of a road movie. However, the film unfolds in the fashion of a *madang kŭk*. For example, it has disjointed episodes and relies heavily on coincidences, consciously neglecting causality in the unfolding of the story as if to incorporate impromptu events, an essential component of *madang kŭk*. Most importantly, the narrative structure follows the way *madang kŭk* is organised. The protagonist is introduced, followed by other characters who represent the oppressed, their dreams are told to the audience, there is a confrontation with the oppressors, the *minjung* fights and wins, they perform rituals for the dead (which heightens the audience's emotional response), and finally both the protagonists and the audience achieve a critical consciousness, a sense of awakening.

The film sets up a *madang kŭk*-style narrative structure from the beginning. Before the credit sequence, a child's narration establishes the film as a fairytale: 'Once upon a time, at the end of the twentieth century there lived a fool named Ttong-ch'il in our country'. Thus, Ttong-ch'il, the protagonist, is introduced – as in *madang kŭks* – walking toward the camera (the audience) while the soundtrack plays traditional Korean dance music. In fact, the way Ttong-ch'il walks resembles the 'cripple dance', one of the many dances included in various mask-dance dramas. At the time the film was made, a traditional dancer, Kong Ok-chin, introduced a set of dances which she named 'cripple dance', as a result of which both she and the dance became very popular. The actor, Kim Myŏng-Kon, who made a film debut as Ttong-ch'il, is an actor who was trained in traditional theatre and *p'ansori*.[11] Also, the narration by a child immediately makes the audience a spectator of a *madang kŭk*, which achieves a distancing effect, as in Brechtian Epic theatre.

In *madang kŭk* as well as in the traditional mask-dance, audience participation is a crucial part of the play. Interaction between the performers and audience and among audience members brings the fun of the impromptu to the play. Since film spectators cannot participate in the story as those of *madang kŭk* can, the film employs such devices as ellipses, jump cuts, and direct address by the narrator to prevent the audience from being just passive observers of the story. Viewing the present from the vantage point of the future is in itself a satire, another characteristic of *madang-kŭk*, since by doing so, the film is implying that the present reality is an absurd comedy. In addition, the use of child's drawings, jump cuts, fast-motion montage sequences and the ironic use of sound are all effective in making *Declaration of Fools* a radically alternative film that is diametrically opposed to mainstream filmmaking.

Ttong-ch'il, who inherited the belongings of the deceased movie director at the beginning of the film, embarks on a journey through the streets of Seoul. He goes to Sinch'on, the university village of the Ehwa Women's University, where he spots a pretty college girl, Hye-yŏng, and instantly falls in love with her. He follows her through several shops around the village and finally decides to abduct her. Accompanied by a fat, naïve and equally moronic taxi-driver, Yuk-tŏk, he succeeds in kidnapping Hye-yŏng. However, it turns out that she is in fact a prostitute who dreams of being a college girl. Also, it turns out she is not a docile woman: she fights off Ttong-ch'il's attempt to rape her in a comic scene in which she defeats the two men with her brilliant tae kwon-do skills. After their defeat, both Ttong-ch'il and Yuk-tŏk become her admirers and follow her to the brothel where they make a living by running errands. However, when Ttong-ch'il attempts to free a rural girl who was abducted and sold to the brothel, the three of them are kicked out of the place. Now, Ttong-ch'il, Yuk-tŏk and Hye-yŏng roam aimlessly from one place to another. It is almost like a silent film for the first third of the running time.

Towards the end of the film, the contrast between rich and poor is made evident in a party scene. The party is held at the hotel where Ttong-ch'il and Yuk-tŏk are working as waiters after Hye-yŏng left them. The party is for rich and influential men, all clad in black tuxedos and ties, accompanied by beautiful women in sexy dresses. To the surprise of Ttong-ch'il and Yuk-tŏk, Hye-yŏng enters the party hall with a rich guy. However, some of the men in the hall recognise her as a prostitute and begin to mock her in front of other guests. Eventually, Hye-yŏng is brutally killed by these upper-class men. In this scene, the rich are portrayed as Westernised and evil; the protagonists, the *minjung*, as innocent victims. The scene of the men torturing and killing Hye-yŏng by forcing alcohol down her throat and then drowning her with forced drink is very long and disturbing. It is intended to arouse anger in the audience, so that when Ttong-ch'il and Yuk-tŏk come to rescue her, the audience will fervently support them. It is significant to note that whereas the torture scene resembles the Biblical story of the degradation of Sodom and Gomorrah, with its disturbing depiction of rich upper-class men's collective violence on Hye-yŏng and their debauchery, the arrival of Ttong-ch'il and Yuk-tŏk is done in the form of a mask-dance, with traditional percussion music drawing attention to them. They are also dressed (or undressed) in the traditional costume of chivalrous robbers. Before they become the brave heroes of the *minjung* by punishing the evil rich, however, they fail to rescue Hye-yŏng before her death.

After defeating the immoral and brutal 'oppressors', Ttong-ch'il and Yuk-tŏk perform a ritual for the deceased prostitute in the open space of a mountain. The landscape, together with the traditional Korean tune, rhythms and body movements, creates a distinctively Korean image on screen. After witnessing the killing of Hye-yŏng, who still had the false dream of joining the rich class, Ttong-ch'il and Yuk-tŏk take off their clothes of servitude and false hope, and dance freely in front of the parliament building. The scene of the two fools dancing together in a spirit of defiance is a very powerful scene that challenges the authority of the government. Then, Ttong-ch'il's rebirth is symbolised by his act of throwing himself from the same rooftop from which the movie director had jumped at the beginning of the film.

The physical disabilities of Ttong-ch'il in *Declaration of Fools* and Tŏk-pae in *A Fine, Windy Day*, represent the marginalised *minjung*, and these disabilities can also be interpreted as a metaphor for the 'imperfect' divided nation. In addition, the silent film quality of *Declaration of Fools* can be read as an allegory of the oppressive regime which prohibited freedom of speech. It also symbolises how the *minjung* has been denied its voice in history. Lee Jang-ho also shows his belief in the *minjung*'s ability to make history. At the end of the film, the child narrator says, 'those with humble hearts are happy. Those who are persecuted for doing the right thing for peace are happy. Because we had ancestors like Ttong-ch'il and Yuk-tŏk, we are happy.' This suggests that the film was a recounting of a history, and that the *minjung* had made a better future for the next generation.

Conclusion

Lee Jang-ho's attempt to find ways to incorporate traditional art forms into his films has a significant meaning in terms of constructing a mainstream *minjung* cinema that is distinctly Korean, both in its subject matter and its style. By concentrating on the differences between the privileged class and the *minjung*, and by paying attention to the suffering of *minjung*, Lee gives a voice to those who had been absent from the official history, and constructs a national identity centred on the *minjung* as its subjects.

Among the four films Lee made in the early 1980s, *Declaration of Fools* stands out as one of the most innovative in the history of Korean cinema. It was filmed without a pre-written scenario and relied heavily on actors' improvisation and interesting experiments with sound: the film has very little dialogue. It relies on occasional voice-over narration and the soundtrack employs diverse music and sound: from the familiar video-game sounds to the traditional farmers' music. *Declaration of Fools* presents a rare case of a truly political film, both in its content and form, in Korean film history. Not even the Korean New Wave films made in the late 1980s and early 1990s, such as Park Kwang-su's *Chilsu and Mansu* (*Ch'il-su wa Man-su*, 1988), Park Chong-won's *Kuro Arirang* (1989) and Jang Sun-woo's *The Lovers of Oomookbaemi* (*Umuk paemi ŭi sarang*, 1990), match the degree of formal innovation that *Declaration of Fools* has achieved.

Minjung cinema developed into a strong political movement in independent documentary filmmaking in the late 1980s and early 1990s. However, after the *minjung* cultural movement lost its momentum in the late 1980s with the collapse of the Soviet block, *minjung* cinema declined by the mid-1990s. The establishment of a civil, democratic government in 1993 contributed to the waning trend of politically charged *minjung* cinema. Also, as the major aims of the democratic movements have been achieved with the establishment of a progressive government, student and civil movements now focus more on environmental issues, women's rights and consumerism. Since the objectives of *minjung* cinema were closely related to the construction of a new national cinema, its urgency as well as its validity seem to have diminished considerably in this age of multinational capitalism, globalisation and transnational cinema that problematise the very notions of fixed national identity and national cinema. However, the fact that minjung aesthetics have produced one of the most unique formal experiments in Korean film history sheds a new light on how indigenous aesthetic principles might contribute to creating an alternative cinema that is very different to the dominant cinema.

Notes

1   I employ the McCune-Reischauer system of romanisation for Korean except for words or names that have their own divergent orthography. Korean names are transliterated in their standard fashion, with the last name first. All the translations from Korean are my own unless otherwise indicated.

2   The authoritarian Chun Doo-hwan regime, which seized power after the bloody suppression of the Kwangju Uprising in May 1980, actively used 'Sex, Screen and Sports' to pacify the growing discontent among the people. Big sporting events, such as the 1986 Seoul Asian Games, 1988 Seoul Olympic Games and the establishment of pro-baseball and pro-soccer leagues, were utilised to avert public attention from politics. The midnight curfew was removed in 1981 and late night cinemas were permitted. Film censorship during this period was extremely harsh concerning political issues but softer on sexual explicitness, hence the proliferation of soft pornographic, erotic movies such as the *Madame Aema* (*Aema puin*) series throughout the 1980s.

3   Social realist cinema refers to those films that realistically depict the everyday lives of people in the lower strata of society including the working class and the urban poor. Films such as *The Stray Bullet* (*Obalt'an*, Yu Hyun-mok 1960) and *A Coachman* (*Mabu*, Kang Dae-jin, 1961) are excellent examples of social realist films of the 1960s. However, this tradition died out during the 1970s.

4   Yoon Kŏn-ch'a's book *Hyŏndae Han'guk ŭi sasang hŭrŭm: chisigin kwa kŭ sasang 1980-90-nyŏndae* (*Contemporary Korean Philosophy and Ideas: Intellectuals and Their Thoughts 1980s-90s*, Seoul: Tangdae, 2000) provides an excellent overview of the philosophical and ideological debates, including the debate surrounding the term *minjung*, among Korean intellectuals during the 1980s and 1990s democratic movements.

5   For a comprehensive examination of the impact of the Kwangju Uprising on modern Korean society, see G.-W. Shin and K. M. Hwang (eds) (2003) *Contentious Kwangju: The May 18 Uprising in Korea's Past and Present*. Lanham: Rowman & Littlefield.

6   The national identity of Korea has been in constant crisis in the twentieth century with Japanese colonial rule (1910–45) in the first half of the century and national division in the latter half of the century. As a 'one ethnicity, one nation', Korean people share a very strong sense of nation in terms of Benedict Anderson's 'imagined community' (1991), and thus, the nationalist movement has struggled throughout the twentieth century to the present day, first, to gain independence, and then to overcome division and reunify the nation.

7   The official history of President Park Chung-Hee's military regime, which lasted eighteen years from 1961–79, was ultra-right anti-communist, and in that period, rapid industrialisation was carried out under the banner of 'modernisation of motherland'. However, in *minjung* historiography, industrialisation only deepened the polarisation between the ruling group and the *minjung*, offering prosperity only to the ruling class and foreign powers. According to Song Kŏn-ho, a dissident journalist, President Park raised the spectre of militaristic, fascist nationalism in conjunction with the development of state capitalism. As an alternative to this 'official' nationalism, Song advocates a *minjung* nationalism that denounces the authority of the two superpowers, who had divided Korea against the will of the people, and their Cold War ideologies (see Choi 1995: 105–7).

8   In his memoir published in the weekly *Cine21*, Lee Jang-ho (1999) wrote that the release of *A Fine, Windy Day* in 1980 served as an opportunity to meet young filmmakers and *minjung* activists. The fans of *A Fine, Windy Day* included aspiring filmmakers, such as Bae Chang-ho, Shin Seung-su, Jang Sun-woo, Kim Hong-joon and Park Kwang-su, all of whom became the leading figures of the Korean New Wave in the late 1980s and 1990s. Bae Chang-ho and Shin Seung-su worked as Lee's assistant directors before making their own social realist films in the early 1980s. At the time, Jang Sun-woo, Kim Hong-joon and Park Kwang-su were members of Yallasŏng, the student film club at Seoul National University. The film club also had a central role in the independent documentary film

movement of the 1990s. Also Lee Dong-chŏl, the author of reportage-type novels such as *Kkobang Villagers* (1981) often came to the theatre to meet Lee Jang-ho. He also introduced Lee to Pastor Hŏ Byŏng-sub who was deeply involved in the urban poor movement. Lee was very much impressed with Pastor Hŏ and all of his films made during this period show his religious influence. Furthermore, Lee also becmae acquaintanced with minjung theatre artists, Im Chin-t'aek, Kim Young-dong and Kim Myŏng-kon, who would all collaborate in Lee's films.

9 In her book, *Contemporary Korean Cinema: Identity, Culture, Politics*, Hyangjun Lee defines the social realist films as 'social commentary films [that] approach individuals essentially as victims of political and historical incidents beyond their control and of the unequal economic structure of the modern Korean society' (2000: 59). Lee argues that the directors of the 1980s saw film as a medium for social criticism and Lee Jang-ho's *A Fine, Windy Day*, *Children of Darkness* and *Declaration of Fools* touched on 'the growing gap between the rich and the poor, class issues and political corruption' (2000: 60).

10 In his book, *Korean Mask Dance* (2005), Cho Dong-il brings it to our attention that the mask dance is a form of drama. He writes: 'Its Korean name, *t'alchum*, literally means "mask dance", referring to only two of the three elements involved, that is, mask, dance and drama; but it still is understood to comprise dramatic elements' (2005: 11).

11 Kim Myŏng-Kon played Yubong, the *p'ansori* singer and the adopted father of Sohwa, in Im Kwon Taek's *Sopyonje* (1993).

Bibliography

Ahmad, A. (1987) 'Jameson's Rhetoric of Otherness and the *National Allegory*', *Social Text: Theory/Culture/Ideology*, 17, 4, 3–25.

Anderson, B. (1991) *Imagined Communities*. New York: Verso.

Cho, D. I. (1979) *Talch'um ŭi Yŏksa wa Wolli* (*The History and the Principles of Mask-Dance*). Seoul: Hong-sŏng sa.

_____ (1997) *K'at'arŭsisŭ, Rasa, Sinmŏngp'uri: Yŏngŭk, Yŏnghwa ŭi Kibon Wolly e taehan Saenggŭk non ŭi Haemyŏng* (*Catharsis, Rasa, Sinmŏngp'uri: Three Principles of Dramatic Arts*). Seoul: Chisik Sanŏb sa.

_____ (2005) *Korean Mask Dance*. Seoul: Ewha University Press.

Choi, C. (1995) 'The Minjung Culture Movement and the Construction of Popular Culture in Korea', in K. M. Wells (ed.) *South Korea's Minjung Movement: The Culture and Politics of Dissidence*. Honolulu: University of Hawaii Press, 105–18.

Choi, I. N. (1979) '*Uridŭl ŭi nŏngk'ul*' (Our Vine), *Ch'unja ŭi Sagye* (*Ch'unja's Four Seasons*). Seoul: Munhak kwa Chisŏng sa, 1979.

Chun, Y. J. (ed.) (1988) *Saeroŭn han'guk yŏnghwarŭl wihayŏ* (*For a New Korean Cinema*). Seoul: Iron kwa silch'ŏn.

Chung, J. C. (1993) *Minjung Munhwa non* (*Theory of Minjung Culture*). Taegu: Yŏngnam University Press.

Ho, H. C. (2000) *Han'guk Yŏnghwa 100 Nyŏn* (100 Years of Korean Cinema). Seoul: Munhak Sasang sa.

Hwang, S. Y. (1979) *Ŏdum ŭi Chasik tŭl* (*Children of Darkness*). Seoul: Hyŏnam sa.

Im, C. T. (1990) *Minjung yŏnhŭi ŭi ch'angjo* (*Creation of Minjung Play*). Seoul: Ch'angjak kwa Pip'yŏng-sa.

Jameson, F. (1986) 'Third-World Literature in the Era of Multinational Capitalism', *Social Text: Theory/Culture/Ideology*, 5, 3, 65–88.

Kim, M. H., ed. (2007) *Korean Cinema from Origins to Renaissance*. Verlag: Communication Books.

Korean Film Archive (2005) *Han'guk Yŏnghwasa Kongbu 1980-1997* (*Korean Cinema Study 1980-1997*). Seoul: Ich'ae.

Lee, J. H. (1999) 'A Fine, Windy Day.' *Cine 21*, 21 December. Available: http://www.cine21.com/Article/article_view.php?mm=005002006&article_id=33701 (accessed on 20 June 2009).

Lee, H. (2000) *Contemporary Korean Cinema: Identity, Culture, Politics*. Manchester: Manchester University Press.

Paik N. C. (1985) *Minjok Munhak kwa Segye Munhak (National Literature and World Literature)*. Seoul: Ch'angjak kwa Pip'yŏng sa.

Shin, G. W. and K. M. Hwang (eds) (2003) *Contentious Kwangju: The May 18 Uprising in Korea's Past and Present*. Lanham: Rowman and Littlefield.

Wells, K. M. (ed.) (1995) *South Korea's Minjung Movement: The Culture and Politics of Dissidence*, Honolulu: University of Hawai'i Press.

Yi H. I. (2001) '1980-nyŏndae han'guk nyu weibŭ e taehan chaep'yŏngka ttonŭn pansŏng (Reassessment or Re-examination of 1980s Korean New Wave Cinema)', in I. Chŏng-t'aek (ed.) *Segye Yŏnghwa-sa Kang'ŭi: Ch'ogi yŏnghwa'esŏ Asia Nyu Weibŭ kkaji* (*History of World Cinema Lectures: from Early Cinema to the Asian New Wave*). Seoul: Yonsei University Press, 309–40.

Yi, H. I. and C. H. Yi (eds) (1996) *Korean New Wave: Retrospective from 1980 to 1995*. Pusan: The First Pusan International Film Festival.

____ (2006) *Han'guk Yŏnghwa Ssitgim (Korean Cinema Washing)*. Seoul: Yŏllin Ch'aek Tŭl.

Yoon K. C. (2000) *Hyŏndae Han'guk ŭi sasang hŭrŭm: chisigin kwa kŭ sasang 1980-90-nyŏndae* (*Contemporary Korean Philosophy and Ideas: Intellectuals and Their Thoughts 1980s-90s*). Seoul: Tangdae.

On How to Tell a Revolution:
Alsino y el cóndor

Robert Dash and Patricia Varas

By the mid-nineteenth century, the ideology of US territorial expansionism in the Western hemisphere was widely subscribed to by many leading public figures. In the most dramatic case of the projection of US power in the mid-century period, the United States engaged Mexico in a war from 1846 to 1848 that resulted in the transfer of sovereignty of nearly one-half of Mexican territory to the United States. With the discovery of gold in California – among the territories that shifted from Mexican to US control in 1848 – interest surged in the building of a Central American trans-isthmian passage that would dramatically reduce the transit time from the US East Coast to its West Coast. Responding to this commercial opportunity, Cornelius Vanderbilt began transporting travellers across Nicaragua in 1853, using its extensive river and lake system.

To support its growing commercial and strategic interests in Nicaragua, US Marines soon followed: 'The first of eleven U.S. interventions … came in 1853 when a contingent of Marines landed on the Atlantic coast to settle a dispute between Vanderbilt's transit company and local Nicaraguan authorities' (LeoGrande 1998: 11). Then, unlike the sending of Marines for brief spells in the nineteenth century, they established long-term presences in Nicaragua from 1912 to 1925 and again from 1927 to 1933. Before the United States departed in 1933, the Marines trained the Nicaraguan Guardia Nacional (National Guard) to ensure a stability that favoured US diplomatic, political and commercial interests and they left Anastasio Somoza García in charge of it. The Somoza family dynasty – father and two sons – ruthlessly dominated Nicaragua until 1979: the pillars of its power were its absolute control of the National Guard, its rapacious command over vast economic resources, its willing-ness to buy off enemies and negotiate political pacts with the bourgeois opposition and the unwavering support of the United States (see Black 1981: 28-45; Gilbert 1988: 4). Early in US/Nicaraguan relations, the Nicaraguan elite became excessively dependent on US diplomatic and economic muscle to maintain a political balance in its favour against more nationalist elements. Writing about other countries in the region but fully describing the situation in Nicaragua, Carlos Castañeda observes that there was 'the sense that the national community [had] been confiscated or sequestered by the "foreigners" and the elite amalgamated into one is undeniable' (1994: 276).

A sweeping political, economic and cultural shift occurred in Nicaragua on 19 July 1979 with the victory of a broad-based insurgency led by the Frente Sandinista de Liberación Nacional (Sandinista National Liberation Front; FSLN) over the Somoza regime. The FSLN, founded in 1961, had adopted Augusto César Sandino, who had fought the US Marines and their Nicaraguan allies to a stalemate during the six-year guerrilla war that ended with the US withdrawal in 1933, as the iconic symbol of its movement. Beyond instituting fundamental political and economic changes, the revolutionary regime introduced and encouraged fresh orientations in traditional artistic practices and the development of new art forms immediately after seizing power (see Ross 1990: 110). The production of cultural artifacts – authentically indigenous as well as new and revolutionary – was to mark the transition from the old to the new order. The Ministry of Culture was created, and through state entities and mass organisations, an explosion of cultural activity – in poetry, music, mural art, artisan work and cinema – characterised the early years of the Revolution. From total *Somocismo* – elitist, aligned with imperialism, repressive, non-indigenous, anti-popular – there was a shift to a revolutionary popular, indigenous, democratic, nationalist, non-aligned and anti-imperialist political culture (see Ross 1990: 120–2). As with Salvador Allende in Chile from 1970 to 1973, Lázaro Cárdenas in Mexico in the late 1930s and Fidel Castro after 1959, the Sandinistas 'made the poor feel at home in their own country and transferred the impression of "foreignness" to the elite [and] for a few scant moments the tables were turned' (Castañeda 1994: 277).

In the closing months of the insurrection against the Somoza regime, the FSLN had established a rudimentary filmmaking unit. With the shift in political power in 1979, film production in Nicaragua surged. While film consumption in Central America can be dated to the early twentieth century, the production of films in Nicaragua had begun only in the late 1970s. 'Before the [Sandinista] revolution, film production in Nicaragua was virtually nil – with the sole exception of the Producine Studios, Somoza's private film company, which specialized in "family albums" for Somoza, training films for the National Guard, and some commercial publicity' (Cortés 2006). The Sandinista regime established the Instituto Nicaragüense de Cine (Nicaraguan Institute of Film; INCINE) on the remnants of Somoza's film production company to produce and disseminate films. INCINE attracted artists from diverse social classes and cultural media, and open discussion and diverse aesthetics marked the institution despite its official links to the FSLN regime (ibid.). INCINE primarily produced newsreels and documentary shorts, reflecting the country's financial and infrastructure constraints, as well as its anti-imperialist goals. Few feature-length and fiction films were produced and thus the production of *Alsino y el cóndor* (1982) by the Chilean director Miguel Littín was notable for being the first Nicaraguan feature film in colour and its most commercially successful film (it was nominated in the United States for the Best Foreign Language Film by the Academy of Motion Picture Arts and Sciences in 1983).

The US film industry's financial power, its potential for mass production and the extensive reach of its widespread distribution networks had facilitated its penetration of Latin America throughout much of the twentieth century. While not constant, the wide reach of the US film industry in the region followed in the wake of and was facilitated by and expressive of the extension of its diplomatic, economic, military and cultural power to the region. The direct backdrop to the development of Nicaragua's INCINE was the rise and fall of 'the new cinema' (*el nuevo cine* in Spanish America, *o cinema novo* in Brazil) that had sunk deep roots in Latin America in the 1950s and 1960s. Following on the heels of the 1959 triumph of the Cuban Revolution, the 'cinema of hunger', the 'imperfect cinema', and the 'Third Cinema' – these labels erroneously pointed to a single regional aesthetic that ostensibly marked Latin America's new cinema, but there was an undeniable sense in which many of the most acclaimed films projected a regional revolutionary utopianism – anticipated that a radical break from the dominant US film industry was both possible and desirable. Very much influenced by the post-World War II Italian neo-realism, the Latin American new cinema was often documentary in style and characterised by low-cost production, location shooting, the expression of cultural nationalism and a socially pertinent discourse (see Aufderheide 1992; Hess 1993: 105–10; King 2000: 66). A general aspiration among Latin American filmmakers for regional cooperation and solidarity in the medium was evident.

Miguel Littín was born in Chile in 1942 and came of age during the effervescence of traditional art forms, popular culture and leftist activism in theatre, music and film in the 1950s and 1960s. He attended the Theatre School of the University of Chile and became a television director and producer, stage director and actor and assistant on several films. Littín joined filmmakers who, strongly influenced by the neo-realist movement, had formed the Grupo Cine Experimental in 1956, expressing a militant commitment to social struggle and to building a new national cinema and cinema forms (see Kovacs 1980: 22; Pick 1987). Salvador Allende named him director of the national production company Chile Films in 1970. The films Littín produced in Chile expressed a politically nationalist and populist point of view and were committed to examining issues of inequality, justice and revolution.[1]

The wave of military dictatorships that swept Latin America's Southern Cone in the 1970s shattered that region's utopian projects, causing many of the key practitioners of the new cinema to cease production, produce inoffensive films, or go into exile. After the *coup d'etat* that ended the Allende regime in September 1973, Littín emigrated to Mexico where his ties to the film community eased his re-entry into the industry. During Luis Echeverría Álvarez's presidential period in office, substantial public financial support was directed towards the Mexican film industry, reviving one of the region's earliest and most influential film industries, one that, subsequent to its Golden Age of the 1940s, had lacked serious filmmaking. During his stay in Mexico, Littín directed *Las Actas de Marusia* (1975), which portrays a massacre of miners in northern Chile in an earlier period and had obvious parallels with the Pinochet years. It was the first Mexican film in many years to be nominated for Best Foreign Language Film by the Academy of Motion Picture Arts and Sciences in 1976 (see Treviño 1979: 26, 31–2); it was also nominated for a Palme d´Or at the Cannes Film Festival and received a Golden Ariel award in Mexico.

At a time when revolutionary projects had been crushed in the rest of Latin America, Central American revolutionary upsurges in Guatemala, El Salvador and Nicaragua from the mid- to late-1970s through the 1980s offered new terrain upon which to practice the cinema of the 1960s (see King 2000: 74). When the Reagan administration entered office in 1981, it quickly identified Central America as a vital element in the East/West Cold War struggle. It established an aggressive policy of supporting pro-US authoritarian regimes with massive aid, training and advising, aiming to weaken and militarily destroy nationalistic and revolutionary regimes and movements in the region (see LaFeber 1984: 271–7). In response, vigorous international anti-interventionist and anti-imperialist movements came to the aid of insurgents in Guatemala and El Salvador and the FSLN in Nicaragua.

A part of the international solidarity movement with the Nicaraguan people, *Alsino y el cóndor* was a financial co-production of Nicaragua, Mexico, Cuba and Costa Rica. It is based on the well-known novel *Alsino*, published in 1920 by the Chilean modernist poet, novelist and essayist Pedro Prado. The thematic backdrop to Littín's film is that of injustice and revolution, but these themes are dealt with indirectly. While some critics see the fashionable Latin American 'magical realism' influencing the film, Zuzana Pick (1987) finds that 'it is a highly personal work that recalls the achievements of Littín's first feature *El chacal de Nahueltoro* (1969)'. Líttín himself said that he wanted to 'make an open film on the movements of struggle in Latin America, because it seems to me that the participation of the North American advisors is much clearer, more obvious now in El Salvador than in the Nicaraguan struggle' (Buchsbaum 2003: 120). Líttín aspired to produce a film that was in part reflective of the broader Central and Latin American struggle and was not just expressive of the singular Nicaraguan experience. On one level, the film is clearly an allegory of political events in Pinochet's Chile (see Aufderheide 1992) where the United States had played a direct and influential role in encouraging and supporting the military coup against Allende. The film retains some of the optimism of the early stages of the new Latin American cinema, that both nationalist and internationalist projects could transform the region's dominance by US imperialism.

Pedro Prado's modernist masterpiece *Alsino* is one of his most innovative and widely acclaimed works. This poem in prose breaks from the traditional *criollista* (regionalist) or realist narrative in vogue at the time. The story of Alsino captures the harsh reality of the Chilean countryside in a lyrical and magical manner. Alsino dreams of flying and to this end he is always jumping off trees and hills. One day he has a great fall and becomes very ill with his broken back developing a hump. After being consumed by a fever, he decides to leave home and wander the world. During his travels and adventures he is constantly made fun of because of his hump. But he will discover that these travails are necessary, as the hump metamorphoses into two beautiful wings. Alsino can now fly and be free, yet he still suffers many misadventures that issue from the shallowness and greed of humankind. His contact with nature is almost Orphic but his knowledge of herbs, which he learnt from his grandmother, does not allow him to save his beloved Abigaíl from death. After becoming famous for his curative powers, he meets Rosa who falls in love with him and pours a potion on his eyes that instead of making him fall in love with her blinds him for life. Alsino decides after all his suffering and loneliness to take his last blind flight by mounting the skies up high and descending down to earth at great speed. Consumed by fire, people on earth mistake him for a falling star.

There are many interpretations of the universal and allegorical meanings inscribed in Prado's *Alsino*. For Lucía Guerra-Cunningham, the novel exemplifies Christian transcendence. Even though Alsino could fly and free himself from worldly ties, as Christ did he must descend back to humankind to affirm his divinity, and Alsino's earthly pains, rendered by those who are in touch with him, confirm his suffering (1983: 33). The end of his mortal body should not be interpreted as a tragedy, according to Guerra-Cunningham, since it guarantees Alsino's spiritual transcendence and immortality (1983: 37).

Another interpretation is that Alsino, a child, undergoes a process of initiation marked by the metamorphosis of his hump into wings through which, like Icarus, he develops extraordinary possibilities. Again, the allegorical interpretation dominates. Alsino is a myth-like character, a universal or archetypal symbol that marks the importance of ritual in the process of becoming a grown up, a fully developed person psychologically and physically. In this manner, Alsino can be any young man who confronts challenges and even death to develop into a man who consorts with nature and has discovered himself (see Aponte 1983: 146).

Nature plays an important role throughout the novel as a romantic component echoed by the lyrical language employed to sing Alsino's triumphs and defeats. The use of mythology also dominates the symbolic structure of the novel. At the same time, however, there is a realist element that directs the detailed descriptions of the geography of the Chilean coastal range in the province of Curicó. Even though Alsino may appear as a rare and immortal being, he succumbs to carnal impulses, feeling sexual desire, falling in love with Abigaíl, becoming drunk, and inflicting violence on others. In *Alsino*, many of the grim aspects of rural life appear: the pervasive poverty, the violent family life Alsino and his brother, Poli, live, and the avarice and ignorance of the people who first believe Alsino's hump will bring them luck and then discriminate against him because of his wings. Others perceive the wings as a potential business venture where Alsino can be exhibited as a freak.

Undoubtedly, Littín would have been familiar with Prado's literary classic and he must have felt that the universal message of struggling and remaining steadfast in order to achieve one's dreams could apply to the struggle of the Nicaraguan people in particular and to the Central American state of affairs in general during the 1980s. Littín retains the name and main character of *Alsino* for his film: the young boy who has a dream and remains restless until he achieves it. There are also other significant elements from the novel that appear in the film: the difficult life of *campesinos* in the countryside; the grandmother who takes care of Alsino and who is known for her curative powers with herbs; Alsino's travels and adventures; his meeting up with the bird seller; the *leonero* (lion hunter); and his first night of love. Overall, Littín has remained faithful to the message of the novel, which is the right to dream and to be free.

This universal message acquires clear ideological intention when brought to the Sandinista reality. If at the beginning of the FSLN project, cinema's main relevance was its 'potential for raising money to purchase arms' (Burton 1986: 70) and as an instrument to increase international solidarity, the FSLN became aware early of the profound importance of cinema in the revolution; cinema was to become a vehicle to recuperate national identity (see Buchsbaum 2003: 98) and 'to document the involvement of the masses during the process of liberation' (Burton 1986: 70).

However, while the Nicaraguan audience's reaction to *Alsino y el cóndor* was generally positive, some Sandinista intellectuals were harshly critical, pointing out that some of the principal characters in the film had non-Nicaraguan (Argentine, Cuban, Mexican and Chilean) accents and appearances and that the portrayal of Somoza's Guardia Nacional using East German trucks (that were supplied only in the 1980s to the Sandinistas) did not take place during the (pre-1979) insurgency (see Buchsbaum 2003: 119). Moreover, while the horrifically brutal behaviour of Somoza's National Guard certainly included several massacres of innocent civilians in the 1960s and 1970s, the film's portrayal of two large massacres of civilians more directly resembles events that occurred in El Salvador early in the 1980s.[2] Finally, the participation of US military advisors in Somoza's anti-insurgency campaign was far less significant than the central role they would later play in the *contra* war that the Reagan administration would launch against the FSLN government in the 1980s and in the US campaign to defeat the leftist insurgency in El Salvador.

The title of the film itself refers to the (Andean) condor, reminding the viewer of Operation Condor, a program – that the United States supported and facilitated – of South American security and intelligence agencies to eliminate left-wing opposition groups in their countries in the 1970s. As Jonathan Buchsbaum points out, the issue for Littín was to make an allegorical statement about the struggle of the Nicaraguan people that could be far reaching and applied to the rest of the region (2003: 119). For some Nicaraguans, this metaphoric outreach created a mix of national and foreign markers that contradicted their reality; 'the dissonances told Nicaraguans that the story wasn't Nicaraguan, and both the associations and expectations provoked by the film led to the rejection of the film by many of those critics' (ibid.).

Littín in *Alsino y el cóndor* has a dual aesthetic and ideological task as he faces two narrative purposes and two very different kinds of audiences. First, he wants to tell a story, universal in origin, but local in scope. Second, he must solve the problem of how to tell a story of the revolution in an engaging manner to Nicaraguans while also reaching out to a broader and less knowledgeable regional and international public in an appeal for solidarity. Littín effectively addresses both publics by opting for a narrative structure that applies a child's point of view, traumatic narrative, oral elements that recall the fable, and a lyrical language – music and sound – that support fragmented images. This narrative approach is unusual in political films. Furthermore, the film succeeds in transforming viewers into active agents who sympathise with the plight of the actors.

Nevertheless, Littín confronts important narrative and filmic challenges in his adaptation of Prado's *Alsino*: how to transform a highly lyrical and fragmented modernist novel into a filmic discourse about revolutionary national identity for an audience with scant cinematic culture? And, how to remain faithful to the Nicaraguan Revolution while making a broader statement about popular struggle in Latin America? Littín uses several strategies throughout the film, among them Alsino's voice-over and his traumatised point of view, to erase the inevitable fissures that appear when transforming a universal and modernist narrative into a political film about the Sandinista Revolution; if he was successful or not in doing so is still up for discussion.

Littín has borrowed from the novel some of its most folkloric episodes, which can turn into a sort of charming fairytale and make for good storytelling: the poor boy who lives with his grandmother, dreams of flying, and perseveres in that dream; the countryside as background with the emblematic tree from which Alsino falls and cripples himself; his adventures in the world; and Alsino's final realisation of what freedom entails. Littín does away with the magical component in the film, as Alsino never succeeds in flying other than in a helicopter, making this desire a highly symbolic and collective feeling that can become true only in an ideological and historical manner through the revolution. Littín adds to the film two emblematic components that become important narrative bridges in the plot: Alsino's drawings and his grandfather's postcards and pictures in a trunk echo as important memories for the traumatised child, and the background of the war locates the narration before the Sandinista triumph against Somoza. He also develops a parallel story to Alsino's that follows the activities of the two US advisers working with the National Guard.

Vladimir Propp's (1968) structuralist approach to the morphology of the fable resonates in Alsino's pursuit of flying. Alsino is obsessed with flying as we can see from his games and conversation with his childhood friend Lucía. After his fall from a formidable tree and after being on the verge of death, Alsino, crippled with a hump (his wound or mark), leaves home to sell the family's old horse, a quest that resembles the hero's. This voyage into the outside world takes place through a series of events with a cyclical structure. He is tested many times as people tease or pity him because of his hump, calling him insulting names. Alsino meets a series of popular characters: the bird seller who dislocates his birds' wings so that they can't escape, the men who get him drunk, and the prostitute with a golden heart who sleeps with him like a mother. The bird seller is an intriguing character whose dress, manner and job reminds the viewer of characters in fairy tales, as he ambulates from town to town selling his birds.[3] But the bird seller exploits Alsino the most, despite also revealing his secret of how to keep the birds from flying away. After promising him 'easy fortune', the bird seller makes him work without pay. Alsino also meets the principal US adviser, who invites him to fly in his helicopter and tells him that if he pursues education then he too may one day fly helicopters. Through these meetings, the film follows Alsino's personal and political growth. Since Alsino could never really fly, his magical power lies in his strong belief that he some day will be able to do so, a metaphor for his freedom. Echoing his name, *al=alas*/wings, *sino*=destiny, Alsino is destined to be free.

Each adventure in the film acquires a mythical tone, orally narrated with prologues and endings full of interjections that remind us of 'tall tales', as well as of the possibility that those could have taken place. As Linda Dégh claims: 'and this is actually correct: the tale – not necessarily the narrated content but its expressed social message – is true' (1995: 37). Each of Alsino's adventures connects the fable world with reality, giving the story authenticity with which the public can identify and sympathise. Stories are important to awaken people to action: 'When authorities are unyielding, storytelling sustains groups as they fight for reform, helping them build new collective identities, link current actions to heroic pasts and glorious futures, and restyle setbacks as way stations to victory' (Polletta 2006: 3).

The villains in this tale are US military advisers and the Somocista army. We see the latter rounding up and massacring villagers, while a US military helicopter, painted with the claws of an eagle (or as the film's title insinuates, of a condor), circles overhead in order to detect and destroy any subversives; all of this takes place in a recurring manner. The principal US adviser offers Alsino a ride in the helicopter and promises him that some day he will be like him, educated and able to fly. But Alsino is well aware that this is not the kind of flight he is seeking; he wants to fly by himself like a bird, rejecting thereby any influence or help from the imperialist forces. Alsino shows an incipient consciousness of the need to exercise one's will, to understand the burden of his chosen mark, the hump, and to continue his development as a subject-in-formation through his adventures and search.

In the end, Alsino reaches a river on his trip back home where he finds the remains of the circus he had seen perform during his travels and witnesses a massacre of civilians by the National Guard. He finds his grandmother dying, his village destroyed, the schoolteacher and Lucía's father killed (because he was a guerrilla fighter) and his tree destroyed by the fallen helicopter of the US adviser which had been shot down by the revolutionary forces. Now alone, Alsino goes in search of Manuel, the *nom de guerre* of a *guerrillero*. He is invited to join the Sandinistas, who accept him with no comments regarding his hump and simply ask the '*compita*' (little companion) his name. Alsino's personal and ideological growth is confirmed when the hunchback with a huge smile full of hope exuberantly raises his Kalashnikov assault rifle – the weapon of choice for third world guerrilla forces – over his head and declares that his name is 'Manuel'. In this symbolic gesture, he chooses to identify himself with the collective struggle against Somoza, fulfilling his true destiny.

The structure of the tale allows the viewer to engage with Alsino's plight. The film's use of music by the Cuban Leo Brouwer, of a poetic language that may sometimes sound odd in the mouth of a young *campesino* boy and of fragmented shots, creates a dream-like quality that is punctuated by the direct shots of the collective massacres and tombs, the floating victims in the river and the war scenes that return the viewer to the cruel reality of the conflict. The point of view and voice-over of Alsino dominate throughout these divergent scenes. Alsino's voice has a robotic quality, lacking any inflection or real emotion, making us realise that this child is no longer surprised by the carnage that surrounds him, as he has become the victim of trauma.

A child's point of view ensures that an innocent perspective, an honesty that tells all and hides nothing, dominates the account. This 'pure' witness, however, is powerless or marginalised by his age. This child is not an agent; things happen to him, as he does not initiate any events. Yet he compensates for his lack of power through his imagination and memory; Alsino yearns to fly and to reconstruct his family and history through the pictures and postcards in his grandmother's trunk. Eventually his true empowerment will come when he joins the revolutionary forces. Tyrus Miller, in his excellent study on European cinema and children's presence as historical witnesses, argues that children can find empowerment not through action but through the passion of their beliefs, which manifest themselves in film through a magnified sensorial experience: 'The intensification of sensory experience that compensates for the loss of active agency and the dream-like indiscernibility of subjective and objective dimensions of the experience point beyond passive witnessing towards a new domain of agency residing in imaginative processes' (2003: 213). We see this happening with Alsino's intense flying dream and obsession that makes him jump from the tree.

The repetitive structure of the tale takes us back to its oral initiation and ritualistic origins. However, there is another important narrative construction that requires a cyclical structure to represent a damaged psyche by a stressful reality: trauma narrative. Anne Whitehead holds that 'one of the key strategies in trauma fiction is the device of repetition, which can act at the levels of language, imagery or plot. Repetition mimics the effects of trauma, for it suggests the insistent return of the event and the disruption of narrative chronology or progression' (2004: 86). Littín grasps the aesthetic qualities of the oral fable, which is firmly established in the community's tradition, and merges it with the effects of trauma, which afflict not only Alsino but also the Nicaraguan nation.

There is an apparent struggle between the repetitious cycle of the fable, which is full of creativity and the attractive recalling of a communal past, and the negative individualist stasis of melancholia and Freudian nostalgia brought about by a trauma that has not been resolved. But in *Alsino y el cóndor*, this tension is resolved because Alsino is a child and thus his personal history is in the making. Alsino is eventually able to differentiate between the specificity of loss (the destruction of his village, the death of his grandmother, his broken body) and the trans-historic universal experience of absence (the inability to fly). Even more, the traumatic memory of historic events characterised by repression, torture and death does not dominate the boy as his imagination and the fable-like events allow him to achieve some understanding of his historical circumstances and prompt him to effective action: joining the armed struggle. Alsino, the child, becomes a symbol of something new, of hope counterposed to the chaotic and violent world created by adults. Children, as Miller sustains, are tools 'to approach artistically the intractable historical situation' (2003: 231).

Alsino y el cóndor is Littín's effort to represent and interpret not only Nicaraguan history but that of the Latin American region as well. Cinema is a compelling means through which events from the past can be rendered to understand what actually happened and to respond to the need of recounting the horrors of war. Littín mixed the traditional tale structure with the more innovative trauma narrative as a legitimate manner of capturing the Nicaraguan revolutionary war and positing the ability to remember it. As pointed out above, however, some Sandinistas were critical of Littín's interpretations as rendered in the film.

Buchsbaum recounts the roundtable discussion that took place among some Sandinista intellectuals in the presence of the Chilean director. What was acerbically criticised 'was not the film's politics but its not adhering to reality' (2003:119). The critics did not argue that the need to experience the event was necessary in order to be able to represent it authentically. They did fear, however, the aesthetisation effects on the war, of making it a 'plot' for the filmic narrative. In a 1987 interview that appeared in *Cineaste*, a Nicaraguan filmmaker asserts that 'we want our fiction films to be part of our reality, not to be fictional scripts conceived from nothing ... We don't want to resort to foreign literature, but to begin from our own reality, from real situations' (see Dratch and Margolis 1987: 28). This position would appear to refer to *Alsino y el cóndor*.

Littín aspires to 'draw on the Nicaraguan struggle and make a more general, even allegorical statement about popular struggle in Latin America' (Buchsbaum 2003:

119). He seems nevertheless, when adapting Prado's *Alsino* to the Nicaraguan reality, to have forgotten one vital premise in filmic discourse: 'unlike the word, the filmic image cannot abstract and generalize' (Rosenstone 1995: 8). Littín's merging of different temporal and geographical episodes and genres may work aesthetically for him. The modernist gesture of bringing together different genres and moments, however, has an outcome quite contrary to Littín's objective. As Hayden White has argued regarding the modernist legacy in film and literature, the event as a building block of history is erased, 'undermin[ing] the very concept of factuality and threaten[ing] therewith the distinction between realistic and merely imaginary discourse' (1996: 18). This is precisely what the Sandinistas criticised; they felt their history had been fictionalised and that there was no mediation to allow the public to distinguish between real and imaginary events. The facts that appear in the film – the massacres, the common executions and tombs, the US involvement, the people's support of the struggle – lose their significant meaning as actual events that happened and rather acquire an allegorical connotation open to the public's interpretation.

One specific criticism made by Nicaraguan critics of the film is worth pursuing in detail. In *Alsino y el cóndor*, the principal US adviser initially appears to wrestle with his conscience, profoundly disgusted by the excesses committed by the National Guard against the civilian population and its general lack of professionalism. Littín, thinking of documentaries he had seen on US Vietnam veterans, claims that he wanted to humanise the 'villains', to present them as full of contradictions and complex feelings (Buchsbaum 2003: 119). Littín's critics felt deeply that the National Guard and US advisers engaged in inhuman behaviour and were completely guilt-free regarding their actions, and that the representation of them in the film was contrary to Nicaraguan reality.

Yet in effect, the two narratives, the fable and the trauma, vie for attention in *Alsino y el cóndor*, producing a shift from the local to a universal and trans-historical story in which Alsino's dream of flying becomes Latin America's aspiration to be free of US intervention and imperialism. Alsino becomes Manuel, an archetype of the *guerrillero* and of any person fighting against postcolonial powers. Littín succeeds in constructing a gripping narrative about the insurgency and the suffering of the Nicaraguan people. Popular audiences in Nicaragua received the film enthusiastically (see Buchsbaum 2003: 118) and internationally it was successfully shown as part of the effort to generate support for the revolutionary project. By mixing two contrasting genres and creating both a realist and fictionalised reality, viewers can approach a bleak moment that otherwise might be overwhelming in the depth of its atrocity.

On the one hand, the structure of the fable responds to the oral tradition of rural Nicaragua. On the other hand, trauma narrative articulates the complex challenge of how to articulate the ineffable consequences of massacres, clandestine burials and torture. Thus, viewers can see, feel, and react to Alsino's story in a more open and personal manner without imposing a single meaning and without falling into a victimisation mode. The viewing public understands through the film that history is constructed by not only facts but also by subjective interpretations and narratives. Littín borrowed Prado's character, whom Gabriela Mistral (DIBAM 2007) had praised as the Chilean fictionalised child,[4] to not only protest but also to raise political consciousness and to launch a call to action against US intervention throughout Central America in the 1980s. Becoming Manuel, the 'Nicaraguan child', Alsino represents and immortalises a whole community on fire. *Alsino y el cóndor* proposes that there are many ways to tell a revolution and that cinema must use as many strategies as possible if it is to successfully engage the public.

Notes

1. These features are evident in his first full-length feature film, *El Chacal de Nahueltoro* (1969), which recounted the horrific murder by a landless *campesino* of his common-law wife and her children. Based on an event that took place in Chile early in the 1960s, the film portrays the marginal and oppressed existence that characterised many of Chile's rural poor in the 1960s.

2. The massacres at the Sumpul River and in the village of El Mozote, both in El Salvador, seemed to have been the direct exemplars for those in the film. 'On 14 May 1980, units of [El Salvador's] Military Detachment No. 1, the National Guard and the paramilitary Organización Nacional Democrática (ORDEN) deliberately killed at least 300 non-combatants, including women and children, who were trying to flee to Honduras across the Sumpul river' and on '10 December 1981, in the village of El Mozote, [El Salvador] units of the [US-trained] Atlacatl Battalion detained, without resistance, all the men, women and children who were in the place. The following day, 11 December, after spending the night locked in their homes, they were deliberately and systematically executed in groups' (United States Institute of Peace 2007).

3. In the novel, the bird seller allows his birds to walk and to follow him as a sort of Hamlin flautist, attracting people with this semi-magical ritual.

4. Thereby joining the circle of other 'national children' such as Sweden's Nils Holgersson, England's Peter Pan, Mark Twain's Huckleberry Finn, and Spain's Lazarillo de Tormes.

Bibliography

Aponte, B. (1983) 'El rito de la iniciación en el cuento hispanoamericano', *Hispanic Review*, 51, 2, 129–46.

Aufderheide, P. (1992) 'Cross-Cultural Film Guide: Films from Africa, Asia and Latin America at The American University'. *American University* website. Available: http://www.library.american.edu/subject/media/aufderheide/alsino.html (accessed on 29 November 2006).

Black, G. (1981) *Triumph of the People: The Sandinista Revolution in Nicaragua*. London: Zed Press.

Buchsbaum, J. (2003) *Cinema and the Sandinistas: Filmmaking in Revolutionary Nicaragua*. Austin: University of Texas Press.

Burton, J. (1986) 'Emilio Rodríguez Vázquez and Carlos Vicente Ibarra (Puerto Rico and Nicaragua): Filmmaking in Nicaragua: From Insurrection to INCINE' [interview], in J. Burton (ed.) *Cinema and Social Change in Latin America: Conversations with Filmmakers*. Austin: University of Texas Press, 69–79.

Castañeda, J. G. (1994) *Utopia Unarmed: The Latin American Left after the Cold War*. New York: Vintage.

Cortés, M. L. (2006) 'Centroamérica en celudoide. Mirada a un cine oculto'. *Istmo: Revista virtual de estudios literarios y culturales centroamericanos*. Available: http://www.denison.edu/collaborations/istmo/articulos/celuloide.html (accessed on 29 November 2006).

Dégh, L. (1995) *Narratives in Society: A Performer-Centered Study of Narration*. Helsinki: Suomalainen Tiedeakatemia.

DIBAM. Dirección de bibliotecas, archivos y museos (2007) *Memoria chilena*. Available: http://www.memoriachilena.com/mchilena01//temas/index.asp?id_ut=alsino (accessed on 28 July 2007).

Dratch, H. and B. Margolis (1987) 'Film and Revolution in Nicaragua. An Interview with INCINE Filmmakers', *Cineaste*, 15, 3, 27–9.

Gilbert, D. (1988) *Sandinistas: The Party and the Revolution*. Cambridge, MA: Blackwell.

Guerra-Cunningham, L. (1983) 'La aventura del héroe como presentación de la visión de mundo en *Alsino* de Pedro Prado', *Hispania*, 66, 1, 32–9.

Hess, J. (1993) 'Neo-Realism and New Latin American Cinema: *Bicycle Thieves* and *Blood of the Condor*', in J. King, A. M. López and M. Alvarado (eds) *Mediating Two Worlds: Cinematic Encounters in the Americas*. London: British Film Institute, 104–18.

King, J. (2000) *Magical Reels: A History of Cinema in Latin America*. 2nd edition. London and New York: Verso.

Kovacs, K. S. (1980) 'Miguel Littín's *Recurso del Método*: The Aftermath of Allende', *Film Quarterly*, 33, 3, 22–9.

LaFeber, W. (1984) *Inevitable Revolutions: The United States in Central America*. Expanded edition. New York: W.W. Norton.

LeoGrande, W. M. (1998) *Our Own Backyard: The United States in Central America, 1977–1992*. Chapel Hill: University of North Carolina Press.

Miller, T. (2003) 'The Burning Babe: Children, Film Narrative, and the Figures of Historical Witness', in A. Douglass and T. A. Vogler (eds) *Witness and Memory: The Discourse of Trauma*. New York and London: Routledge, 207–32.

Pick, Z. M. (1987) 'Chilean Cinema: Ten Years of Exile (1973–83)', *Jump Cut: A Review of Contemporary Media*, 32, 66–70. Available: http://www.ejumpcut.org/archive/onlineessays/JC32folder/ChileanFilm (accessed on May 1, 2007).

Polletta, F. (2006) *It Was Like a Fever: Storytelling in Protest and Politics*. Chicago: University of Chicago Press.

Propp, V. (1968) *Morphology of the Folktale*. Trans. L. Scott. 2nd edition. Austin: University of Texas Press.

Rosenstone, R. A. (1995) 'Introduction', in R. A. Rosenstone (ed.) *Revisioning History: Film and the Construction of a New Past*. Princeton: Princeton University Press, 3–13.

Ross, P. (1990) 'Cultural Policy in a Transitional Society: Nicaragua 1979-89', *Third World Quarterly*, 12, 2, 110–29.

Treviño, J. S. (1979) 'The New Mexican Cinema', *Film Quarterly*, 32, 3, 26–37.

United States Institute of Peace (2007) *Truth Commissions Digital Collection. Reports: El Salvador*. Available: http://www.usip.org/library/tc/doc/reports/el_salvador/tc_es_03151993_casesC.html (accessed on 27 July 2007).

White, H. (1996) 'The Modernist Event', in V. Sobchack (ed.) *The Persistence of History: Cinema, Television, and the Modern Event*. New York: Routledge, 17–38.

Whitehead, A. (2004) *Trauma Fiction*. Edinburgh: Edinburgh University Press.

Storytelling and Postcolonialism

Telling Stories About Unknown People in Faraway Countries: US Travelogues About Mexico in the 1930s and 1940s

Isabel Arredondo

Film travelogues of the 1930s and 1940s were seen as opportunities for the audience to travel. In *Zapotec Village* (1941), for instance, the narrator comments: 'We are visiting a village; only Zapotec live here.' By using the term 'visiting', the narrator invites the audience to participate in a virtual voyage to the faraway world of the matriarchal Tehuantepec, where women approve marriages and assemble their own trousseaus.[1] Jeffrey Ruoff defines travelogues as films whose main purpose is to travel in space and time (2006: 13), and distinguishes four periods in the production of travelogues. The second period, which begins in 1905 and ends before World War II, is characterised by a strong interest in ethnographic issues (2006: 1). This chapter discusses US travelogues from the second period that portray life in remote indigenous villages in Mexico, analysing the travelogues' narrative strategies and examining the social context in which they were shown.

Since the 1980s, ethnographic writing has been scrutinised within the academy. For instance, James Clifford's *The Predicament of Culture: Twentieth-Century Ethnography, Literature, and Art* (1988) disputed ethnography's claim to objectivity, proposing that this methodological strategy included assumptions and specific narrative strategies. Clifford supported his claim by analysing the narrative structures of travel and ethnographic accounts. Some scholars have also claimed that other academics have imposed their own meaning when collecting tales and stories from other cultures, which is seen as colonising practice. In *Native American Life-history Narratives: Colonial and Postcolonial Navajo Ethnography* (2007), Brill de Ramírez and Susan Berry suggest that in their attempt to be objective and scientific, collectors of tales distort their meaning, a claim that was already suggested in Harold Scheub's *Story* (1998).[2] The same claim has been made about travellers to distant places. In '"The Whole World Within Reach": Travel Images Without Borders' (2006), Tom Gunning analyses travelogues filmed in the first decades of the twentieth century, and presents the act of recording images while travelling as a colonising and imperial practice in which the traveller appropriates images of another culture and brings them back home as a trophy. With these images, I propose, the traveller makes stories which, as Scheub says, are 'at the heart of the way humans see themselves, experience themselves within the context of their worlds' (1998: 21). This chapter draws on the critical approaches to ethnography and travel, and on Scheub's understanding of storytelling, to propose that travelogues are storytelling sessions for US audiences. The most important questions in this regard are: What stories do travelogues tell, and what do these stories mean in the context of the US audience of the 1930s and 1940s?

To consider these questions, I have selected two groups of travelogues from the 1930s and 1940s as case studies. The first group was made with the footage shot for a film to be called *Qué viva México!*. In 1930, US novelist Upton Sinclair, through the Mexican Trust Fund, backed a trip to Mexico made by three Russians: Sergei Eisenstein, Eduard Tissé and Gregory Alexandrov. Initially, the group was going to make a travelogue, and with that goal in mind, the three Russians travelled to the Isthmus of Tehuantepec, Yucatán and Central Mexico. Travelling by car, train and on foot, the group shot many images, among them scenes of Mexican festivities and religious celebrations.[3] However, upon their return from Mexico, Eisenstein was not allowed to edit the film, as originally planned, and part of the footage was made into travelogues.[4]

The first group of travelogues examined here had different creators. Wanting to recover the Mexican Trust Fund's investment, Sinclair hired Sol Lesser to use the part of the footage that contained ethnographic images to make the travelogue *Death Day* (1933). By the late 1930s, when the price of holding the *Qué viva México!* film stock and paying for the insurance became burdensome, Sinclair began to sell the film stock by the foot. In 1939 he sold footage to the Bell and Howell Company. They hired William. F. Kruse and Egon Mauthner to edit six educational films: *Mexico Marches*, *Conquering Cross*, *Idol of Hope*, *Land of Freedom*, and *Spaniard and Indian*, which were collected under the title *Mexican Symphony* (1939). In the same year Bell and Howell also edited a separate travelogue entitled *Zapotec Village*. Archival research shows that while Sinclair might have helped Lesser with the writing of the voice-over narration for *Death Day*, he most likely did not participate in the writing of *Mexican Symphony* or *Zapotec Village*.[5]

Industrialist Harry Wright (1876–1954) made the second group of travelogues studied in this chapter. A wealthy US businessman who lived in Mexico most of his life (though without learning Spanish), Wright was also an avid global traveller who made his own amateur travelogues, built his own private theatres and owned one of the largest private collections of 16mm film of his time.[6] He hired photographer Edwin Forgan Myers to travel to indigenous communities in Oaxaca, Chiapas, Quintana Roo, Puebla and Hidalgo to shoot material for sixteen travelogues. In the introduction to Wright's travelogues, Myers is presented as an adventurer who faces many perils in exploring remote locations. The locales portrayed in Wright's series were often accessible only by a mule ride of several days.

Wright's travelogues were shot in 16mm between 1939 and 1941 and were organised into two series: *The Harry Wright Ethnographic Series: Indian Tribes of Unknown Mexico* and *Harry Wright's Mexican Indian Series*.[7] By looking at his series side by side with the ethnographic films in his collection, such as J. G. Swafford's *Malayan Ceremonials: Strange Customs in the Malayan Archipielago* (1930) and *Bits of Africa: Railways, Cotton Plantations and Copper Mines* (1930), one can conclude that Wright had some of the same assumptions and used similar strategies to those used in other US travelogues and ethnographic films of the period.[8]

Narrative strategies of travelogues

Influenced by literature and ethnography, travelogues from the 1930s and 1940s are episodic, non-narrative films organised around a place. Unlike fictional films, the travelogue does not follow a dramatic storyline or cause-and-effect organisation, but 'brings together scenes without regard for plot or narrative progression' (Ruoff 2006: 11). Indeed, Jennifer Peterson has argued that the characteristic that sets travelogues apart from other types of films is their organisation around a place; in travelogues she says: 'the trip is the organizing principle that structures the film' (1998: 2). Sinclair mentions the importance of the trip to give shape to the travelogue in a letter that he sent to Eisenstein on 16 December 1930, while Eisenstein was still in Mexico. In the letter, Sinclair writes: 'You want some kind of story on which to string your pictures, and I find myself thinking continually of a Mexican lad brought up in a mountain-village […] He could see various aspects of Mexico: he could go from the mountains to the jungles, visit cities, etc' (cited in Geduld and Gottesman 1970: 32). Despite the inclusion of the narrative, the different places the boy visits are the main objective of the film; place is the regulating principle of travelogues, and everything else is subordinated to it.

Travelogues from the 1930s and 1940s were much influenced by literature, borrowing narrative strategies from novels. Ruoff explains that 'during the hegemonic period of the studio system, the travelogue kept alive the loose narrative aspects of the picaresque in movies' (2006: 11). In the same letter from Sinclair to Eisenstein mentioned above, we can observe loose aspects of a picaresque technique, in which a picaro has adventures that lead him to different places. The novelist proposes that the boy: 'for some reason or other, is impelled to go out and see the world in search for something. In the course of the search he will, of course, meet some girl, or maybe more than one, and be impelled to go back to the place where the girl is staying' (cited in Geduld and Gottesman 1970: 32). In Sinclair's letter, the love of a girl gives the picaro a reason to move from place to place. However, the picaresque strategies are always to be subordinated to the main goal of the travelogue: showing the audience different places and people in distant countries.

Travelogues tend to be episodic, following the picaro's adventures in different places. This aspect surfaces in Eisenstein's response to Sinclair. The filmmaker responds to the 16 December 1930 letter, saying that, 'the difficulties are just in that the picture is *not* a "travelogue" ... in which scenes, bits and episodes are following just the railroad order of stations' (ibid.; emphasis in original). The Russian director is aware that travelogues are organised according to episodes, which he pejoratively describes as 'the railroad order of stations'.

Travelogues are also influenced by ethnography. As opposed to literature or picaresque films, where the body of the traveller is present, in ethnographic films, the body of the traveller/ethnographer disappears from the film. The influence of ethnography explains why, in some travelogues, the different episodes of the trip become independent, and are presented as separate elements of an ethnographic series. Despite the fact that in Wright's ethnographic series Myers is introduced at the beginning of the films and also appears on screen in several episodes, his trip from community to community is omitted. This omission, however, does not disturb travelogues' organisation around space. Each episode follows the movement of Meyer as he enters the community he is visiting. The first shots tend to be panoramic views of the community accompanied by an off-screen voice telling the viewers the general characteristics of the specific community being observed. For instance, *Otomi Indians Poison Their Fish* begins with panoramic views of a community in Puebla's Sierra Norte, followed up by shots of women weavers whom Meyer encounters on the outskirts of the community. As he passes by, the voice-over announces that what we are seeing are 'ancient tribal customs and industries'. Afterwards, the camera is stationed at the river to witness the ceremony of fishing. The audience sees a group of Otomi males as they create a barricade in the river, gather mexcal leaves, pound the leaves to pulp and put the pulp in the river to blind the fish. In the Otomí episode, as well as in other episodes, the body of Meyer disappears from view leaving only a first-person commentary. The practice of not having a dialogue but a first-person narrative is linked to the development of sound technology and to travelogue conventions.

The voice of the traveller/lecturer

As previously stated, travelogues from the 1930s and 1940s have a distinctive voice-over narration. This is a result of difficulties in recording sound, stylistic conventions in travelling accounts and the influence of ethnography. As synchronised sound developed in the 1930s, studio-made films incorporated diegetic sound, music and dialogue. This was not the case, however, for travelogues and films shot in remote locations. When talking about the unfinished film *The Forgotten Village* (1941), John Steinbeck explains that 'sound recorded at the scene [the Mexican pueblo of Santiago] was impracticable' (Steinbeck et al. 1941). Even in the late 1930s, sound equipment was so heavy that it could not be taken to remote villages, as the villages were only accessible by mule or on foot; for that reason, sound was incorporated in post-production. In the 1940s, Wright added sound in Hollywood studios to the footage that Myers took in the mid-1930s in Mexico,[9] and sound was also incorporated during post-production in the *Qué viva México!* travelogues.

While voice-over narration is partly a product of the technological difficulties of sound recording in the 1930s and 1940s, this practice can also be related to the conventions of travelling accounts. Burton Holmes (1870–1958), one of the most famous early travelogue makers, collected his images in the summer and gave lectures in the winter.[10] In some cases, travelogues maintain the first-person narrative of the adventurer. In Wright's *Rain Fiesta of the Tzotil Indians*, filmed in Huixtán, Chiapas, for instance, the voice-over complains that he has been waiting a long time for the celebration to begin. This comment is intended to be Meyer's personal observation; the sentiment expressed in the voice-over coincides with that of the adventurer who visited the Tzotil.

The voice-over narration in travelogues from the 1930s and 1940s is also a vestige of the voice of the travelling lecturer in an educational setting. For the most part, travelogues were not exhibited in commercial theatres but in educational milieus. In the late 1800s and early 1900s, before mass tourism was available, and at a time when knowing about the world was considered cultural capital, travelogues were used as educational tools (see Ruoff 2006: 2–6). In the earliest sessions, the lecturer used photographs made into slides ('magic lantern shows') to illustrate the lecture. In the first decades of the twentieth century, the voice of the lecturer giving the presentation accompanied film clips. Holmes, for example, engaged in this practice while touring the US giving lectures about his expeditions. With the incorporation of the commentary of the lecturer into the soundtrack, lecturers disappear. Thus, the voice-over commentary of travelogues is a convention originating from the narration given by the travelling lecturer who used to be present at the time of exhibition.

In some cases, the voice-over is subjective. *Zapotec Village*, for instance, incorporates a personal narrative together with ethnographic information. As the camera shows a necklace of flowers similar in shape to a necklace of coins which is typically worn by married women from the Istmus of Tehuantepec, the voice-over comments: 'Rosa is getting married. She does so because she is very hard working and she has been able to make money to buy pieces of gold for her necklace.' The voice-over refers to the custom among Tehuana women of preparing a necklace of gold coins as part of their trousseau, but it does not use the distant voice that characterises the objective ethnographer.

Other travelogues employ an objective and distant voice-over narration, typical of ethnographic films. Travelogues from the 1930s and 1940s incorporate ethnographic information into their accounts, and thus it is not rare that some travelogues mimic the objective voice of the ethnographer as well. The voice of the ethnographer uses the third person to present its observations as objective, and asks the audience to regard its commentary as the truth. In *Idols of Hope* (1941), the voice-over begins by situating the images shown within a specific geographical space: the península of Yucatán; then, it proceeds to show parallels to other cultures, explaining that Mayan culture 'is comparable to that of Egypt and Greece'. Afterwards, it moves to Mayan history, explaining that Chichen Itza was built 70,000 years ago by master builders who, through their observatory, could see the 'changing position of the sun'. In his analysis of narrative strategies used in ethnographic writing on Africa, James Clifford uses the term 'scientific ethnography', which he describes as 'a discursive position that understands Africa, its peoples and its cultures' (1988: 169). In the travelogues compiled in *Mexico Marches*, the voice-over that dominates reproduces the claim to objectivity and intimate understanding of the people being filmed that characterises the voice of the ethnographer.

In the preface to *The Forgotten Village, with 136 Photographs from the Film of the Same Name*, a book in which John Steinbeck discusses his unfinished film *The Forgotten Village* (1941), he mentions the production problems the crew faced and explains that 'the most difficult problem of all was the method for telling the story to an American audience … the usual narrative method did not seem quite adequate. It was decided finally to use the method of the old storyteller' (Steinbeck et al. 1941). With this quote, Steinbeck explains that they decided to use a voice-over commentary, 'the method of the old storyteller', instead of a dialogue. Although Steinbeck does not mean to say that the voice-over commentary is a story, I find his comment suggestive, because how can we use the method of an old storyteller without telling a story?

Tales about diverse modernisation

Travelogues in general, and US travelogues about Mexico in particular, are tales about diverse modernisation. We can trace this idea back to Sinclair's letter of 16 December 1930. Referring to the picaro Sinclair recommends Eisenstein create, he writes:

> Such a boy would be brought up in the midst of the Indian superstitions. Perhaps you will come upon some aspect of these religious rites which might cause a youth to go journeying. He might be cast out for breaking some taboo… Or he might revolt against some cruel or senseless tribal rite and go away to seek something better. That would give him occasion to visit churches and see what the Christian rites were. He might also come into contact with modern science and American ideas and ways … he might inspect them all, and go back to his native home a sadder and still more uncertain man… I am inclined to think that to portray an Indian boy in contact with the new currents in

Mexico and shrinking back from them bewildered, will be about as safe a theme as you can choose. (Geduld and Gottesman 1970: 32–3)

Sinclair's proposed tale centres on the conflicts brought by modernisation; it is a story about a boy who comes from 'superstition' and 'taboo' and encounters 'modern ideas', 'new currents in Mexico', 'sciences' and even 'American ideas'. Interestingly, Sinclair's tale of diverse modernisation shares many similarities with Steinbeck's *The Forgotten Village*; in the 1930s a boy is forced to leave his Mexican village, ruled by backward ideas, and faces the outside modern world.[11]

Although none of the travelogues from the 1930s and 1940s studied here have a narrative similar to the one Sinclair and Steinbeck wrote, the same presumptions about diverse modernisation are present in the voice-over narration of travelogues. In *Mexico Marches*, for instance, a travelogue depicting Mexico's search for 'progress', the voice-over narrator comments that Oaxacan potters, silversmiths and fishermen use technologies 'as primitive as that of England before the Industrial Revolution'. Likewise, the cultures in *Spaniard and Indian* are presented as cultures that do not participate in 'progress'. While the audience is shown images of the boats in Xochimilco, the narrator comments, 'they still push their boats just as they did before the Conquest'. Similar comments appear in Wright's series; for example, the narrator states that 'the Tetzal women used identical looms when the first whites arrived as those used today'. In Sinclair and Steinbeck's stories, as well as in the commentary of travelogues, there are two diverse worlds: the modern, technologically developed world of those who speak and observe, and the backward, technologically deficient world of those who, without the power to speak, are observed.

Emotions

What does the tale about diverse modernisation tell us about the emotions of the makers of travelogues and those of the US audience travelogues are made for? My question is heavily influenced by Scheub's way of looking at storytelling. While discussing African stories, he argues that the true meaning of the story is not in the narrative itself, but in elements that we might have considered peripheral, such as rhythm, emotion, pattern and trope. He writes: 'But narrative is not story. Story is the totality of activities that comprise storytelling performance, each of which is a crucial ingredient' (1998: 47). Following Scheub's views, my question focuses on emotions which Scheub considers 'the soul of storytelling' (1998: 21).

One of the most salient emotions travelogues address is the anxiety created by places that are unknown to the US audience. Remnants of this anxiety can be seen in the way in which Mexican indigenous communities are portrayed as dangerous. In *The Tetzal Have Strange Customs*, for instance, Tetzals are portrayed as backward and cruel, and in *The Cruel and Barbarous Triques* the voice-over says that in Trique territory horses are attacked by vampire bats at night 'leaving inch-long marks in the horse's neck'. The commentary about horrific nights in Trique territory blurs the separation between the real and the fantastic, something that is also present in the introduction to Wright's series. During a display of art-deco drawings of Cortés and Moctezuma, the voice-over mentions the Aztec practice of human sacrifice, claiming that the dead were fed to the animals in Moctezuma's zoo, 'where arms and legs protruded from the cages'. This fictionalised account of Moctezuma's world exposes Wright's draw on fantasy to captivate his audience. At the same time, the account is also a reflection of the feeling of fear caused by unknown people living in other parts of the world.

From strange to familiar

To calm the anxiety produced by unknown peoples, the voice-over commentaries of travelogues from the 1930s and 1940s about Mexico use comparisons to make the 'strange' cultures of Mexico fit into familiar categories. In *Idols of Hope*, the commentator compares Mayan culture to ancient Egypt and Greece, and in Wright's series, the Amuzgos are like Apaches, the Tetzal like South Paws and the Mixtec women like Balinese because they expose their chests. The voice-over also brings up similarities between Mexican festivities and behaviours and their US 'counterparts'. In *Death Day*, the observer finds that the Mexican celebration of All Saints Day is fundamentally the same as Resurrection Day, Memorial Day and Halloween; in *The Strange Amuzgos*, the narrator states, 'They greet each other much as we do, except they say' and he gives the local salutation. Another strategy meant to present Mexican indigenous life as familiar is to give personal names to the people portrayed in the footage. In *Zapotec Village*, while the film shows images of two young Zapotec women, the voice says 'One of the most common girls, Rosa, is getting married. Anastasia envies her.' By naming the Zapotec women with two invented names, William F. Kruse and Egon Mauthner give this travelogue a very familiar tone.

One of the reasons why I chose to look at travelogues as a storytelling practice and to look at the emotions that arise from viewing them is to counter travelogues' tales of diverse modernisation. Underlying the commentary is the presumption of the United States' technological advantages and the country's superior status in comparison to the other cultures. This is taken as a sign of the intelligence of the North American whose voice is heard, and therefore of the correctness of his disparaging assessment of Mexican culture. Despite their claim to objectivity, travelogues function as invented tales that construct their own discourse.

In his book *Griots and Griottes* (1998), Thomas A. Hale describes at length the functions of the *griot*, an African storyteller. These functions include genealogist, historian, adviser, spokesperson, interpreter and translator, teacher and exhorter. Travelling lecturers and their descendants, travelogue commentators, fulfill some of the same functions as the *griot*, such as historian, educator, interpreter of other cultures and exhorter of US culture. Furthermore, travelogue sessions, like storytelling sessions, have performative elements. Upon the travellers' return, the images they collected were shown in academic or related environments. Ruoff suggests that the events at which travelogues were shown were a type of performance. By introducing the film and speaking about its content, the lecturer became the star performer, and the film a show (2006: 4). Travelogue exhibitions are storytelling sessions whose main function is to interpret for the audience a 'world beyond reach', a world that was too far away for the audience to have personal knowledge. The *griot* and travelogue lecturer help their respective communities to understand who they are in the world. The *griot* tries to make sense of time for the audience, bringing back the past and making it meaningful to understand the present (Scheub 1998: 21). The lecturer tries to make sense of the geographical space that surrounds his North American audiences, bringing the unknown home to make sense of the world that surrounds them.

Conclusion

While the narrative strategies of travelogues are diverse and, influenced by literature and ethnography, range from the personal account of a traveller and/or lecturer to the distant observation of an ethnographer, they also have a trait in common: they use a story of diverse modernisation to organise the physical and mental universe that surrounds the audience. By looking at travelogues as a form of storytelling, this chapter has questioned travelogues' use of a scientific observer's commentary to legitimise their colonisation of other cultures. Travelogues are seen as tales used by North American society to encourage its growing political power; the voice of the scientific ethnographer of the travelogue from the 1930s and 1940s is intended to calm the audience's fear of the communities beyond reach by assuring them that the US has a technology that surpasses that of the community being studied, and this very technology gives the US a position of moral superiority.

Notes

1 The book that Jeffrey Ruoff edited, *Virtual Voyages: Cinema and Travel* (2006), suggests that travelogues are a way of travelling virtually.

2 'Over the course of the last few decades, many ethnographers have been redirecting their work away from what Susan Pierce Lamb describes as the "linear paradigm [that] manifest itself in separating self from the data base, in the preoccupation of being objective"' (de Ramírez and Berry 2007: 25).

3 Afterwards Eisenstein expanded the project and decided to pair up ethnographic and dramatic footage in an avant-garde film to be called *Qué viva México!*

4 The complex set of reasons why Eisenstein was not allowed to edit his film go beyond the scope of this chapter, but can be found in Geduld and Gottesman (1970) and in many other books on Eisenstein's films.

5 I would like to thank the Lilly Library at Indiana University in Bloomington, Indiana, for having granted me the Everett Helm Visiting Fellowship to consult the Upton Sinclair manuscript collection in 2009. When reading Sinclair's correspondence to different people, I found little information about the editing of *Death Day*. It is doubtful that Lesser, who has the credit as the director of the film, wrote the voice-over; the information found in Sinclair's correspondence shows that Lesser's main skill was distribution, and there is no evidence that he wrote scripts. There are also reasons to believe that Sinclair would prefer to have his participation in *Death Day* concealed. During June and July 1932, Sinclair participated in the editing of *Thunder Over Mexico*, a fictional film made with the footage shot by Eisenstein. We know that on 13 June 1932 a rough-cut of *Thunder Over Mexico* was shown to Sinclair's close friends at Lesser's office in Santa Mónica. However, in July of the same year, Seymour Stern, backed up by Agustín Leyva in Mexico, began a strong international campaign against Sinclair on Eisenstein's behalf. Given the animosity against Sinclair, it is very possible that the novelist did not want to be associated with editing *Death Day*, although it is unlikely that Lesser had the skills to write the script and edit the film. It is very possible that *Death Day* was conceived by Sinclair, who may have written the voice-over, but that the film was cut and distributed by Lesser, who Sinclair trusted and who became the novelist's friend for life. After 1933, Sinclair withdrew his participation from any editing of the footage shot by Eisenstein. The international campaign against Sinclair had badly damaged his reputation and in 1934 he lost his campaign as Democratic governor of California and his candidacy for the Nobel Prize in Literature. After these unsuccessful attempts, Sinclair went back to writing and lost interest in the *Qué viva México!* footage.

6 Wright also directed the Churubusco Country Club and the Cinema Club of Mexico, a subsection of the Amateur Cinema League.

7 The footage was shot after 1935, when Kodachrome colour came to the market. Using the edge marks and archival references found in Mexico City's Country Club, Acosta Urquidi dates the production of the series between 1939 and 1941 (2008). The footage was made into two series, edited at different times in the early 1940s. He believes that the *Indian Tribes of Unknown Mexico* was edited first because in it, the credits appear over a coloured landscape (typical of the 1930s). The *Harry Wright's Mexican Indian Series* was edited later. According to Acosta, it was edited before 1945 because Edna McCawley, Wright's first wife who died between 1940 and 1946, does not appear in the credits (2006: 2).

8 His films were later to become the Harry Wright Collection at the US Library of Congress. The Collection is a testimony to Wright's interest in entertainment; it includes vaudeville, cartoons and, most importantly, 16mm travelogues.

9 Acosta (2008) believes that Wright himself recorded the voice-over narration in the ethnographic series.

10 Extensive information about Holmes can be found here: http://www.burtonholmes.org ('Burton Holmes, Extraordinary Traveller').

11 I thank Jesse Lerner for pointing out this similarity to me.

Bibliography

Acosta Urquidi, M. (2006) *Descripción de contenidos de las copias en Cineteca Nacional de 39 elementos fílmicos en 16mm de la colección Harry Wright en El Library of Congress.* Mexico City: Cineteca Nacional.

_____ (2008) personal communication with the author, March.

Clifford, J. (1988) *The Predicament of Culture: Twentieth-century Ethnography, Literature, and Art.* Cambridge, MA: Harvard University Press.

de Ramírez, B. and S. Berry (2007) *Native American Life-history Narratives: Colonial and Postcolonial*

Navajo Ethnography. Albuquerque: University of New Mexico Press.

Geduld, H. M. and R. Gottesman (1970) *Sergei Eisenstein and Upton Sinclair: The Making & Unmaking of ¡Qué Viva México!*. Bloomington: Indiana University Press.

Gunning, T. (2006) '"The Whole World Within Reach": Travel Images Without Borders', in J. Ruoff (ed.) *Virtual Voyages Cinema and Travel*. Durham, NC: Duke University Press, 25–41.

Hale, T. A. (1998) *Griots and Griottes: Masters of Words and Music*. Bloomington: Indiana University Press.

Mauthner, E. and W. F. Kruse (1941a) *Mexican Symphony*. New York: Museum of Modern Art.

____ (1941b) *Zapotec Village*. New York: Museum of Modern Art.

Peterson, J. (1998) *World Pictures: Travelogues and the Lure of the Exotic, 1896–1920*. Unpublished PhD Dissertation, University of Chicago.

Ruoff, J. (2006) 'The Filmic Fourth Dimension: Cinema as Audiovisual Vehicle', in J. Ruoff (ed.) *Virtual Voyages: Cinema and Travel*. Durham: Duke University Press, 1–21.

Scheub, H. (1998) *Story*. Madison: University of Wisconsin Press.

Steinbeck, J., R. Harvan Kline and A. Hackenschmied (1941) *The Forgotten Village, with 136 Photographs from the Film of the Same Name*. New York: Viking.

Wright, H. and E. Meyers (1935–1945a) *The Harry Wright Ethnographic Series: Indian Tribes of Unknown Mexico*. Washington, D.C.: Harry Wright Collection at the Library of Congress Broadcasting and Recorded Sound Division, Motion Pictures.

____ (1935–1945b) *Harry Wright's Mexican Indian Series*. Washington, D.C.: Harry Wright Collection at the Library of Congress, Broadcasting and Recorded Sound Division, Motion Pictures.

Memory and Tradition as a Postcolonial Response in the Films of Kyrgyzstan's Aktan Abdykalykov

Willow Mullins

The Kyrgyz filmmaker Aktan Abdykalykov uses his trilogy of films about growing up – *Sel'kincek* (1993), *Beshkempir* (1997) and *Maimil* (2001)[1] – to invoke stories that are glimpsed rather than fully narrated, that mediate both local traditions and national identity. He does not attempt to recreate the great Kyrgyz stories, the legends of the hero Manas. These stories are already told by others. Nor does he look for tradition in a pre-contact or pre-colonial past. Intensely situated in the subtle navigation of memory and tradition as integral parts of the everyday, his project is more complex:

> *Kurak* is a technique of making patchwork blankets. You remember that during our funerals, these bits and pieces of cloth are given away… The family buys lots of fabric, then tears it apart – approximately one elbow-length – and gives the pieces away to everybody who comes to bid farewell to the deceased. This is how bits of different fabrics are collected in a household. Our mothers and grandmothers sew a *kurak* from these pieces of cloth. In essence, a *kurak* accumulates the memories of dead people – it becomes a patchwork of remembrance. For myself, I named *Beshkempir* a patchwork of my childhood. The film is constructed according to this principal [sic]. There is no linear story in it but there are fragments of my memories, my impressions, and when you put it all together, you get a *kurak*. (Abdykalykov in Abikeeva 2003)

Filmed in the first decade after independence from the Soviet Union, Abdykalykov's films are invested in a process of telling and re-telling personal histories to both mediate the ruptures caused by, first, Russian and Soviet imperialism, and then Soviet collapse, and to construct Kyrgyz national identity in much the same way as someone might sew together a *kurak*. A major part of this identity formation and maintenance centres on the role of memory and the use of the traditional in forging a bridge between the present and the past. Repeated throughout the trilogy, these themes, when situated within the context of Kyrgyz history, suggest the potential for a postcolonial reading of Abdykalykov's films that reveal the filmmaker as a story-teller, employing technology to fulfill traditional functions of reasserting group identity.

A central theme in postcolonial discourse is the attempt to actively remember and record histories as a way to mediate the rupture in historical and cultural continuity caused by colonialism. Stuart Hall has argued that postcolonial identity is an ongoing production, 'always constituted within ... representation', whether oral narrative or film; such identities are constructed not through uncovering but rather '*re-telling*... the past' (1989: 704–5, emphasis in original). This process of remembering and recounting memories and representing them in film seems to drive Abdykalykov's work. In Ella Shohat's refiguring of the postcolonial from Hall, she remarks:

> For communities which have undergone brutal ruptures, now in the process of forging a collective identity, no matter how hybrid that identity has been before, during, and after colonialism, the retrieval and reinscription of a fragmented past becomes a crucial contemporary site for forging a resistant collective identity. A notion of the past might thus be negotiated differently; not as a static fetishized phase to be literally reproduced, but as fragmented sets of narrated memories and experiences on the basis of which to mobilize contemporary communities. (1992: 109)

Similarly, Chadwick Allen (2002) has suggested that identities are intricately co-productive with a project of remembering and are rooted in cultural specificity. The history of colonialism reveals an imposed history and relationship to memory, tradition and modernity, and it is these issues which play out in modern Kyrgyz film. The complexity of the relationship to the past deserves attention for it points not only to the importance of remembering and retelling to help form a cohesive identity but also refiguring the past as something that is continually being negotiated and rein-vested with new meanings.

Abdykalykov produced his trilogy as a semi-autobiographical exploration of growing up. Each film encapsulates a moment in the life of a boy as he navigates increasing maturity, family, friends and the world in which he lives, beginning in early childhood with *Sel'kinchek*, exploring puberty in *Beshkempir*, and finally on the cusp of adolescence and adulthood in *Maimil*. Crucially, unlike the more typical researches into the past which focus on recreating plots from the great Kyrgyz epic, Manas, or adapting the novels of Kyrgyz writers, Abdykalykov's films are intensely personal stories. Profoundly rooted in the everyday, all three films are heavily focused on tradition and the ties and responsibilities of both family and community. By depicting three moments of exploration into and negotiation of personal identity as it relates to community, tradition and modernity, Abdykalykov attempts through his films to begin to fill the vacuum he felt was created, first by colonialism and then independence through a recollection and reinterpretation of the past. His choice to tell his stories in the abstract, with another protagonist, extends his personal story to larger questions of Kyrgyz identity. Stressing both the didacticism and intergenerational investment of storytelling and group identity, Abdykalykov casts his son as his own representative in the films. By making this move – endowing the personal with symbolic weight for the community – the filmmaker takes on the larger functions of the storyteller in part by offering images from his own life, as well as the retelling of personal memories, as a source and a model for a larger process of identity production through cultural memory.

Creating memory/Creating identity

Film and media can provide a powerful way to negotiate the rupture created in a colonial context[2] and a venue for the forging of new national and personal identities. The modern Kyrgyz Republic may be just such a context and Abdykalykov's films are engaged in just such a process. The relationship of Kyrgyzstan to the Soviet Union undoubtedly was in many ways a colonial one, but the specific histories and power structures which mark this relationship both engage and challenge postcolonial theories developed with particular reference to other places, specifically in India, the Caribbean and Africa. While the extent to which postcolonialism is applicable in Central Asia generally and Kyrgyzstan specifically is beyond the scope of this chapter,[3] some of the ideas developed in connection with postcolonial discourse can provide helpful insights for reading Kyrgyz film – in addressing ideas of rupture and continuity, the formation and maintenance of identity, and the uses of tradition and its relationship with modernity. Because postcolonial discourse requires historic and cultural specificity, it is necessary to root this discussion with brief overviews of both Abdykalykov's trilogy and Kyrgyz history.

Abdykalykov's trilogy consists of three separate views of childhood, from the perspectives of three different boys of different ages. The medium-length *Sel'kincek* starts off this set of films, documenting a child's first experience of unrequited love and the movement towards adulthood. This black and white film, which is rarely shown in the West, focuses on a boy who happily pushes an older girl on a swing until she falls in love with a sailor home from his post who takes her away. Both the boy and the man who had taken turns pushing her on the swing are devastated by her departure. While the man falls into lethargy, the boy deals with his despair first by drawing pictures of the girl on the swing and later by stealing a large shell the sailor had brought home as an exotic souvenir and hiding it in the mountains. The film has no dialogue, relying instead on long takes to provide the audience with insight into the characters and the images of the shell and the swing to evoke eroticism and the sense of loss. Abdykalykov's use of images and framing, not only here but throughout the trilogy, reflect his training as a painter.

Set in the 1960s, *Beshkempir*, the second film of the trilogy, is the coming-of-age story of a boy who discovers that he has been adopted through a traditional ceremony. Here the rupture of colonialism is signified by the rupture of adolescence and adoption. Much of the film follows Beshkempir and his friends, all around ten to fourteen years old, as they play in their rural village, stealing honey, hiding from girls, and covering themselves in mud. Through the taunting by another boy, Beshkempir learns that he was adopted, and thus much of the film explores the importance of tradition in forming identity as the boy seeks to understand who he is in the face of distant parents and the death of his beloved grandmother. The film is mostly shot in black and white, but certain objects and scenes appear in colour. For example, a shot of the girl Beshkempir has a crush on walking around the corner from behind some trees is entirely in colour; similarly, a close-up of his grandmother's wool, spindle and jewellery lies in colour on a black and white kerchief he holds following her death.

The trilogy's final film, *Maimil*, offers one final look at adolescence on the cusp of adulthood. Like the previous two, this film also follows the protagonist – called the Chimp by his friends for his large ears – through his daily life. The Chimp is waiting for his final papers to report for mandatory military service, and the film covers the period between his physical exam and his entering the military. During this time, he helps work on the railroad through his small town, spends time with friends, suffers heartache and attempts to negotiate the conflict between his mother and his alcoholic father. This is the only film that is shot entirely in colour. My arguments will focus on the second and third films as the most nuanced and available. In order to explore why the production of identity is so crucial for these films, however, it is necessary to understand how Kyrgyzstan has been construed politically and culturally.

Contemporary Kyrgyz questions of identity can be imagined as a result of at least two ruptures – one at the beginning of Soviet control and one at the end. The first rupture built over time through longstanding relations with Imperial Russia but both climaxed and dramatically changed character during the early period of Soviet rule. Russia proved itself an imperial power as early as the eighteenth century, conquering large areas of Asia, all centrally governed from St. Petersburg.[4] Central Asia was important both geographically and economically for Russia; controlling Central Asia meant controlling the Silk Road, still the quickest overland trading route between China and Europe. Central Asia was also a crucial battleground for the Great Game, as Russia sought to expand south and the British Empire pushed north from India.

While Russian imperialism in most of Asia focused on resources and strategic benefits and seems to have lacked some of the civilising mission of other imperial nations such as Britain, following the Russian Revolution in 1917, the Soviets were heavily invested in creating a new culture which would unite the widely diverse peoples and cultures beneath its administrative control – what Gayatri Spivak in her brief consideration of the former Soviet states as postcolonial called 'an articulated ideal [of] "scientific socialism"' (2006: 830). The process of Sovietisation of Central Asia was not an easy one – the Bamaschi Revolt violently opposed Soviet rule until 1934. Central Asians primarily felt the effects of Soviet control in newly imposed Western relationships to the land[5] as well as ideas about what constituted appropriate gender roles and cultural and nationalistic expressions. Thus the beginnings of the Soviet Union culminated in a rupture that began a century earlier with imperial Russia – one that redefined land use, governmental systems, cultural expression and identity.

The Soviets materialised as a government partly through war and expansion into the East, yet the process of Sovietisation in Central Asia required a new way of thinking about national culture construction. In order for the Soviet system to work, a new single Soviet identity had to be imposed onto all of the various groups represented in the Union. The sense of communal identity that the Soviets set out to instill, however, could not be found in the past, since no Soviet past existed, but rather was created through an intense focus on the future through mechanisation and an imposition of Western-styled histories, nationalisms and understandings of land. This new cultural identity served to support Soviet administrative needs as well, since it both required and encouraged the forced settlement of traditionally nomadic Kyrgyz and other Central Asia peoples.

The Soviet collapse in 1991 caused a second rupture, requiring another attempt at nation building and the formation of a traditional identity but this time from within the Kyrgyz culture itself.[6] Abdykalykov has commented that independence created a vacuum of uncertainty, left by an uncertain relationship to communism and to independence. His remarks underscore the ambivalence with which many Kyrgyz viewed both Soviet rule and independence. The new nation-building intended to fill this space focused on a reinterpretation of tradition and history in which modernity and position within a global system became important stakes. The first step of this process centres necessarily on retelling histories as a way to find and confront identities that may be fragmented, to remember the past in ways politically and personally engaged. Abdykalykov's films embrace this process of active remembering through their cinematography, structure and symbolism.

By shooting the first and second films in black and white, Abdykalykov visually situates them in the past.[7] Yet this move also allows him to comment on that past's relationship to the present by suggesting that even a personal, individual past cannot be remembered precisely or in full. *Beshkempir*, however, complicates this simple reading through the use of particular objects that appear in colour periodically throughout the film, such as the bright bird held in the boy's hand. These moments of colour point to another kind of memory – the fragments of our pasts that remain clear but decontextualised. The colourised objects are startling, especially later in the film as the audience becomes more accustomed to the black and white cinematography.

The objects become almost hyperreal against the more subtle background, begging to be given meaning but also for the depth of that meaning to be questioned. The audience is unsure whether to trust the reality of these objects or the stories of the past that animate them, but ultimately the veracity of both objects and narratives is less important than their function in defining identity.[8] These objects become markers of narrative, the physical remnants of memory, which can only be understood through the recontextualisation provided by the rest of story, in this case the rest of the film. Like souvenirs, they require a narrative to give them meaning and provide a basis for storytelling.[9] Abdykalykov uses memory to give voice to fragmented narratives that help to provide continuity across rupture and ultimately to forge a collective identity – one which must deal with the Soviet past.

By piecing narratives together and retelling the past, Abdykalykov is able to comment on a history shaped by Soviet communism and the extent of its influences on the everyday. As often as not, these influences seem secondary to the more immediate concerns of the characters. In *Beshkempir*, the Soviet government barely seems present at all; while in *Sel'kincek*, the sailor wears the uniform of the Soviets, which inspires the awe of the girl, but the importance of his role seems to lie less in his allegiance to the military than in his ability to impress the girl. The trilogy's final film, *Maimil*, however, is framed by the institution of required Soviet military service – beginning with the Chimp's physical exam by the military and ending with him awaiting his superior officers as they move towards him down the aisle of the train filled with new recruits. This period of time seems like a hiatus between adolescence and adulthood, before 'real' life begins. Of course, this is an illusion, however, as the life the Chimp lives during this time is very real, particularly as he must deal with his parents' separation due to his father's alcoholism and his own nascent love life. Yet again, the effects of the Soviet period on day-to-day existence seem comparatively small though intensely present all the same. All of these films seem to resist passing judgement, reflecting Abdykalykov's own ambivalence about the Soviet period.

For Abdykalykov, depicting lived experience and remembering the past function on both a personal and a metonymic level. The films are all largely autobiographical, most notably in their emotional content, although subplots and character development are drawn from other sources as well as the filmmaker's own life. The intensity of the autobiography is heightened through Abdykalykov's casting of his son, Mirlan, to play the lead role in all three films. Further, in the third film, *Maimil*, the filmmaker uses mirrors to symbolise the process of both recollection and the search for and confrontation of identity. At its most poignant, the mirror even reveals identities that the characters do not want to face, such as at the moment when the Chimp's alcoholic father looks at his own image in the mirror, and rejecting himself, turns it face down (see Abdykalykov in Dönmez-Colin 2003: 17). But mirrors also offer the possibility of new perspectives in the film, questioning the larger truths. Because they are autobiographical, it is tempting to extend the symbolism of the mirror to the trilogy as a whole – the films as a mirror for the filmmaker. Yet because the films are not documentaries, they can be read not only as personal stories but as a collective exploration of the past and renegotiation of cultural identity. As Abdykalykov has said: 'Although this trilogy is autobiographical, the term shouldn't be taken literally, because it encompasses not only my own fate, but that of the people around me' (Abdykalykov in Holloway 2001). Abdykalykov's three boys, all aspects of one experience of growing up, fill in not only for himself but become representative of Kyrgyz identity itself – three connected stories representing the possible memories of an entire people. Much of this connection is made through the depiction of cultural traditions. The filmmaker's investment in showing Kyrgyz tradition not only helps to establish the world of the characters but serves to remind a Kyrgyz audience of their connection to that world. It is this very investment that turns Abdykalykov from memoirist to cultural storyteller.

Such a process of reclamation of history and more specifically tradition has similarities to the reformulations and constructions of identity found among many postcolonial peoples as described by Frantz Fanon's (1961) three stages. Indeed, Central Asian film scholar Gulnara Abikeeva has placed Abdykalykov's films fully in Fanon's second stage – a period during which a postcolonial people turn to the past as a source for positive representations – because of the way he has engaged in portraying tradition.[10] This assertion bears out in Abdykalykov's filmic uses and representations of Kyrgyz tradition.

Beshkempir, in particular, is heavily laden with images of tradition, using them to set off two of the most defining moments both in the film and its protagonist's life. The film opens with the ceremony in which the five elderly *ejes*[11] allow the baby Beshkempir to be adopted as they sit on *kurak*, the traditional Kyrgyz quilt; the film's climax centres on a traditional funeral, held in a felt yurt, at which Beshkempir must take on the culturally sanctioned role of putting his grandmother's affairs to rest. Beshkempir's relationship to tradition is ambiguous and must be negotiated after his grandmother, the family member to whom he is closest, dies. Through his grandmother's funeral, Beshkempir is forced into an acute awareness of the ties he has to his family, social bonds which become more important than the blood bonds he feels he does not have. Moreover, as he stands with the other boys in mourning outside of the yurt where her body lies, Beshkempir learns from his father that his grandmother has named him as the head of the family, and he must perform the rituals of putting her life in order. He must take on this traditional identity, whether or not he is ready, and to do so he must acknowledge his own identity as part of a family and a culture.

Abdykalykov posits this question of what it means to be a family in a way that resonates with what it means to be a nation. For both, there is a need to remember but not be constrained by the past, to be aware of oneself as an individual and as a member of a larger community. The grandmother's death, like the end of the Soviet Union, uncovers narratives that reveal the fragmentations which undercut daily life, requiring a reinterpretation of the past. Abdykalykov seems to suggest that it is through engaging with the past and the fragmentation in individually and culturally productive ways that a community, or even a nation, can move forward. Yet Abdykalykov's work goes well beyond the more simplistic 'recovery' of a mythologised past which would seem to be suggested by Fanon's second stage of the creation of national identity – a glorification and nostalgia for the past. For as much as these films are engaged with tradition, they are also consciously negotiating the role of modernity as well, both in terms of the Soviets' investment in modernisation and in positioning independent Kyrgyzstan as engaged in the contemporary global world.

Modernisation, as represented by settled agrarianism, science and industry, became an underlying theme of many of the Soviets' programs. Following the Western binary which pits modernity against the traditional,[12] the call to embrace technology and industry served to draw people in the new Union together by focusing on the similarities between people as human beings, particularly through their relationship to labour and science, while erasing the differences highlighted by culture. As Shirin Akiner describes:

> Under Soviet rule, Central Asia underwent an intensive process of modernization. In effect, the region was wrenched out of Asia and thrust into Europe. Traditional culture was either destroyed or rendered invisible, confined to the most intimate and private spheres. In the public arena, new national identities were created, underpinned by newly fashioned languages and Western-style literatures and histories. (1997: 261–2)

This process meant that not only were Western concepts of land being imposed but so were Western ideas of what constituted equality, work, relaxation and daily function, including dress and gender roles, which were extremely bound in tradition for predominantly Muslim Central Asia.

Abdykalykov's youths are aware of the kind of modernisation imposed by the Soviet administration as well as its effects on daily life. Its influence is most clear in *Maimil*, in which the whole film is framed by the main character's medical examination by and induction into the Soviet army and he spends the intermediary days helping repair the railroad, whose engine and cars all bear the Soviet crest. For *Beshkempir*, however, the Soviet modernisation recedes behind more immediate concerns of family and growing up. Instead, Beshkempir participates easily in a kind of global modernity, represented by the films he sees in the village and his friendship with the older boy with a bicycle who shows them. Yet it is this relationship to modernity through peers and media which his parents contest, perhaps because of their uncertainty about its ultimate source. During the 1960s, when the film is set, a genre of Soviet films developed to foster the settlement of ethnic Russians in Central Asia by depicting it as a land of opportunity through colonising narratives based in tropes similar to Manifest Destiny in the cause of American western expansion, including 'cowboy-and-Indian' style narratives featuring the Red Army[13] (see

Grenall 2005). When both his parents refuse to give Beshkempir money to see a film being shown locally, his grandmother gives him the price of admission without being asked. The scene serves a double purpose, both situating the rural Kyrgyz village in relation to a large global community through film and positioning Beshkempir in relation to that world and to the media which bring it to him. Abdykalykov has said that this film was primarily about showing traditions 'so that people could remember' (Abdykalykov in Dönmez-Colin 2003: 18), but this sequence begins to hint at his later concerns of integrating the new nation into the world by exposing Kyrgyz youth to what that world has to offer. One way this exposure is accomplished is through the use of film and video, thus media seem to highlight for Abdykalykov the ways in which the traditional and the modern coexist and build on each other. Indeed, Beshkempir's grandmother embodies the usefulness of both. While at the moment of her death, she requires that he fulfill the traditional roles of the son, in her life, she promotes his engagement with the modern, as represented by film. Both modernity and tradition serve their purposes.

Given this movement between the traditional and the modern, Fanon's second stage does not seem to offer as useful a description of Abdykalykov's work in constructing identity. More helpful for my reading is Shohat's description of 'forging a collective identity' taken in conjunction with Brown's idea of 'the redemptive power of memory', thus allowing for a construction of identity that incorporates the complexities of traditional identities in discussion with the present and future (Shohat 1992: 109; Brown 2004: 236). Because Abdykalykov's films are both personal memories and fragmentary, they offer spaces for the audience to contribute their own memories, thus creating a national identity that is necessarily collective and in conversation with the past. These openings appear not only in the disparate storylines of each film and the almost snapshot quality of these stories within the films but also in the cinematography itself as seen in the moments of colour in *Beshkempir*.

Abdykalykov uses his trilogy to explore the past, but he does so in a way that challenges a continuous linear understanding of the past, replacing it with not only three distinct films, each with its own characters and narrative stakes, but also with images stitched together within the films as well. *Beshkempir* is highly ethnographic in the ways it depicts the boys and life in the village. Rather than using multiple narratives to draw the film together, however, the filmmaker relies on multiple images, which he compared to a patchwork quilt in the interview quoted above. This concept of the *kurak* pulls together nostalgia for home, family and comfort, with memories of times and people who are gone. A close-up of the *kurak* opens the film. The camera pulls back to show Beshkempir's adoption ceremony, in which the women express their hopes for him. The model of the *kurak* also helps to explain Abdykalykov's cinematography – his movement between black and white and colour, splicing the two types of film together as one might sew together new and old fabrics or brilliant prints against duller ones. The metaphor of the *kurak*, which visually drives *Beshkempir*, extends to the whole trilogy – three narratives pieced together to form a whole.

This metaphor hints at a deeper level of collective identity production through the invocation of personal memory where the boundaries between the personal and the cultural are blurred. Abdykalykov thus evaluates and reinscribes memory, tradition and modernity in terms of their usefulness for creating identity in the present and future, replicating one of the central roles of the storyteller.

Filmmaker as storyteller

In 1954, folklorist William Bascom, seeking to form a bridge between the fields of anthropology and folklore, chose to focus on the functions that folklore serves in a community in his address to a joint meeting of the two disciplines. Bascom outlined four major functions of folklore: to entertain, to educate the audience in cultural norms and standards, to elicit conformity to those standards and to validate the culture 'justifying [the] rituals and institutions to those who perform and observe them' (1954: 332–5). These functions, particularly stories' ability to teach and to validate a culture, are precisely what make storytelling so useful to the project of identity construction described by both Hall and Shohat and exemplified in Abdykalykov's films.

The kind of identity production that occurs at the end of colonialism turns to the traditional for source material precisely because of the ability of stories to define and reaffirm cultural standards and norms. Abdykalykov similarly draws on the traditional as a way to reassert a range of identities: his own, his characters' and his cultures'. Abdykalykov has stated that he was consciously engaged in just such a process of returning to and honouring tradition: 'I gave prominence to Kyrgyz traditions in my earlier films so that people could remember' (quoted in Dönmez-Colin 2003: 18). As I have described, the traditional appears again and again in Abdykalykov's films through images, events and even structure. Yet his storytelling goes beyond a search for and reclamation of tradition.

Instead, the filmmaker is validating culture at the level that most people experience it, daily life, and during a time period that much of his audience can remember, the 1960s. His focus on the everyday validates lived experience, showing the ways in which those experiences create and recreate identity on a daily, if not a moment by moment, basis. By situating his films in the relatively recent past, rather than the age of epics and heroes, Abdykalykov authenticates the collective memory. Thus the filmmaker performs the functions of a storyteller – giving voice to the past, proclaiming the validity of a cultural experience that both acknowledges and denies the influence and importance of the Soviet period. To extrapolate from Bascom (1954), one of the primary functions of the storyteller is to assert cultural identity, and this function becomes all the more important in the postcolonial context. Stuart Hall has stated that 'identities are the names we give to the different ways we are positioned by, and position ourselves within, the narratives of the past' (1989: 706). Abdykalykov offers three such possible narratives through his trilogy, and thus at least three relative positions of self not only to the past but also to the larger culture. By presenting the deeply personal as stories, he creates a path for his Kyrgyz audience to recognise the importance of their own histories in the production of postcolonial identity that is necessarily multiple and ongoing.

Abdykalykov's trilogy about growing up is centrally invested in redefining Kyrgyz identity in the wake of colonial rupture through tradition and memory. Kyrgyzstan, along with the other post-Soviet Central Asian states, is in a unique position – it is attempting to reassert a specific cultural identity at the same time that it must create itself as a nation-state. As it engages with global economies, Kyrgyzstan must negotiate global modernity in a way that makes sense given the nation's specific history. This new nationhood makes the creation of a specifically Kyrgyz identity that much more important. As represented by these films, the Kyrgyz are coming to terms with the legacy of the Soviet Union and the ruptures which it created through an intensely postcolonial process of re-membering and re-presenting themselves. Abdykalykov's storytelling offers a process of collective identity production and a model for working through narrative possibilities to shape and reshape the past and the future.

Notes

1 I have chosen to use the Kyrgyz titles for these films. They are also known by their English titles as *The Swing*, *The Adopted Son* and *The Chimp*, respectively.

2 The concept of mediating the rupture caused by colonialism comes from Faye Ginsburg's work 'Indigenous Media: Faustian Contract or Global Village?' (1991). Ginsburg has remarked on the power of media 'to transcend boundaries of time, space, and even language … to mediate, literally, historically produced social ruptures and to help construct identities that link past and present in ways appropriate to contemporary condition' (1991: 94). I will be drawing on this concept of using film to mediate colonial rupture throughout.

3 Postcolonial scholar Gayatri Spivak (2006) has argued that the former Soviet states were subject to a form of colonialism, although not the same kind of colonialism practiced by Britain and other Western European nations. As a result, the countries which gained independence following the fall of the Soviet Union are now largely postcolonial. Spivak is cautious to note, however, that because the form of colonialism was specific to the Soviet Union, postcolonial discourse must be adapted accordingly to make sense in the post-Soviet context. Nancy Condee (2006), responding to Spivak, goes further to suggest that whether or not the former Soviet states are now postcolonial depends largely on how one defines the relationship between each of these states and the Soviet government, which employed often radically different strategies in different places. The applicability of both colonial and postcolonial discourse to Kyrgyzstan is a matter of debate among not only postcolonial scholars but also Central Asian scholars and the Kyrgyz themselves. For the purposes of this chapter, postcolonial discourse provides some useful ideas, but like Spivak and Condee, I believe it is necessary to remain culturally and historically specific.

4 Movement between Russia and the Mongolian and Central Asian plateaus is much older, however, and the territory between present-day Kiev and Moscow in the West and Ulan Bator in the East has been variously held over the centuries by Scythians, Mongols, Huns, Turkmen, Chinese and Russians, to name a few (see Grousset 1970). During the nineteenth century, Central Asia served as

both pawn and battleground between Russian, Chinese, and British powers, all of whom saw the territory as a buffer zone to the imperial aspirations of the others, namely the British, Ottoman Turks and Chinese.

5 The relationship to the land is distinctly different between traditionally nomadic peoples and traditionally settled agricultural peoples. First, the administrative division of Central Asian lands was based on linguistic groupings with an aim to create new administrative districts that contained a single lingual majority. Thus Uzbek speakers formed a majority in Uzbekistan, Tadjik speakers a majority in Tadjikistan and so on (see Akiner 1997: 267). To some extent, however, these divisions were as arbitrary as any other – all of these new regions still contain a large number of individual tribes, who may or may not be nomadic or share cultural traits with their neighbours. Not only was the division of land into administrative states at issue, but Sovietisation also involved collectivisation during this period and the redistribution of land from a capitalist to a communist system. However, Marxist communism was reacting against a Western capitalist understanding of land relations based on the agricultural model. So while the predominantly nomadic Kyrgyz were not being required to conform to capitalist land relations, they were nonetheless being settled into both a bureaucratically defined state with borders established by the Soviet government in Moscow and a sedentary agricultural lifestyle. This is not to suggest that agriculturalism is a Western concept, but rather that the way in which it was deployed in this context had Western roots.

Kate Brown has argued 'that nation itself [as a concept and construction] worked in a colonial pattern as a formula to replace localized identities and cultural complexities, which made modern governance so difficult in places' (2004: 11). These constructions meant that borders which had previously been in constant flux were now solid, and that the new nationalities these borders were meant to contain were not based on indigenous concepts of group identity but on 'standardized notions of nations' (2004: 229). Moreover, the new nations created by the Soviet Union were based on Western relationships to the land, which assumed individual or state ownership of land under a Westphalian understanding of the nation-state. Such land relationships presuppose an indigenous population who are tied to a specific territory which is discreet from surrounding indigenous groups, in other words, a nation (see Brown 2004: 10). Such a construction breaks down among traditionally nomadic peoples, who travel through intersecting areas depending on the time of year, making the importance of nailing down nomadic peoples all the more pressing to the new government. The newly imposed divisions of land, in addition to the nomadic settlement became culturally defining in their own right and have continued to produce effects to this day, notably in countries like Pakistan and Afghanistan.

6 Nancy Condee refers to 'Soviet colonizers who have withdrawn – either physically or in terms of a systematic failure of power and knowledge – leaving behind some distinct group to engage in the cultural reclamation project of nation building' (2006: 829–30).

7 Although *Beshkempir* is set in the 1960s, which is well after the invention of colour film, the connection between the past and black and white film is both strong and often unheeding of film history.

8 Jan Brunvand (1999) has pointed out in his discussion of urban legends that it does not matter whether or not they are true, but whether or not people respond to them as though they were true, e.g. one may not believe that there has ever been a killer who has hidden in the backseat of a woman's car but might still glance at the back seat every time they get in the car to see if anyone is there. I am following a similar logic here in discussing memory – in terms of memory's function in establishing identity, what matters is how an individual or, I would argue, a community, constructs the past. Needless to say, the stakes are much higher here, particularly in a postcolonial context where the official history under the colonial administration may be notably different than the lived experience of the colonised.

9 The ability of the souvenir to encapsulate and serve as a marker of experience which is restored through narrative is the subject of Susan Stewart's *On Longing* (1993) (see particularly pages

135–50).

10 Fanon describes three stages in the creation of national identity at the end of colonialism. The first stage involves assimilation to the colonising power, the second turns to the past as a source for positive representations, and during the third, the colonised becomes a revolutionary. While Fanon's schema is useful in some ways, it does not deal adequately with the diverse ways in which people relate to and invoke tradition, particularly in conjunction with rather than opposition to modernity. For a brief discussion of Fanon's stages, see Abikeeva (2003) or Hall (1989).

11 *Eje* is a Kyrgyz term of respect for an older woman. It translates roughly to 'auntie'.

12 In this construction, modernity is associated with industrialised economies, while tradition represents the beliefs and daily practices of non-industrial culture. As many authors, including bell hooks, Stuart Hall and Kimberley Lau, have pointed out, this is a limited paradigm that serves to reinforce a colonialist understanding of the Other as traditional and therefore not developed and childlike. Nonetheless, it remains a powerful underlying framework in current Western culture.

13 The film *White Sun of the Desert* (Vladimir Motyl, 1969) probably best exemplifies this mentality. It was a comedy adventure film that was hugely popular in Russia after its release. The plot follows a Red Army officer who has been stationed in Central Asia and is set to guard the harem of a fugitive native chieftain. Apparently, it is traditional for this film to be screened to Cosmonauts and dignitaries the day before the launching of any Soyuz spacecraft.

Bibliography

Abikeeva, G. (2003) Special Issue on Central Asia. *Kinokultura*. Available: http://www.kinokultura.com/CA/A1centralasia.html (accessed on 15 December 2009).

Akiner, S. (1997) 'Between Tradition and Modernity: The Dilemma Facing Contemporary Central Asian Women', in M. Buckley (ed.) *Post-Soviet Women: from the Baltic to Central Asia*. Cambridge: Cambridge University Press, 261–304.

Allen, C. (2002) *Blood Narrative: Indigenous Identity in Native American and Maori Literary and Activist Texts*. Durham , NC: Duke University Press.

Bascom, W. (1954) 'Four Functions of Folklore'. Presidential address to the American Folklore Society. *Journal of American Folklore* 67(266): 333-349.

Brown, K. (2004) *A Biography of No Place*. Cambridge, MA: Harvard University Press.

Brunvand, J. (1999) *Too Good to Be True: The Colossal Book of Urban Legends*. New York: W. W. Norton.

Condee, N. (2006) 'The Anti-Imperialist Empire and After: In Dialogue with Gayatri Spivak's "Are You Postcolonial?"', *PMLA*, 121, 3, 829–31.

Dönmez-Colin, G. (2003) 'Secrets in the Looking Glass: An Interview with Aktan Abdykalykov', *Cinemaya*, 58, 15–20.

Fanon, F. (1961) *The Wretched of the Earth*. New York: Grove.

Ginsburg, F. (1991) 'Indigenous Media: Faustian Contract or Global Village?', *Cultural Anthropology*, 6, 1, 92–112.

Grenall, R. (2005) 'Russians left behind in Central Asia'. *BBC News Website*. Available: http://news.bbc.co.uk/1/hi/world/asia-pacific/4420922.stm (accessed on 23 November 2005).

Grousset, R. (1970) *The Empire of the Steppes: A History of Central Asia*. Trans. N. Walford. New Brunswick, NJ: Rutgers University Press.

Hall, S. (1989) 'Cultural Identity and Cinematic Representation', in R. Stam and T. Miller (eds) *Film and Theory: An Anthology*. Malden, MA: Blackwell, 704–14.

Holloway, R. (2001) Miamil (The Chimp). *Cannes Daily*. Available: http://www.filmfestivals.com/cgi-bin/cannes/film.pl?id=3015&site=us (accessed on 15 December 2009)

Shohat, E. (1992) 'Notes on the "Post-Colonial". *Social Text* 31/32: 99-113.

Spivak, G. (2006) 'Are We Postcolonial? To the Teachers of Slavic and Eastern European Literatures', *PMLA*, 121, 3, 828–9.

Stewart, S. (1993) *On Longing*. Durham, NC: Duke University Press.

'Postcolonial Beaux' Stratagem: Singing and Dancing Back with Carmen in African Films

Yifen T. Beus

The treatment of 'Otherness', such as appropriating non-Western subjects and exoticising them for popular consumption, has been a common manifestation of colonial storytelling. Nonetheless, since the second half of the twentieth century, many postcolonial nation states began to reclaim their rights to (re)write their own national narratives through this very model of writing 'Otherness' as one of the most effective strategies of writing back to the Western centre. One such story is Carmen. A friend of the French Romantic writer Prosper Mérimée mentioned to him on his first trip to Spain a trivial drama of jealousy and murder, which formed the foundation of the famous story. Mérimée's personal interest in the Gypsy people and the language also inspired subsequent literary publications on this very subject. As a result, in his 1845 novella, he re-tells this Spanish love story through which a subtle French nationalism also surfaced.[1] Thirty years later, Georges Bizet adapted the story into a Romantic opera, and since then Carmen as an archetype serves as the pivotal symbol of free spirit and rebellion.[2]

Two African films, *Karmen Geï* (2001) directed by Joseph Gaï Ramaka of Senegal and the South African *U-Carmen eKhaylitsha* (2004) by Mark Dornford-May, a British director, utilise the motif of Carmen and intertextuality as rhetorical tropes, navigating between the colonial and postcolonial story spaces. Both films as political cinema, in an act of returning the gaze, display self-reflexivity about the politics of storytelling and representation. Both films have a significant musical component: *Karmen Geï* employed locally as well as internationally famous musicians to star in the film and for the music score, while *U-Carmen eKhaylitsha* is the very first film in the Xhosa language, using local vocal performers of the Dimpho Di Kopane Theatre Company and following Bizet's score and narrative quite faithfully while mixing in African songs and dances set in the shantytown of Khayelitsha. In this chapter, I examine how the adaptation and thus appropriation of a Western Romantic novella and opera serves as a powerful political tool in a gesture of writing back while creating a contemporary as well as a prophetic African story. I will condition my analysis within the discussion of how the directors, taking on Mérimée's and Bizet's strategies in introducing the drama, mobilise the audience's gaze particularly in the opening sequences.

In contrast to the light-hearted Restoration comedy *Beaux' Stratagem* by play-wright George Farquhar (1707), the title of this chapter ironically takes on the dark side of the play to suggest a narrative strategy, albeit as subtle as the 'gentlemen's scheme', which is indeed a trick to deceive an enemy, disguised in songs and dance. It is a ruse of the directors, as postcolonial artists, to take on the stratagem established in the opening of both Mérimée's and Bizet's *Carmen* and attack back by surprise, using the enemy's own tools, in this case, Carmen as a cultural icon and cinema as a popular mass medium.

Using the tactic of singing and dancing back is significant for the following two, if not more, reasons. Firstly, from the anthropological, sometimes even regarded as scientific, perspectives of early Western ethnographers, the African was portrayed as a barbarian or cannibal typified in some kind of dance rituals, posing an image of threat and fear to Western colonists. Secondly, a much more benign depiction of the African as the noble savage, the exotic and naked jolly native, jumping up and down, again singing and dancing as evidence of the natives' social life, replaced the blood-thirsty and threatening savages. These polarised portrayals were typical in the West's representing the natives during the height of colonial exploration and expansion.[3] By appropriating and thus re-writing a famous Western story about a non-Western, exotic *femme fatale*, the African Carmen is able to use the same cultural specificity as portrayed in colonial writing to deconstruct the whole myth of this 'primitive' dance and to construct a new story that is African in its very essence, while recognising the obvious hybrid nature of the medium itself – the Carmen archetype represented through the camera lens. What Carmen is capable of doing is luring others' gaze towards her. And sure enough, the seduction of a voyeuristic gaze in the films also comes from the erotic and inviting dance of Carmen, orienting the audience to follow the camera as it switches perspectives from one to another, identifying the gaze and perspective for the spectator as it moves along.

As Ann Davies points out in her introduction to *Carmen: From Silent Film to MTV*, commentators have often referred to Carmen as myth due to the timelessness of her story, which can tap into all sorts of socio-political concerns in different historical times and geographical locations, ranging from sexual and ethnic Otherness to class and labour issues (2005: 1–2). Thus, structuralist Claude Lévi-Strauss's (1949; 1983) notion of myth is applicable here to the understanding of the workings of Carmen stories by positioning her as an age-old cultural icon. The issues mentioned above have been manifested in the eighty or so versions of cinematic adaptation alone (up until the publication of this chapter), expanding a near century-long timeframe and covering geographical and cultural areas beyond its 'original' France and Spain to include Asia and Africa.[4] This broad interest in the Carmen theme reveals her universal appeal in the historical development of cinema as an art form and medium for social commentary; it also transcends the immediate Spanish/Gypsy geo-cultural mores to resonate similar connotations in other cultures. Readily embodied in these variants of the Carmen story are codes and customs shared by both readers/audience of the 'original' story and those of later renditions or adaptations which demonstrate the cross-cultural and intertextual applications (including operas, songs, films, fiction, musicals, and so on) the Carmen myth renders.

Lévi-Strauss (1949) sees myths as stories that can have a very specific historical context as well as be ahistorical, transcending time and space, and thus can be translated, re-told, reduced, expanded and even altered without losing their fundamental structure. Likewise, this is how a kinship between different Carmen authors (composers and filmmakers alike) and spectators can be formed, and how they communicate with each other with a common interpretative semiotic property of Carmen in the Straussian sense by using the same mythèmes (which function like phonemes in a language system) as basic structural elements in (re)telling these variants of the same stories, in this case using Carmen's attributes as mythological or legendary tropes and motifs.

Carmen's 'independent sexuality as a source of danger' (Davies 2005: 4) is one of these shared codes, or 'mythèmes', in defining what is essentially Carmen-esque, a code that cuts across Bohemian cultural locality and Western literary history diachronically (in terms of the various historical moments when these stories develop over time and receive interpretive significance) and synchronically (in relation to the scattered incarnations of the Carmen narrative at any given historical period when variants of the same stories are created and told). This image has come to signal an 'authentic' *femme fatale* stereotype common in popular culture, cinema in particular. Even pop diva Édith Piaf sang of the enchantment Carmen evinces on the cinema screen in her chanson 'Carmen's Story' (1962):

> Dans le grand studio
> De cinéma,
> Sur le plateau,
> Tout le monde est là,
> Les deux vedettes et les acteurs,
> Metteur en scène et producteur,
> Décorateurs, et assistants
> Et puis la foule des figurants.
> On va tourner la première scène

Du nouveau film d'après Carmen
Et quelqu'un crie : 'Silence! On tourne!'
Carmen's story! Carmen's story!
(from her 1962 album *Les Amants de Teruel*)

Notably, Piaf exclaimed at Carmen's power in commanding the attention and gaze of the spectator including those who make the film such as directors, producers and crew members even before the opening scene commences. Both *Karmen Geï* and *U-Carmen eKhaylitsha* utilise the common themes of seduction and betrayal, and yet rework them into contemporary African struggles of class and gender inequality while retaining the force of a protagonist who navigates and transcends these pro-scribed social boundaries in search of a new order by mobilising her positionings and maximising her agency at will. The Carmen in both films claims such subjectivity through her role as storyteller, dancing and singing counter narratives that separate them from Mérimée's or Bizet's versions.

One can find the self-reflexive parallel in the opening moments of all four versions of Carmen by Mérimée, Bizet, Ramaka and Dornford-May. In the opening paragraph of Mérimée's novella, the narrator, ostensibly the author himself using the first-person singular subject, poses questions concerning a location called Munda:

I had always suspected the geographical authorities did not know what they were talk-ing about when they located the battlefield of Munda in the county of the Bastuli-Poeni, close to the modern Monda, some two leagues north of Marbella. According to my own surmise, founded on the text of the anonymous author of the *Bellum Hispaniense*, and on certain information culled from the excellent library owned by the Duke of Ossuna, I believed the site of the memorable struggle in which Caesar played double or quits, once and for all, with the champions of the Republic, should be sought in the neigh-bourhood of Montilla. Happening to be in Andalusia during the autumn of 1830, [this happens to be when Mérimée first travelled to Spain] I made a somewhat lengthy excur-sion, with the object of clearing up certain doubts which still oppressed me. A paper which I shall shortly publish will, I trust, remove any hesitation that may still exist in the minds of all honest archaeologists. But before that dissertation of mine finally settles the geographical problem on the solution of which the whole of learned Europe hangs, I desire to relate a little tale. It will do no prejudice to the interesting question of the correct locality of Monda.

This 'little tale' is the love story between Don José and Carmen. This framing device sets up the theme of Carmen not as a story of passion, love and death, as it is often interpreted, but one of ambiguity and liminality, which will even deserve an aca-demic investigation into this place called Monda for 'all honest archaeologists' sake' by promising to publish a dissertation to clear all doubts. It in fact foreshadows the central concerns of this version of Carmen, as David Ellison argues: 'Carmen has been misread as a work of mere exoticism, of exciting and seductive *dépaysement*, whereas the seductive overlay masks the unsettling dis-placements of the uncanny' (2003: 73). It is indeed a much more ambiguous textual drama than the surface theme suggests. It also presents Otherness with a theme of uncertainty. Spain is the author's/France's Other, Ellison suggests.[5]

It is also an Orientalist discourse concerning conflict of cultures through a dichotomy of the national vs. the regional, as Don José and Carmen are respectively Basque and Gypsy living in Spain (see Ellison 2003: 81–3). As the story progresses, in chapter three Don José refers to Gibraltar, the location where most parts of the story takes place, as 'finibus terroe' (end of the earth), a place 'full of ragamuffins from every country in the world, and it really is like the Tower of Babel, for you can't go ten paces along a street without hearing as many languages'. Mérimée's attempt, as an ethnographer, to sort out this linguistic and cultural chaos, turns out to be an impossible task, as the opening of the novella suggests: it is more than an uncertainty of location as the story also deals with protagonists whose origins are untraceable like the Gypsies. Thus this self-reflexive ambiguity conveniently frames the story the narrator was about to tell, about Carmen, and separates the novella itself from the grand Carmen myth, reminding the reader that this might only be a version of the story based on the research or the version the narrator heard. This framing device functions like a reflexive digression as in Cervantes' narration about the Basque in the ninth chapter of *Don Quixote*. In fact, Mérimée heard of this story while travelling in Spain through a secondary source. The separation, and thus disclaimer of the narrator from the Carmen story through the frame, also cautions the reader about the exoticism and sensual nature of the story. It is the politics of such narratology that narrates and at once critiques itself, asking the reader to look carefully at the protagonist's traits and credibility of the story details.

The first act of Bizet's opera also opens with such an invitation to gaze into the characters through a chorus of idle soldiers observing people on the street, repeating these lines numerous times: 'on regarde passer les passants' (watching passers-by pass by) and 'Drôles de gens que ces gens-là!' (What funny people these are!). With this introduction, the audience enters into the world of drama from the soldiers' perspective, first of all to observe these funny people coming and going on the street. A few minutes later, as Micaëla enters the stage, the gaze of the soldiers as well as the audience, falls upon her as they flirt with her. The location is supposedly the streets of Sevilla. As Bizet's conservative audience of the 1870s listened and watched in the Opéra-Comique, a 'subsidized theater, an honest theater', there was controversy and shock after its première over Carmen's loose morals on the stage with such comments as: 'once they [referring to women of dubious morals] have sunk to the sewers of society they have to do so again and again; Carmen is the daughter [of these] in the most revolting sense of the word … the veritable prostitute of the gutter and the street-corner.'[6] Jean Henri Dupin, a friend and fellow librettist of Henri Meilhac (who co-wrote *Carmen* with Ludovic Halévy) even made such frank and unfavourable critique the morning after the première: 'The music goes on and on. It never stops. There's not even time to applaud. That's not music! And your play – that's not a play! A man meets a woman. He finds her pretty. That's the first act. He loves her, she loves him. That's the second act. She doesn't love him anymore. That's the third act. He kills her. That's the fourth! And you call that a play? It's a crime, do you hear me, a crime!'[7] But there was absolutely no problem with characters travelling in and out of the Spanish locale, speaking French, with its clichéd colourful props of 'daggers and roses, castagnettes and seguidillas, soldiers and contrebandiers, tobacco factories and ventas, fortune-tellers and picadors, assignations and duels' (Ellison 2003: 74). But for twenty-first-century audiences, Susan McClary argues, these soldiers in the opening scene both 'naturalize spectatorship and situate us as part of the dominant (French) social group that watches the colorful antics of the local (Spanish) inhabitants from the safety of the sidelines' (1998: 116). Nevertheless, the question remains: once these soldiers disappear, whose perspective do we assume? Who are these 'funny people on the street?' The identity of us as well as the relationship between us and the characters become ambiguous.

Likewise, the narrative of *Karmen Geï* follows the Carmen prototype: it is all about love and death, with an undercurrent of rebellion in search of freedom. The Senegalese Karmen here is turned into a political martyr not without the myth's usual exotic as well as local colours: 'lavishly visual, hypnotically musical ... blend of sensual fantasy',[8] sabar drumming, a *griot* singing at a wedding, saxophonist David Murray's jazzy scores, Julien Jouga's choir, as well as voices of famous local singers like El Hadj Ndiaye and the blind diva Yandé Codou Sène. *Karmen Geï* also explores the forbidden topic of lesbianism, making the politics of the film even more controversial and yet much more up to date and even avant-garde using a past myth to cast the eternal symbolism of the Carmen archetype. The seduction of this Senegalese Karmen also functions at two levels: firstly, as a reflexive manouevre to invite the audience into a cinematic world through an active gaze at the central character as the story unfolds through her dance in the opening sequence, and secondly as a symbolic move to engender a gaze back to the embodiment of Carmen, to liberate her from the classical shell of sexual exoticism by turning her into a universal *tour de force* which can navigate between classes and even genders to serve as socio-political critique.

Karmen Geï opens similarly with an ambiguous voyeurism as Karmen dances to a group of female inmates in the Kumba Kastel prison. Mostly in medium close-ups of Karmen's legs, feet or torso, and occasionally a few long shots of her full body, the spectator follows her fragmented body parts. Moments later, the perspective is identified as coming from Angelique, the female warden for whom Karmen dances. A series of shot/reverse-shots takes place, exchanging eye-lines between the two women. Eventually, as Angelique succumbs to Karmen's seduction, she also gets up and joins in, duelling with the sensual Karmen. As the crowd cheers, Angelique becomes part of the spectacle, rendering her subjectivity to the crowd and the spectator. The exchange of positionings signifies an ambiguous power struggle. The fair-skinned Angelique, a Christian herself, standing for the colonial power who imprisons Karmen and other local women, commits suicide after realising that she cannot possess Karmen's body or soul. Karmen, on the other hand, exercises her sexual power to get out of jail, seduces men to work for her, smuggles illegal goods and, during a powerful dance sequence at the wedding of her lover and a military chief's daughter, critiques the corruption of government officials, acting as a *griot*, a traditional West-African storyteller. She is the only one who freely travels between gender and class boundaries. And yet, from reading the tarot cards, she is also quite aware of what lies in the future for her – death, instead of love, as her dialogue toys with the sounds of the original French words: 'l'amour' and 'la mort'.

Karmen has become a *'femme fatale'* and *'femme libre'*, whose freedom comes at the price of death. As Ramaka shot the film on location in the coastal town of Joal and the historic Gorée Island, a centre of the Atlantic slave trade in the eighteenth century, memories and reminders of slavery and its price were obvious and appropriate in embodying the theme of emancipation and circumventing the traditional gender and class hierarchies in Karmen's rebelliously free character. Towards the end of the opening sequence, the women chant about Karmen's strength in overthrowing the colonial as well as patriarchal orders: 'You attract men and you make women undo their robes... Be careful! Hide your women, hide your men. Karmen has come! She who creates havoc is here!' She serves as a destabilising force in the diachronic evolution of the myth. As a narrative stratagem, utilising the cultural heritage of the former empire in a seemingly self-exoticising gesture, Karmen's erotic dance is her first self-reflexive move from the very beginning of the film towards the reclaiming of subjectivity in postcolonial storytelling.

While Ramaka's Karmen controls the film's narratology through her liberal (literally and symbolically) body movements and her narration as a *griot*, both disguised in a transgender performance, Dornford-May uses *mise-en-scène* and cinematography in his opening sequence to deconstruct the notion of gaze and problematise spectatorship. Before the overture of Bizet's opera begins, the film opens with images of neon lights flickering the credits and winds howling in the background. Then a male narrator's voiceover speaking Xhosa introduces Carmen to the audience:

> In Spain, for a woman to be thought beautiful, she should have thirty positive qualities. Or, to put it another way, it must be possible to apply to her three adjectives, each of which describes ten parts of her person. For example, three that are dark: dark eyes, dark eyelashes [*A woman's face, appears faintly centre screen as the credits end, and the black background changes to an extreme close-up of flames with their hissing noises barely heard*], dark eyebrows. Three that are delicate: her hands, her lips, her hair, and so forth. [*The camera begins to zoom in slowly on the face of Carmen.*] My woman could not lay claim to such perfection. [*Carmen's full medium close-up appears in focus, looking straight into the camera, seemingly into the spectator, as the camera continues to zoom in.*] Her eyes were slanting but remarkably wide, her lips were full but finely chiselled, her hair,

rather coarse and black with a sheen like a raven's wing, was lovely and shining. Not to weary you with too long a description, I will sum her up by saying that for every fault she had a quality perhaps more striking from the contrast. She had a strange wild beauty, a face that was disconcerting but unforgettable. Her eyes, in particular, had an expression at once alluring and fierce that I had never seen on any other human face.

By referring to Spanish standards and pointing out the criteria for describing 'his' woman, an African, Xhosa-speaking beauty, the audience immediately sees the 'dislocation' or rather, 'relocation' of the Carmen myth, which necessitates a willing suspension of disbelief in performing a well-known Western opera in South Africa. However different 'his' Carmen might be from the Spanish one, they had the same irresistibly alluring quality, a Straussian mythème that defines the Carmen-esque and naturally attracts the gaze of the spectator. Just when the audience looks attentively at the emerging image of Carmen, she in fact stares straight (back) into the camera, returning the gaze at the audience. Although such a gaze back is mediated through the camera lens, it creates a multiplicity of the very act of looking– the director/camera operator looking at the actress, Pauline Malefane, whom the audience perceives as a character, and who in turn is seemingly doing the looking at the spectator outside the dramatic illusion. This unstable and indeed flexible subjectivity of seeing breaks down the conventional subject/object binary of domination and consequently creates multiple layers of action and a resistance to fixed meanings. Hence such a story space allows the reconfiguration of the traditional author/reader/object relationship by calling into question the cinematic framing and the boundaries of the subject/object paradigm. It is a self-reflexivity that invites the spectator to be the co-maker of meanings. Film viewing thus becomes an intellectual activity in the Brechtian sense that calls for an educational engagement, preventing the spectator from a sit-back-and-relax experience.

No sooner has the narrator finished this lengthy description of Carmen, now in an extreme close-up with only her eyes and nose in the frame, and the spectator has comfortably fixed his/her eyes on Carmen than the camera pulls away at variably accelerating speeds, showing Carmen in a fiery orange-red dress, sitting and posing in a photo studio named 'Photo Me'. Such a name toys with the notion of subjectivity in still photography contrasted with the mobility of cinematography, typically defined as 'writing in movement'. As the camera moves faster away, some instruments and noise are heard. The camera speeds up backwards towards the audience, and zigzags through the township showing all facets of life, alternating long and medium-long shots, and revealing the very nature of cinema – its capability of recording past images and projecting them repeatedly at various speeds as if in a moment of playback. This very cinematic characteristic compresses the diachronic and synchronic workings of the Straussian mythèmes of the Carmen icon into film sequences that at once summarise the consistent qualities of Carmen throughout different historical times and locations and manifests the modernity and fluidity of her archetype in twenty-first century Khayelitsha. This is turn locates Carmen within a geo-social framework to critique gender, class, ethnicity and labour issues.

At the end of the camera's animated speed-away, the cityscape of Khayelitsha appears in an extreme long shot. Carmen, dressed in a light blue polo shirt, dark jeans, red sneakers and, most notably, a bright red jacket tied to her waist, emerges from a distance and walks briskly towards the audience, who now can hear women singing. The narrator's woman turns out to be a contemporary township girl working for the 'Gypsy Cigarette Factory'. She is matter-of-factly late for a rehearsal at the factory's women's choir, which causes a stir among its members. However, she nonchalantly ignores others, and this free-spirited display of disregard of public opinion augurs her other archetypal character traits: willfulness, feistiness, independence and most notably, untameability. 'Gypsy' here as a brand name not only replaces the nineteenth century exotic ethnicity in Mérimée's and Bizet's works, but it also serves as a clichéd motif for loose morals and unruly behaviour. When the choir finally resumes practice, the familiar overture begins, and the camera again weaves through the township, showing a street sign that says 'Welcome to Seville, Site D, Khayelitsha, Nando's'. While the crew and cast are from South Africa, the filmmaker's highlighting the Nando's brand as a global fast-food chain specialising in chicken dishes with Portuguese flavour certainly exposes his effort to internationalise and at once localise the production.

Co-funded and produced by Spier Films and Nando's, who has fashioned its own history of Portuguese exploration, the film's predominantly South African identity also strives to find a boundary-crossing niche by meticulously translating the lyrics from English (originally from the French, of course) to Xhosa.[9] Shooting on location, the director intended for the Carmen story to be as universally local as it could be:

> It was an easy step to make. We're a South African company and the politics and eco-
> nomics of the story work in a South African township as they worked originally in the
> slums of Seville. Her desire to establish an independence, if you like, from what men
> want her to be works very well within a South African context. One of the things we
> still struggle with in South Africa is a male-dominated society, as I'm sure existed in
> the nineteenth-century Spain. So in those ways, those decisions weren't very difficult to
> make. They were very easy to make. (Q&A with Director Mark Dornford-May')

If transferring a myth from Spain to France, then from France to South Africa can be as free from the usual obstacles faced by most adaptations (such as contextual incompatability, language barriers and cultural differences) as Dornford-May suggests, Carmen has certainly proven to be one of the most flexible and adaptable stories. The archetype of Carmen transcends the diachronic signification of the story. As demonstrated above, despite textual and generic differences in these four versions and through extracting cultural specificities synchronically, this archetype is able to serve as an effective rhetorical trope. It self-reflexively displays the workings of a traditionally gendered gaze and turns it into a stratagem within the postcolonial story space to function as a political cinema commenting on the nuances and politics of representation through adaptation.

Notes

1   One final chapter was added in the 1846 edition, using Mérimée himself as the narrator to 'prove' claims and knowledge of the gypsies. Mérimée even did a watercolour of Carmen, which appears on the cover of the 1973 Garnier-Flammarion edition of *Les Ames du Purgatoire* and *Carmen*.

2   The French version used here is Guallimard's 1974 *Nouvelles complètes, tome 2: Carmen et treize autres nouvelles* while the English translation by Lady Mary Loyd is available at the Gutenberg Project website: http://www.gutenberg.org/files/2465/2465-h/2465-h.htm.

3   Alison Griffiths' *Wondrous Difference: Cinema, Anthropology, and Turn of the Century Visual Culture* (2002) analyses early ethnographic films that depict 'exotic' places and cultures, which reflected the colonial perspective and rhetoric about foreign locations and established the 'canon' of images of the empire's 'Other.'

4   *Carmen on Film: A Cultural History* (2007) by Phil Powrie, Bruce Babington, Ann Davies, and Chris Perriam is the most up-to-date and comprehensive project that covers the entire history of the Carmen genre.

5   Ellison's essay highlights three textual issues concerning the Carmen narrative as an unsettling *tour de force*: the multiplicity of 'Carmen' in terms of locality, the first paragraph's function in setting up the self/other dichotomy, and the Orientalist discourse of *Carmen*.

6   'Critical Reception' in *New York City Opera Project: Carmen* enlists major criticism on the production of Bizet's *Carmen* in the days following the world première of the opera in Paris <http://www.columbia.edu/itc/music/NYCO/carmen/reception.html>.

7   As above.

8   This description is found at Kino's promotional material for the DVD version of the film, quoting reviews from *The Nation* and *Variety*; http://www.kino.com/video/item.php?product_ id=853.

9   The chain's website features and describes a masala of culinary flavours and influences as well as sea stories to showcase its international outlook. See http://www.nandos.com/.

Bibliography

Bizet, G. (1875) *Carmen*. Directed by H. von Karajan. Available on DVD, Deutsche Grammophon, 2005.

Cervantes, M. (1950) *Don Quixote*. Trans. J. M. Cohen. London: Penguin.

'Critical Reception' (2003) *New York City Opera Project: Carmen*. Available: http://www.columbia.edu/itc/music/NYCO/carmen/reception.html (accessed on 5 February 2008).

Davies, A. (2005) 'Introduction', in C. Perriam and A. Davies (eds) *Carmen: From Silent Screen to MTV*. Amdterdam: Rodopi, 1–8.

Ellison, D. R. (2003) 'The Place of Carmen', in F. G. Henry (ed.) *Geo/Graphies: Mapping the Imagination in French and Francophone Literature and Film*. Amsterdam: Rodolpi, 73–85.

Griffiths, A. (2002) *Wondrous Difference: Cinema, Anthropology, and Turn of the Century Visual Culture*. New York: Columbia University Press.

Karmen Geï (2001) Directed by J. G. Ramaka. Canal + Horizons. Available on DVD, Kino Video, 2005

Lévi-Strauss, C. (1949) *The Elementary Structures of Kinship*. Trans. J. Bell and J. von Sturmer. Boston:

Beacan Press.

____ (1983) *Structural Anthropology*. Trans. M. Layton. Chicago: Chicago University Press.

McClary, S. (1998) 'Structures of Identity and Difference in Bizet's *Carmen*', in R. Dellamora and D. Fischlin (eds) *The Work of Opera: Genre, Nationhood, and Sexual Difference*. New York: Columbia University Press, 115–29.

Mérimée, P. (1974) *Nouvelles complètes, tome 2: Carmen et treize autres nouvelles*. Paris: Gallimard.

____ (1973) *Les Ames du Purgatoire*, Carmen. Paris, Garnier-Flammarion.

____ (2006) *Carmen*. Translated by Lady Mary Loyd. Gutenberg Project. On-line. Available: http://www.gutenberg.org/files/2465/2465-h/2465-h.htm (accessed on 15 April 2008).

Piaf, É. (1962) 'Carmen's Story' in *Les Amants de Teruel*. Available on CD, Paris: EMI France (2003 release).

Powrie, P., B. Babington, A. Davies and C. Perriam (2007) *Carmen on Film: A Cultural History*. Bloomington: Indiana University Press.

U-Carmen eKhayelitsha. (2004) Directed by M. Dornford-May. Spier Films. DVD, Koch Entertainment, 2007.

'*U-Carmen eKhaylitsha* Q&A with Director Mark Dornford-May and Pauline Malefane' (2006) *Phase 9 Website – Tartan Films*. Available: http://www.phase9.tv/moviefeatures/ ucarmenekhayelitshaq&a-markdornfordmay&paulinemalefane1.shtml (accessed on 13 April 2008).

Telling Women's Stories

Heard/Symbolic Voices:
The Nouba of the Women of Mont Chenoua and Women's Film in the Maghreb

Zahia Smail Salhi

In her book *Ses voix qui m'assiègent* (1999), Assia Djebar ponders the question of women and the function of writing. It is undeniable that even though the tradition of writing in the Middle East and North Africa region predates the advent of Islam, women were historically excluded from the realm of writing and assigned the role of oral narrators who told/narrated stories and history/events instead of writing them. This state of affairs automatically strips women of positions of power in the form of scripture, which – unlike the oral word – immortalises the voice, into the position of the subaltern raconteurs who only spoke within the walls of their homes. Maghrebi women have always been made to believe that they should only speak in whispers and were told that their voices should not be heard by strangers as they belonged to the private rather than public spheres.

As such, across the history of the region, women passed over their knowledge to the next generation of women and to male children through oral narration. The most disconcerting aspect of this function, however, is that after the written word, and the male word, women's narration occupies only the last position. Djebar remarks: 'After all, if Scheherazade did not narrate at every dawn, but wrote, perhaps she would have needed only one night, and not a thousand nights to liberate herself' (1999: 77).[1] This suggests that one written word bears more power than a thousand spoken words. Furthermore, the transmission of the inherited word does not confer authorship on women. Instead they remain the eternal transmitters of the word and the faithful guardians of the collective memory, which they relate in the past tense, in the third person and often in a hyperbolic manner.

This form of expression does not allow space for expressing the self nor for speaking in the first person. While this serves well the purpose of transmitting the past and folk heritage, it becomes problematic when women not only witness important events they would like to report but actually play a role in these events. With regard to the Maghreb, this becomes particularly true in the case of women's roles in wars of independence.

How are these women going to transmit their experiences? Is oral transmission a suitable tool to carry over the heroic stories of women of the likes of Djamila Boupasha and Hassiba ben Bouali, the heroines of the Battle of Algiers, and other heroines whose stories may not have survived to the postcolonial period? Is not oral transmission a risk to the veracity of these stories? Do we not run the risk of hyperbole and turning the reality into myth and legend?

All of those risks highlight the magnitude of women's need for a transition from the function of oral narrators to that of writers, an evolution which can only be achieved through women's literacy and education.

Maghrebi women between the written and the spoken word

The schooling of women in the modern Maghreb only started under French colonial rule. This privilege, as far as female children are concerned, was only given to a restricted minority of urban girls amongst whom we find Assia Djebar, whose entrance to school in the late 1930s was due to her father being a primary school teacher in a colonial French school. Djebar and the very few Maghrebi women of her generation who were schooled knew for sure that their access to French education positioned them in the category of the lucky few women who, unlike the vast majority of their compatriots, were given access to the masculine world. She clearly explains that when she left home (the private world of women which Fatima Mernissi [1999] calls 'the harem') she left her feminine self there behind the shutters where she also left her secluded and veiled mother, and when she entered the school vicinity with her father she equally entered the world of men and therefore leaned towards the masculine side in herself (Djebar 1999: 73). In this context the masculine and feminine divide symbolised power on the one hand and domesticity on the other, and obviously in this case, the first dominated the second.

What emerges from Djebar's move from the world of the mother to that of the father is a third position of a woman who is educated and therefore cannot be dominated/ domesticated as she possessed the written word and could actually read and write. In fact, I would argue that the woman who could read and write enjoyed more power than men as she possessed two levels of language, the oral as well as the written, and gained access to both worlds, that of the inside and that of the outside, which Djebar expresses with a tone of joy in the following words, 'Porte ouverte vers le dehors, vers les autres, vers le monde entiré [An open door to the outside, to the others, to the whole world]' (1999: 74).

Well aware of this privilege, Djebar and the women of her kind became conscious of their duty towards their women folk; to be in this position meant to become their spokesperson '*Porte-parole*'. Djebar explains how her illiterate women compatriots who did not possess the written word became the bearers of the oral, of the inherited word and the inherited memory, making them thus the '*Porte-mémoire*'. This position of '*Porte-mémoire*', instead of empowering women as one might expect, resulted in their subjugation, condemning them to the role of the guardians of cultural heritage, a role which the nationalists of the postcolonial period across the Maghreb, but especially in the cases of Algeria and Morocco, used against women rather than to their advantage.

It must be highlighted that against a fierce colonial campaign of acculturation, women in the Maghreb stood as the guardians of the collective memory which they not only continued to safeguard in the vicinity of the private sphere but also passed over to future generations, thus surviving a 132-year-long period of colonialism/acculturation. In the absence of an official history and culture, people became attached to the oral roots of history, which were preserved and kept alive by women who in their anonymity nurtured the collective memory.

This safeguarding of the national identity on the cultural level was going hand in hand with the women's participation in the nationalist movement in the 1940s and the armed struggle for independence in the 1950s and 1960s. While the first role was assured by the women who stayed at home, the non-educated and the '*Porte-mémoire*', the second became the role of the new generation of educated women who worked or attended universities,[2] the '*Porte-parole*'. The heroism and war experiences, and in some cases experiences in captivity and torture and often rape by the colonial soldiers as experienced by this last category of women, could not become material for collective memory in the form of narrated stories. A thick veil of silence was imposed on their stories in order to protect the honour of their male folk.

My argument here is that while these newly educated women quickly moved into areas which were not designated as their own, especially in terms of joining the ranks of the freedom fighters in the bush, society as a whole was not quite ready for this change. Yes, on the surface these women were glorified for their revolutionary roles especially by the international media and by humanists such as Frantz Fanon (2001: 41), Jean Paul Sartre and Simone de Beauvoir (see de Beauvoir and Halimi 1962) who described their work as the hallmark of a national revolution's potential to liberate women. And yes, the nationalist movement and the National Liberation Army (Armée de Liberation Nationale; ALN) were happy to have them in their ranks as a form of publicity for the Algerian cause. It has to be underlined, however, that their roles on the fighting front soon became problematic as women's new status as warriors not only altered the patriarchal concept of the division of labour between the genders, but also challenged the wider power of patriarchy, threatening to erode its privileges.

What made the presence of these women amongst the freedom fighters most problematic was the type of relationships they could engage in with these new women whom they called mothers and sisters at first, as if to free them from posing a sexual threat which could distract the male fighters. But it is specifically this sexual side that resulted in more problems, as when these women fighters were arrested they were almost automatically raped. Djebar testifies:

> Before the war of liberation, the search for a national identity, if it did include a feminine participation, delighted in erasing the body and illuminating these women as 'mothers', even for those exceptional figures who were recognized as women warriors. But when, in the course of the seven years of the national war, the theme of the heroine becomes exalted, it is exactly around the bodies of young girls, whom I call the 'fire carriers' and whom the enemy incarcerates. (1992: 144)

It is surprising to notice that the traumatic events lived by these new women were quickly covered with thick layers of silence – a silence shared by everyone including the survivors of rape. A silent consensus was reached amongst everyone about this particular aspect which in reality is only part of the general suffering endured by the women war prisoners. However, in order to cover the shame caused by rape, the whole story has been sacrificed, which ultimately resulted in effacing the stories about the heroic participation of women in the Algerian war of independence. Brigitte Weltman-Aron remarks:

> The unveiling of women's tortures is apprehended as an unbearable infringement, not on women's bodies any more, but on their symbolic location within culture, which affects in turn men's own position. If, so goes the dream, that location had remained undisturbed, it would have preserved women. This construction is a dream in the sense that the 'preservation' of women is mythical, not actualized pragmatically, at least never in that totalizing gesture. The effect for women, however, of the wish to preserve, or the urge to veil them, is to shut out woman's possibility of seeing and of speaking, that is more generally, of testifying, above all about her own participation in history. (2000)

As a consequence of this imposed silence, the emancipatory movement of Algerian women, which culminated in joining the ranks of the war of independence, and which was seen by many as a challenge to patriarchy and old ways of life, was purged in its early days. As soon as independence was achieved, patriarchy resurfaced and claimed its traditional place in society. To consolidate its position, women were sent back to the private sphere. Their historical roles in safeguarding tradition and cultural heritage were glorified while overshadowing their roles in liberating the nation, which if highlighted could promote the liberation of women on the one hand and the weakening of patriarchy on the other. Highlighting the image of the woman fighter would also allude to men's inability to fight on their own; soliciting the help of women to liberate the nation could only signify men's weakness, while as culture has it, it is part of men's role to protect their women, honour and nation.

Sending women back to their homes was also a way meant to minimise their possibility of testifying about their participation in history. This became quite obvious in the early years of independence when the re-writing of Algerian history was launched by male members of the revolution, excluding the women who contributed to its making from the re-writing process. This exclusion from the writing of official history is backed up with images in the media, which glorified male heroes of the war of independence while relegating women to secondary roles as helpers and supporters of the revolution rather than real actors.

Images of Algerian women in film

The first feature film to have focused on Algerian women in the war of independence was made by Egyptian director Youssef Chahine in 1958, following the arrest and torture of Djamila Bouhired in 1957. His film *Jamila al-Jaza'iriyya* (The Algerian Jamila) was and remains the first and only feature to date focusing solely on the heroism of Algerian women during the 1954 revolution, exemplified in the film's protagonist, Djamila Bouhired.

As one of the heroines of the Battle of Algiers, Djamila was arrested and tried for being responsible for the deaths of many French settlers. After extensive torture which included her deflowering with a glass bottle, she was convicted and sentenced to death in July 1957. Jacque Verges, a French lawyer and humanist who believed in the Algerian people's right for self-determination, took Djamila's defence and waged an extremely effective public relations campaign. Under the overwhelming pressure of world public opinion, the execution was postponed, and in 1958 Djamila was sent to prison in Rheims (see Abul Husn 2003).

Chahine's film turned Djamila's heroism into the stuff of legend, as she stood firm against her oppressers and wrenched the hearts of an entire nation (see Salhi 2004b). During the verdict delivered on 26 April 1957, she told the magistrate, 'By killing us, remember it is your country's traditions of freedom that you assassinate, it is its honour that you compromise, and it is its future that you endanger' (quoted in Daoud 1996: 140).

Although *Jamila al-Jaza'iriyya* was hailed throughout the Arab world and the Eastern bloc countries, the film was banned by the Algerian government for many decades. Even though many believe that the reason for the ban is Djamila's marriage to Jacque Verges, who after all was a French man, I believe the reason to be the film's point of view as it centred on and glorified women's heroism. Another reason is because the film highlighted the rape of Djamila as part of the torture to which she was subjected. As mentioned above, a thick veil of silence was cast on the rape issue as it signified an assault on the clan's honour.

The first film to illustrate Algerian women of the revolution in the postcolonial period is Gillo Pontecorvo's, *La Bataille d'Alger* (*The Battle of Algiers*, 1965). The film's success lies in the way it depicts the transition of Algerian women from being veiled and secluded to becoming war heroines during the Battle of Algiers, and in the way it re-enacts with remarkable fidelity the events of this battle in which women played a major role and points out with a high degree of objectivity and realism the damage caused by the war to both coloniser and colonised.

Financed by the Algerian authorities, the film has as its central focus the war veteran Yacef Saadi, the military engineer of the Battle of Algiers who played his own role in the film. By the end of 1956, he had assembled in a meticulously organised hierarchy of some 1,400 operators. These included a good number of young Algerian women, chief among whom were Hassiba Ben Bouali, Zohra Drif, Djamila Bouhired, Malika Koriche, Fella and Samia Lakhdari.[3]

The film depicts the female heroines of the Battle at a meeting with Yacef Saadi in one of his secret hideouts in the Casbah.[4] The three women were assigned the task of placing three bombs in the heart of the European quarters in Algiers. The camera shows them as they transform themselves into European-looking girls by cutting and colouring their hair, wearing make-up and summery European dresses. 'Each was given a small bomb of little more than a kilogramme prepared by Yacef's bomb-maker, a twenty-four-year-old chemistry student called Taleb Abderrahmane [...] The girls concealed the bombs, set to go off at one-minute intervals from 18.30 hours, inside their beach bags under a feminine miscellany of bikinis, towels and sun-oil' (Horne 1977: 185–6).

The camera portrays the three girls as doing their utmost to pass for Europeans; when one of them is stopped at a checkpoint by a courteous soldier: 'I'd like to give you a real going over, but it's not so easy here!', she responded coquettishly: 'that could be, perhaps, if you often come to Saint-Eugéne beach' (Horne 1977: 186). This scene illustrates the audacity and skill of the woman-warrior who crossed the checkpoint to deposit her bomb in the Milk-bar, a particularly popular spot for the settlers on their way home from the beach.

Although the heroines suffered revulsion at their tasks, urban terrorism was then the only possible option left for the National Liberation Front to retaliate to the extreme violence of the colonists, namely the enormous bomb deposited in the Rue Thèbes in the heart of the Casbah, resulting in carnage killing seventy innocent civilians, and the execution by the guillotine in Barberousse prison in Algiers of Ahmad Zabana and Ferradj.

Although the motor in the Battle of Algiers was definitely the women, who not only deposited all the bombs but also facilitated the movements of the male fighters (see Fanon 2001: 41), Pontecorvo's film shows them as helpers and not as leaders. In the film they speak very little and only take action when they are given orders. The focal point of the film is not the role of women but the bravery of men like Ali la Pointe, the central hero, who was killed at the end of the film, and the tact and intelligence of heroes like Yacef Saadi and Larbi ben Mhidi whose discourse and voice dominate the movie and provide it with its philosophical line of argument. The voices of the female heroines, on the other hand, are non-existent throughout the movie and elsewhere in the public sphere.

A good example is when the camera zooms in on the three characters, namely Hassiba ben Bouali, a young boy and Ali la Pointe, who are in the same hideout, the camera's focus is mainly on Ali who is the only one whose voice is heard. The viewer has not heard Hassiba saying anything at all or passing a message to other women; in silence she followed Ali to the hideout and in silence she died.

Despite the fact that *The Battle of Algiers* may be criticised for the lack of agency granted to the female heroines and their being voiceless, films made by Algerian male film directors have never portrayed women in the revolutionary roles they played during the war.

Misrepresentation and betrayal: Women in the national war film

In the post-independence period, 'film was seen as forming a key part of the Algerian liberation struggle and in the mid-1960s the new Algerian government played the major part in the organization of all aspects of cinema, maintaining a monopoly on production, distribution and exhibition' (Leaman 2001: 446). This explains the thematic focus of virtually all filmmaking in the 1960s and 1970s on the Algerian revolution, a subject of vital concern to the first generation of Algerian filmmakers, many of whom had been active in the revolution.

What is overwhelming in these films is the machismo that is manifest in all war films. War heroes were glorified and their bravery over-stated. Such productions offered the public a restoration of the national pride which a long history of colonialism had completely repressed. Manhood and honour often constitute the focal point of these movies. What is also surprising is the total effacement of the female war heroines from these movies to the point that a less educated viewer would never know that these women actually played active roles in the revolution. As to the more educated viewer, these movies cast doubt on the portrayals of these women in the works of Fanon, Halimi and others. Two very contrasting images conflict in the mind: one propagated by the national media and another found in books.

None of the war films depicted women in the roles they actually undertook during the war; they were never shown as being fully responsible agents who played active parts in the revolution. Instead they were shown as helpers, and even then they were not portrayed as individuals, but rather as a group. This state of affairs depicts the general attitude towards women in post-independent Algeria. In Naomi Sakr's words, 'media representation of women matters because it is linked to women's status, which is determined in turn by national laws' (2002).

Furthermore, the misrepresentation of Algerian women in the colonial media as exotic attractions was replaced by other misrepresentations in the national media:

not portraying women in the roles they played, while at the same time the imagination of ordinary people was being filled by orally transmitted stories of heroism and courage displayed by the likes of Djamila Boubacha and others, creating more mystification around these women. Miriam Cooke remarks: 'We read about women whom Simone de Beauvoir and Frantz Fanon lionized in the 1960s, but whose voices were rarely, if ever heard. Without their voices, these women remain abstract heroines who had sprung up, Venus-like, from the maquis' (2001: 30).

In his film *L'Opium et le baton* (1969),[5] Ahmed Rachedi depicts the suffering undergone by the rural communities during the revolution, and focuses on a group of male heroes as central characters. To the viewer of the film, women only appeared as a group together with the children and the elderly, who were unable to join the ranks of the revolutionaries. The only woman that *Opium and the Stick* singles out is Ferroudja, sister and wife of fighters. She was arrested and questioned and under torture let out important information about the whereabouts of the fighters.

The film portrays the women not only as passive agents but also as negative characters who actually betrayed the revolution; had Ferroudja not given in to torture the heroes would not have been trapped by the French army. Ferroudja's betrayal, if one can describe it as such, cannot be compared with the courage of the Algerian Djamilas, such as Djamila Boubacha[6] and Djamila Bouhired or other Algerian heroines who resisted the most hideous kinds of torture and compromised their own lives in order to save those of their comrades. Clearly, despite its success as one of the best Algerian war films in terms of technique and acting, gender representation in this film is a slap to the Algerian women's heroism and history of nationalism.

Other war films, such as *Le Vent des Aurès* (*The Wind from the Aurès*, 1966) and *Chronique des années de braise* (*Chronicles of the Years of Embers*, 1975) by Lakhdar Hamina, also did not focus on the roles played by the women fighters. Although unlike most Algerian films dealing with the struggle for independence, *The Wind from the Aurès* put a female protagonist in the spotlight, the film only reproduced the traditional image of the suffering mother. She was lonely after her husband was killed, and her only son was held captive by the French army. Torn by the loss of her loved ones, the indomitable mother went from one detention camp to another in search of her son, until she eventually died electrocuted on the barbed wire surrounding the camp where her son was incarcerated, vainly trying to reach him (see Leaman 2001: 457).

Despite her obstinate search for her son, Hamina's protagonist is not a positive war heroine. The drive behind her search was not the revolution, but her motherly feelings for her son. This state of affairs contradicts the government's programme for the political and economic promotion of women in the early years of independence. Negative stereotyping in the media undermines the message that women's rights are integral to national development, a message propagated by the government in the 1976 national charter.[7]

Djebar and the restitution of women's gaze, voice and memory

In her collection of short stories, *Women of Algiers in their Apartment*, Djebar questions, 'what do we have as a "story" of our women, as feminine speech?' (1992: 144).

Although her literary career started with her novel *La Soif* (1957) when she was in her early twenties, and all her novels have centred on the women of Algeria, Djebar realised that the women in question did not have a voice. While it is true that as a woman who could write, she faithfully carried out her duty as the spokesperson of her women folk, Djebar soon became conscious that writing about these women was not enough, because what she was doing was conveying their voices rather than allowing them to physically express their voices and make them heard.

It is at this point that the need for a new medium became urgent, as the voices in question needed to be recorded and heard in all their originality. Through this active process of communication, a change of attitude was gradually taking place as new forms of discourse resurfaced and replaced as well as challenged the old. Furthermore, making these women speak plays more than one role; in addition to making them heard, Djebar was making them remember and by remembering she was empowering them and helping them regain confidence in their abilities to fulfill more than just the role of the '*Porte-mémoire*'. Most importantly, this act of remembering was allowing them to revisit and tend a wound which was forced to be hidden while untreated. For reasons to do mainly with the honour of the clan, women survivors of rape were never given the opportunity to overcome their trauma. The violence they were subjected to was never shared with anyone including their close relatives and partners. Instead they were encouraged to erase the whole story from their memory and suffocate the untreated wound.

For Djebar, the restitution of her compatriots' memory, and therefore their voice, was also an opportunity for her to re-emerge from a decade of self-inflicted literary silence during which she battled with the questioning of her role hitherto as a spokesperson of her women folk in the language of the ex-coloniser, and the bad linguistic polemic taking place in the early years of independent Algeria whose politicians were rejecting all French colonial legacy including the use of French as a medium of writing.[8] In fact, the new nationalist honour-based discourse drowned out all other discourses and voices in order to allow itself prominence.

During this decade of literary silence, Djebar examined the place of women in Algeria under the patriarchal nationalists, finding women's bodies and minds imprisoned by physical walls and mental veils. At this point she started a different kind of war to that against colonialism. It was a war against oblivion and against a narrow type of patriarchal nationalism which glorified manhood at the expense of sacrificing women's place in history and society, silencing their voices.

In her quest to retrieve her literary voice, Djebar worked on restoring the severed voices of the women of Mont Chenoua. Through liberating their discourse, she sought to liberate their gaze and voices, which emanate from their material bodies. To come close to these women, for and about whom Assia Djebar writes, she needed to resort to the language they spoke and understood – the language of their excised voices and shattered memories, which I would like to highlight here as 'mother-tongue'. I would argue that the return of Djebar to her mother-tongue, which she symbolically sought in her mother's village in the Mont Chenoua, is a Fanonian return of the disillusioned intellectual to their people. Spending long hours close to these women, listening to their stories and recording their voices, and more importantly them leading their lives, afforded Djebar a linguistic as well as a cultural immersion.

She expressed her ardent desire to come close to her mother-tongue as the umbilical cord that tied the women to each other; 'I decided to catch the sound, to get hold of the crude language' (Djebar 1999: 178), and to do so, she settled upon the idea of writing for the cinema as the most appropriate tool to give voice and reality to these women's struggles and frustrations, as well as to restore their place in the national discourse about Algerian history, from which they were tenaciously excluded. In 1978 Djebar, who until then was known as a Francophone novelist, took up the movie camera to shoot a film on Algerian women. Her act marked an important political and symbolic breakthrough of liberation and empowerment, despite the fact that it came at a relatively late stage in post-independence Algeria. She reveals:

> In my films, I have experimented with the different versions of the Arabic language in Algeria. I had an Arabic soundtrack and a French soundtrack for *Nouba*. I lived immersed in the language of the hinterland, an experience that ran quite contrary to the current efforts to impose a version of classical Arabic upon the land, an 'Arabisation from above' that has become, for me, the linguistic equivalent of war. Official Arabic is an authoritarian language that is simultaneously a language of men. (1992: 176)

She believes that women's cinema, whether in the third world or in 'the old world' always comes from *un désir de parole*: a desire for the word, 'it is as if "turning" to cinema was for women, to film with closed eyes, yet with the mobility of the voice and the body, the body not gazed upon, therefore not passive but rediscovering its autonomy and innocence' (1999: 166).

This leads to the conclusion that for Djebar, cinema is a liberating tool which restores the mobility of the voice and the body of the women in question. Not only of the women in the film but also of Djebar herself, who after a decade of literary silence, finally found her voice. Unlike the novel, cinema brings the author closer to her people, and at the same time it restores their truncated voices and revives their shattered memory as well as recording and immortalising their gestures and postures, as they tell their stories.

La Nouba des femmes du Mont Chenoua[9]

When Djebar's film *The Nouba of the Women of Mont Chenoua* was released in 1978, as the first film by a woman in the Maghreb, Algerian journalists commented on the great difficulties of reading it, and the viewers' failure in becoming 'engaged' or 'taken' by the film. Djebar remarks: 'My film was vilified by almost all the cinema critics in Algiers, because they could not find in it the optimism of social realism. It won, however, the International Critics Prize at the Venice Film Festival' (1999: 6).

In his book *Experimental Nations*, Reda Bensmaïa, voicing the views of other critics, described the film in the following terms: 'The film seems to take a perverse pleasure in thoroughly disappointing any desire on the viewer's part to tie up loose ends or to reach closure' (2003: 83). This can be contrasted with Djebar´s words:

> I am aware that this is a difficult film. As I said I wanted to make a research film. I do not think, however, that it is inaccessible. I did not want to fall into populism by choosing a simplified production and narrative based on certain clichéd characters. The aim of my work is to restore the authentic voices of ordinary women, and help them regain their sensibility in order for them to become able to express themselves about their everyday concerns … at the level of the narrative I had to decide when history should be turned into fiction and when to insert the documentary slots. (1981: 105)

That the critics vilified *The Nouba of the Women of Mont Chenoua* can be explained not just by the break with the tradition of social realism as Djebar claimed, but also because it came from a film with an entirely different perspective: (i) the film affords the women it represents the central stage while the men are relegated to the periphery; (ii) it focuses on the feminine first-person narrator, 'I', which was denied to women in preceding national films; and (iii) it propagates a strong feminist message, because restoring women's voices and memory empowers women and genders war narratives, which in turn genders the nation.

Furthermore, whereas the national war films, which were and still remain much favoured by Algerian viewers, often portray a linear story, with a focus on two fighting groups, while highlighting the heroism and suffering of the revolutionary fighters, the only war scenes portrayed in *The Nouba of the Women of Mont Chenoua* are flashbacks composed of war footage. There is no chauvinism, no villains and no heroes. What matters most is that the women of Mont Chenoua come to terms with their lived traumas of yesterday, as a cure to empower them to face the future.

The Nouba of the Women of Mont Chenoua offers viewers none of the classic narrative perspectives that would enable them to close the circle and enter fully into the subject matter of the film. What made it more difficult for the public to engage with the film is its polyphonic aspect: there is not one voice but many voices and there is not one story but four different storylines: (i) the story of the main protagonist Lila:

fiction and war footage; (ii) the stories of the women of Mont Chenoua: reality; (iii) the stories women storytellers tell the children: folk heritage; and (iv) the legend of the pigeons incorporated into the film, as a sample of the repertoire of Maghrebi folktales. These four threads are knitted carefully throughout the film by the unusual structure, in the form of a *nouba*, a classical form of Maghrebi, Andalusian symphony, in which women play active parts either as the main singers of the *nouba*, or as part of the orchestra.

A musical *nouba* is made of a number of movements, which may differ from one to another, and all these movements are played by the same orchestra, and often each movement would be sung by a different member of the orchestra, with the finale being sung by the whole orchestra. While a traditional *nouba* would voice several melodramatic accounts of failed love and longing that are not necessarily interlinked thematically, *The Nouba of the Women of Mont Chenoua* encompasses stories by various women, with the main protagonist's story as the backbone to which the other stories are linked.

The film is thus divided into six movements of ten to twelve minutes each, which in turn is similar to the movements of the musical *nouba* which can be enjoyed as separate movements/songs. Djebar explains: 'each one of the six movements of *The Nouba of the Women of Mont Chenoua* has its own unity. Thus, you could view the film in sections of ten to twelve minutes each. This technique allows the broadcasting of the film as a documentary' (1981: 107). On choosing this musical structure for her film, Djebar clarifies: 'this comes as a result of my empathy with popular culture, which inspired me on various forms to structure the film upon. These *noubas* have existed for four centuries as a collective heritage. I also played on the word *nouba*, which means: a story that people tell one after another' (ibid.).

The story of Lila

The film opens with an indoor sequence portraying Lila who has finally found her voice, as she repeatedly says: 'I speak, I speak, I speak', which undoubtedly symbolises Djebar's finding of her lost voice after a decade of literary silence. Like the author, Lila sets out on a mission to restore the lost voices of her women compatriots. Furthermore, by turning away from the camera and refusing to be gazed upon, Lila challenges the image of Arab women as the mute objects of Orientalist and colonial media.

This betrays Djebar's excitement at the potential the camera offers for a distinctive reversal of the female gaze; at the same time as the camera zooms in on Lila, the latter turns against the wall, and declares: 'I do not want to be gazed upon.' All that the viewer is left with is the back of her head, but what matters most is the recovered voice of the woman and not her image.

In the background, Ali, Lila's husband, is symbolically confined to a wheelchair, and while she speaks he is silent and powerless, especially when she tells him: 'I do not want you to gaze at me.' He is portrayed as calm, silent and passive, characteristics that are usually attributed to women in the Maghreb, and while Lila is constantly on the move, by car, boat or on foot, his space becomes restricted. There is a reversal of space too in this film; in the Maghreb the private sphere of the home is usually designated as the women's space, while the public space is that of men. Lila moves freely between the two spaces, and does not seem to be blocked by any boundaries.

At home, Lila interacts very little with Ali, which betrays a relationship at crisis point. She is almost entirely detached from him, as they do very little together. What seems to keep the relationship going is their little girl Aisha, who interacts equally with both parents, and brings a stream of life to the desolate and almost empty home. It is with Aisha that Lila finds her moments of joy, such as when they play on the bed, when they are bathing, and most importantly, when Lila tells her child the stories told to her by the women in the village; the camera adapts the female role of transmitting the cultural heritage across the generations.

At night Lila is constantly tormented by nightmares of the not-too-distant past of the war of independence; this is when the film incorporates war footage in black and white, which gives Lila's fictitious story a touch of realism. These war scenes inform us that the lived traumas of the bloody events of the revolution are still in the subconscious of people, and the remedy to overcome these traumas is certainly not the silence that was largely observed by Algerians as a way of forgetting the horrors of the past. Rather, as the film suggests, the people should go through the labour of mourning and anamnesis, which may result in a reconciliation with Algeria's horrific past.

One should highlight at this point that during the Algerian war, those who lost loved ones for the revolution were not supposed to mourn them. Instead, women were expected to ululate, a cry of joy that symbolised the transition of the deceased to paradise. Mourning a martyr was also deemed inappropriate as the price for the nation's independence had no bounds.

On the human level, however, these losses are traumatic. Although Lila is silent about the losses of both her parents and brother as martyrs, she is haunted by the war that rendered her an orphan at a young age. Her return to the village, and her search for signifiers that resuscitate certain patches of childhood, are vital elements for her to reconstruct a personal history from tatters. Moreover, re-appropriating her ability to speak is indispensable if she is to overcome the traumas of the past in order to fully interrelate to the present and the future.

The stories of the women of Mont Chenoua

For Lila, the women of Mont Chenoua symbolise her return to her native village. They represent the umbilical cord that ties her to her past, her history and her culture. They are also the silent witnesses and actors of the revolution. To the younger generation of Algerian women, the recurring and tormenting question is why did these women keep silent? Why did they give up their revolutionary roles to return to the traditional roles that bind them to the private sphere? One might even wonder whether they have really contributed to the revolution. These women are in fact the main target of *The Nouba of the Women of Mont Chenoua*, the women whose silenced voices Djebar wants to restore. In the film, they are portrayed not as weak characters, as one might expect, but as proud women who, like all the women of Algeria, have played a crucial role in the revolution. What surprises the viewer is their confidence, their spontaneity and their eagerness to tell their side of the story.

With the mediation of Lila who visits them in their houses and asks them specific questions, the stories of the women of Mont Chenoua unfold. The camera not only records their voices, but also their gesture and posture as they tell their stories, and most importantly the camera moves to the places where the story events took place as landmarks of memory, with the women pointing at various spots which they carefully link to their narratives.

One of them points to the fields she ploughed in order to feed the revolutionary fighters, another points to the locations where Zuleikha, the female martyr of the village, was operating. Following the martyrdom of her husband, Zuleikha, Lila's mother, joined the *maquis* to fight the invaders. After her arrest she was killed and her body was dumped in the city square. Another woman told Lila about the martyrdom of her brother, who, before his death, came to ask her to bury his body for he feared being eaten by jackals. The same woman lost her three sons in battle, yet, she told Lila with pride, 'I shall not weep' and this image of the defiant woman is contrasted in the film with that of a father who wept as his wife told Lila the story of their thirteen-year-old daughter who became traumatised as she witnessed the martyrdom of her brother from the tree top where she was hiding. Unable to overcome her trauma, she remained on the same tree for the rest of her life.

As such, stories, and sometimes fragments of stories, of remembrances, of things buried in the memory and never spoken of, testimonies from the immediate or distant past are told again and again to finally come together like the pieces of a jigsaw, to assemble a shattered memory of the revolution. Bringing these narratives together in one film creates a unity, a group memory of women, not only as a cure from the traumas they underwent, but most importantly to empower them to claim their place on the map of independent Algeria.

In her book *Autobiographical Voices*, Françoise Lionnet highlights this empowering aspect. She insists on these women's 'need to find their past, to trace lineages that will empower them to live the present, to rediscover the histories occluded by History' (1989: 25). Moreover, internalising and keeping silent over their traumatic experiences means never overcoming the nightmares of yesterday, and never crossing the barrier of history that keeps them confined to the past. Making these women tell their stories allows them to revive their revolutionary spirit of yesterday, so that they may continue in the same vein today, but most importantly, so that they become the role models for younger generations of women.

Women's roles as storytellers

In addition to the importance of women's oral transmission (of her-story) in the project of rewriting national history (his-story), Djebar also gives women's role as transmitters of cultural heritage, 'Porte-mémoire', its due merit. Although this particular role of women, to which Maghrebi governments seem to confine them, is often considered negative by critics, The Nouba of the Women of Mont Chenoua takes a different perspective on women's role as 'Porte-mémoire' and specifically as storytellers.

In the film, Lila cherished the memory of her grandmother who not only told her fascinating folktales, but also the history of her tribe in her very own words. In the absence of a living person who witnessed Algeria before the invasion and occupation (which lasted 132 years), its history as a free country only lived in the memory of the grandmothers who made sure they transmitted it to their granddaughters. Djebar writes, 'my former mother-in-law ... was able to show me that a woman's memory spans centuries – just one woman. She would talk of an obscure, forgotten old woman she used to know who used to talk of the old days. This is precisely how Algerian women "relay" the past: they tell the (his) story of colonisation, but tell it otherwise' (1992: 170–1).

At one stage the camera zooms in on a little girl sitting close to her grandmother who in the posture and gesture of a traditional storyteller counts and recounts a story in a cage-like bed. The camera then moves swiftly to the floor where several other women sitting on mats tell groups of children sitting in a circle around them the oral history of their tribe, reproducing and immortalising images of how stories were narrated in the past. These women speak in whispers, with the camera focussing on their gestures, while we hear the voice-over of Lila who identifies with the little girl sitting close to her grandmother, 'that was her, that was me. Me as a little girl, in the bed! Every night, my grandmother would tell me the story of our tribe, its history, in her own words!' (1992: 171).

The camera then moves to shots from the nineteenth century, when the French invaded the country, and captures a group of women who were running towards a cave, which recalls the events of the ruthless 'fumigations' of rebel tribes in the Oued Riah caves when women, children and oxen were trapped forever. In other words, Djebar pays due respect to the 'Porte-mémoire', who with their tireless telling and retelling of the history of the nation before its invasion made it possible for Algerians to dream of a free Algeria despite the density of the long colonial night.[10]

The legend of the pigeons

As part of the history of the tribe, the film incorporates a mythical version in the form of the story of the pigeons. The mother of Djamila, as Lila calls her, tells the story of

Sidi Abdel Rahman, the saint ancestor of the tribe, who came from the Orient as a shepherd. When it was later discovered that he was a man of learning who knew the sacred word of Allah, a mosque was built for him to teach the *Qur'an* to the children. The story swiftly moves to the legend of the pigeons and how, thanks to the benediction of their saint, the people did not have to work. In his house there were magical jars whose contents never disappeared, until the day when his seventh daughter-in-law, who, driven by curiosity, dared and uncovered the jars which then freed the pigeons they contained. The chain of oral transmission of this legend reached the younger generation of Lila's daughter, who replied to her mother when she told her the story, that she could hear the pigeons flying over her house.

The end of *The Nouba of the Women of Mont Chenoua* draws all four narrative strings together through a Saharan song which directly addresses the viewer. The warm voice of the male singer is accompanied by a summary of the film, through images of the people who in their turn contributed to its construction. Like the musical *nouba* all the members of the chorus are brought together in the finale.

The song transmits a note of optimism, as well as a 'proper' celebration of independence by the women who have now come to terms with their traumas and risen with confidence to celebrate a well deserved freedom. The ending offers a clear sense of relief which represents the joy of Lila and the women of Mont Chenoua, who have finally managed to overcome the traumas of yesterday by overcoming silence and becoming conscious of their storytelling gift as an empowering tool which gave them prominence over the male nationalists.

Conclusion

From Djebar's venture in *The Nouba of the Women of Mont Chenoua*, it becomes clear that what she is trying to say is that the national history narrative should not just be made up of famous people. It is undeniable that the names of the heroines of the battle of Algiers are known to the world through the images propagated by the international media in the 1950s and 1960s, and despite the efforts of the successive governments of Algeria to overshadow these heroines across the various national media (mainly film and representations in museums and public places), their names inhabit the national memory.

What *The Nouba of the Women of Mont Chenoua* highlights is that history should be a compilation of the narratives and testimonies of the makers of that history which include both men and women, both heroes and ordinary people who, despite their anonymity, ensured the continuation and success of the national revolution; they are the women who cooked, washed, sewed, kept vigil, transported messages in the most intimate parts of their bodies, hid and transported the funds of the revolution – all at the risk of being discovered by the colonial soldiers, raped and tortured in the most hideous manner. They are also the ones who stayed behind to face the colonial army's reprisals following an attack by the revolutionary fighters.

These women were not given space in the war narratives and national history, which were traditionally thought to be solely a male domain. Their vital contributions were not considered as central to the revolutionary work, but were seen as marginal and often taken for granted, as were the works they would be doing in ordinary times. Marie-Aimé Hélie-Lucas explains:

> If a man carried food to the armed fighters at great personal risk, he was called a 'fighter'. A woman doing the same was called a 'helper'. If a man risked his life to hide armed fighters or wanted political leaders, he was called a 'fighter'. A woman doing the same was simply performing the female task of 'nurturing'. Nor was she considered a fighter when she collected fuel or food for the fighters, or carried their guns, or guided them through the mountains. She was merely helping the men. (1990: 106)

Consequently, women's version of the history of Algeria, as well as their war narratives were dismissed or at best left in the margins of modern Algerian history, and their voices were destined to an eternal silence and general amnesia. Annedith Schneider elucidates: 'Traditional accounts of war define it as a masculine enterprise and war narratives thus as the work of men. Such accounts have been used to justify a special role for men within the nation, as wartime experience supposedly makes them eminently qualified to be not only military but also civilian leaders' (2003: 1).

The value of *The Nouba of the Women of Mont Chenoua* lies not only in restoring oral transmission to its rightful place, but most importantly in challenging the established order that war narratives are the work of men alone. Even more fundamentally, it represents a symbolic opportunity for women to restore their excised voices and memories and empower them to face the challenges of the contemporary, independent Algeria. What Assia Djebar achieved through this film is the re-writing of the story of the Algerian revolution, interweaving official, written histories of Algeria with the oral stories of ordinary women who participated in the struggle for independence. Valorising women's contributions in non-military roles and acknowledging their sacrifices, these latter stories imagine women as central to national history and suggest a vision of nation building that might include both men and women.

As such, Djebar successfully substitutes silence with voice, oblivion with memory, and voicelessness with speech. She has rightly become the spokesperson '*Porte-parole*' of the sequestrated women, writer-witness of a historical era, the writer stimulating the memory of the grandmothers, the '*Porte-mémoire*', who shakes the archives of history.

Notes

1   All quotations from this source are translated by the author.
2   For more details on the Algerian feminist movement and the new roles played by women in the

Algerian war of independence see Salhi (2009).

3   For the first time in October 2004, fifty years after the revolution, the Algerian daily *El Watan* published a whole page with a photograph of the young women who participated in the Battle of Algiers and a testimony by Fella. See Bensalem (2004).

4   Casbah is the old medieval part of Algiers, which, during the colonial period, was inhabited solely by Algerian families. French settlers inhabited the European quarters in the centre of Algiers which was built by the colonists.

5   The film is based on Mouloud Mammeri's 1965 novel of the same title.

6   For a detailed account of the ordeal of Djamila Boubacha, see Simone de Beauvoir and Giséle Halimi (1962).

7   For further details see Salhi (2004a).

8   For a lengthy discussion of this point, see Salhi (2008).

9   Assia Djebar, *La Nouba des femmes du Mont Chenoua* (1978). The film won the International Critics Prize at the 1979 Film Festival in Venice. Before the production of *La Nouba des femmes du Mont Chenoua*, Djebar worked as an assistant director on a number of productions. In 1973 she directed her own adaptation of Tom Eyen's play about Marilyn Monroe, *The White Whore and the Bit Player* (1964). Along with teaching history at the University of Algiers, Djebar also taught theatre and film. In 1982, Djebar made *La Zerdaou les chants de l'oubli*, a documentary about the history of the Maghreb between 1912 and 1942.

10 A similar metaphor is used by Mohammed Dib in the trilogy *Algeria* (1952–57), where Oum El-Kheir, the oldest woman in the tribe still remembered when Algeria was free.

Bibliography

Abul Husn, M. (2003) 'Woman of Distinction: Djamila Bouhired, the Symbol of National Liberation'. *Al-Shindagah*, November-December. Available: http://www.alshindagah.com/novdec03/womanof distinction.htm (accessed on 02 March 2003).

Bensalem, S. (2004) 'Portrait d'une moudjahida poseuse de bombes', *El Watan*, 31 October, p.16.

Bensmaïa, R. (2003) *Experimental Nations, or the Invention of the Maghreb*. Trans. A Waters. Princeton: Princeton University Press.

Cooke, M. (2001) *Women Claim Islam: Creating Islamic Feminism Through Literature*. London: Routledge.

Daoud, Z. (1996) *Féminisme et politique au Maghreb: Sept décennies de lutte*. Casablanca: Editions Eddif.

De Beauvoir, S. and G. Halimi (1962) *Djamila Boubacha: The Story of Torture of a Young Algerian Girl which Shocked Liberal French Opinion*. London: Deutsch/Weidenfeld and Nicholson.

Djebar, A. (1957) *La Soif*. Paris: Julliard.

_____ (1981) 'J'ai recherché un language musical', interview in M. Berrah, V. Bachy, M. ben Salama and F. Boughedir (eds) *Cinémas du Maghreb*. Paris: Editions Papyrus, 105–9.

_____ (1992) *Women of Algiers in their Apartment*. Trans. M. de Jager. Charlottesville: University Press of Virginia.

_____ (1999) *Ses voix qui m'assiègent: en marge de ma Francophonie*. Paris: Albin Michel.

_____ (2003) 'Idiome de l'exil et langue de l'irréductibilité'. *Retour remue.net: auteurs contemporains*. Available: http://www.remue.net/cont/djebar01.html (accessed on 02 March 2003).

Fanon, F. (2001) *L'An V de la révolution algérienne*. Paris: La Découverte.

Hélie-Lucas, M.-A. (1990) 'Women, Nationalism and Religion in the Algerian Liberation Struggle', in M. Badran and M. Cooke (eds) *Opening the Gates: A Century of Arab Feminist Writing*. Bloomington: Indiana University Press, 105–14.

Horne, A. (1977) *A Savage War of Peace: Algeria 1954–1962*. London: Macmillan.

Lionnet, F. (1989) *Autobiographical Voices: Race, Gender, Self-Portraiture*. Ithaca: Cornell University Press.

Leaman, O. (2001) *Companion Encyclopedia of Middle Eastern and African Cinema*. London: Routledge.

Sakr, N. (2002) 'Seen and Starting to be Heard: Women and the Arab Media in a Decade of Change', *Social Research*, Fall. Available: http://findarticles.com/p/articles/mi_m2267/is_3_69/ai_94227143/ (accessed on 04 May 2009).

Salhi, Z. S. (2004a) 'Algerian Women, Citizenship and the Family Code', in C. Sweetman (ed.) *Gender, Development, and Citizenship*. Oxford: Oxfam Publications, 27–35.

____ (2004b) 'Memory, Gender, and National Identity in the Work of Assia Djebar', *Moving Worlds: A Journal of Transcultural Writings*, 4, 1, 17–30.

____ (2008) 'Between the Languages of Silence and the Woman's Word: Gender and Language in the Work of Assia Djebar', *International Journal of the Sociology of Language*, Special Issue on 'Language and Gender in the Mediterranean Region', 190, 79–102.

____ (2011) 'Algerian Women as Actors of Change and Social Cohesion', in F. Sadiqi (ed.) *Women as Agents of Change in the Middle East and North Africa*. London: Routledge, 149–72.

Schneider, A. M. (2003) 'Building the Nation: Narrating Women and the Algerian War', *Gender Debat/tl/ed*, 5. Available: http://www.genderforum.uni-koeln.de/debattled/Schneider.html (accessed on 24 November 2004).

Spivak, G. (1985) 'Can the Subaltern Speak?: Speculations on Widow Sacrifice'. *Wedge* 7-8(Winter/Spring): 120-130.

Weltman-Aron, B. (2000) 'Veiled Voices: Fanon, Djebar, Cixous, Derrida'. *Tympanum* 4, 15 July. Available: http://www.usc.edu/dept/comp-lit/tympanum/4/weltman_aron.html (accessed on 20 January 2005).

Women's Stories and Public Space in Iranian New Wave Film

Anna M. Dempsey

After the Islamic Revolution of 1979, Iranian cinema reflected the regime's insistence on the invisibility of Western visual and cultural mores – especially those associated with the sexually mature or maturing female. Yet, though Iranian directors in the 1980s and early 1990s largely complied with government standards, filmmakers did indirectly challenge government censorship (see Naficy 1995). To bypass censors, directors used young people to comment on Iranian politics and culture. Abbas Kiarostami's *Where is My Friend's House?* (1987), for example, employed children as direct observers of the restrictive conditions under which Iranians lived and filmmakers operated. 'Children,' as one critic notes, are 'freer than adults,' and could be viewed by these filmmakers 'as everyone's alter egos' (Sadr 2002: 235, 228).

With changes in the governing body and the loosening of political and cultural restrictions in the first decade of this century, a more complex and nuanced form of Iranian cinema has emerged. This is particularly true regarding gender. Though post-Revolutionary filmmakers also employ girls and boys as cinematic narrators, they depict male/female relationships in a far more explicit fashion than that of their predecessors. As this chapter argues, the directors of the contemporary New Wave films *The White Balloon* (Jafar Panahi, 1995), *The Girl in the Sneakers* (Rasul Sadr Ameli, 1998), *The Circle* (Jafar Panahi, 2000) and *The Day I Became a Woman* (Marziyeh Meshkini, 2000) present viewers with a multilayered, textured portrait of the public position and the myriad choices available to young women and girls in contemporary Iran.

As Lindsey Moore observes: 'one of the remarkable features of recent Iranian film is its allegorical use of gendered tropes, in particular the (in)visibility and (im)mobility of women in social space' (2005: 1). This chapter illustrates this by focusing on how Iranian New Wave films use public space to comment on the position of women in Iranian society. In *The Girl in the Sneakers*, *The White Balloon* and *The Mirror* (Jafar Panahi 1997), young female protagonists move through urban landscapes that are gritty greenless spaces marked by clogged roadways, bus exhaust fumes and anonymous rushing pedestrians. These non-distinct streets are reminiscent of those in a postwar Italian neorealist film. Shohini Chaudhuri and Howard Finn observe that contemporary Iranian film adapts the 'spatial indeterminacy' or 'disconnected spaces' of European neorealist cinema to Iranian cinematic forms (2006: 394, 396). As in the films of Roberto Rossellini or Vittorio de Sica, Iranian New Wave directors portray the public square as a dystopic space in which no genuine public exchange occurs. In contrast to the disenfranchised characters in Vittorio de Sica's *Bicycle Thieves* (1946) however, Iranian female figures have little agency. While the boys in *Bicycle Thieves* and *Shoeshine* (Vittorio de Sica, 1946) and the freedom fighters of postwar Rome (*Rome, Open City*, Roberto Rossellini, 1945) affect the power dynamics in the public square, Iranian cinematic females are consigned to the fringes of the city. They inhabit the sidewalk's edge, a nighttime transient-filled park, the roadside gutter, a paved road by a beach and other liminal spaces that underscore their marginalised, ephemeral presence.

Panahi's young female protagonist in *The White Balloon*, for example, glides through the street throngs as though she were simply a shadow. Almost no one, despite the child's evident efforts, seems to notice her. As with the orphaned children of postwar Italy, she appears to be at the mercy of the dominant adult forces which surround her. Yet unlike an innocent Western girl who is alone in a city – and to which many of us would supply an inevitable tragic ending – this persistent child eventually and competently negotiates urban power relations. Though the narrative begins with her ostensibly futile quest to find and retrieve the lost money her mother gives her to buy a goldfish, at the end of the story the child emerges triumphant and unhurt (see Sadr 2002: 232). The director depicts childhood, and Islamic girlhood in particular, as far more complex and contradictory than Western assumptions about youth or gender might suggest. More importantly, he employs a narrative framework in which no conclusion to the story is evident – a convention common in Iranian cinema. Panahi's gender and narrative frameworks are also evident in the Iranian New Wave films discussed in the remainder of this chapter: *The Girl in the Sneakers*, *The Circle* and *The Day I Became a Woman*.

Sadr Ameli's *The Girl in the Sneakers* tells the story of fifteen-year old Tadai who is chastised and humiliated – including a dehumanising physical examination to establish her virginity – for speaking with a teenage boy, Aideen, in a public park. As a punishment, her parents forbid her to see him. Despite this, Tadai runs away from home in a desperate attempt to get in touch with Aideen. We accompany her on her 24-hour quest through the streets of Tehran. During the daylight hours, she meanders on narrow pedestrian paths that parallel frenetic street traffic. To enable viewers to see the city through her curious and frightened eyes, the director immerses us in the confusion, noise and smells of a Tehran that could be almost any developed city. Because no architectural, cultural or historic marker distinguishes the cinematic urban centre through which Tadai wanders, viewers are equally disoriented by this overwhelming urban landscape. Sadr Ameli depicts the city as a disjointed set of 'disconnected spaces' much like the European neorealist filmmakers used after World War II (see Chaudhuri and Finn 2006: 396). Thus, viewers must search for a familiar marker or object upon which to focus attention.

The telephone (and the tone of the voices associated with it) represents just such an object and is the viewer's primary material link to the comfortably familiar. Moreover, it is the literal and metaphoric thread that shapes Tadai's quest and with it the cinematic narrative. In the film, the determined but naïve girl repeatedly stops to telephone Aideen's home, only to be rebuffed by his mother or sister. We witness her frustration and subsequent desperate attempts to solicit the help of a middle-aged man who has been quietly watching her. Though she innocently accompanies the stranger to his home – where viewers are tempted to supply the inevitable tragic ending – Tadai escapes unharmed and wanders Tehran's congested streets once more. Surprisingly, she seems to be safest while immersed in an urban landscape which functions as a metaphoric parent for the adolescent girl. Like the headscarf she wears, the impersonal public square of the daytime hours cloaks her in a mantle of invisibility. As Andrew Horton concludes, 'landscapes are not passive but operate as part of the intricacies of social relations, including identity formation' (2003: 75). In *The Girl in the Sneakers*, the daytime urban chaos protects the female protagonist's anonymity and allows her to assert her independence – an independence that depends, nevertheless, on the benevolence of the adults she encounters.

Once night begins, the cityscape changes. Despite Tadai's efforts to obtain a hotel room, her status as an unaccompanied young woman prevents her from finding any accommodation. She is forced to wander the streets again where she encounters the marginalised but colourful night-time inhabitants of Tehran. It would seem that they emerge during the evening hours as though from behind the 'veil' that shrouds them from the city's daytime residents. For example, Tadai encounters a street child and an ostensibly homeless mother and infant while on her journey. The woman is revealed to be a charlatan who offers to help Tadai find accommodation in a shuttered kiosk. After Tadai objects, the woman takes the young girl to her homeless colony in a city park. While the woman and the other denizens of this space initially appear somewhat menacing, they welcome Tadai into the carnivalesque, marginalised world they inhabit.

This cinematic place exemplifies what Michel Foucault has referred to as a heterotopia. For Foucault, heterotopic spaces are the opposite of our unreal, utopian projections. Though he regards psychiatric clinics, prisons and brothels as exemplars of heterotopias, he also notes that a heterotopia is 'as perfect, meticulous and

well-arranged as ours is disordered, ill-conceived and in a sketchy state. This heterotopia is not one of illusion but of compensation' (1997: 356) for what we lack.
Such spaces represent actual places which are marginal to society and in which the
Other resides. In this regard, the colourful cinematic night-time park where Tehran's
prostitutes, petty thieves and homeless inhabitants gather could be regarded as a
compensatory space for those marginalised in the sexually segregated, puritanical
daytime world. Though it seems unlikely that this park's night-time card-playing
residents can kidnap a recalcitrant teenage youth and force him to converse with
his waiting girlfriend, they do so. In the film's concluding scene, Tadai meets the kid-
napped Aideen in this Foucauldian compensatory space. Her final decision to walk
away from him and into the night-time streets seems as romantic and as improbable
as the colourful lights which frame their meeting. Nevertheless, though idealised, we
should regard the setting in which it occurs as real. Sadr Ameli frames an imaginary,
but tangible, heterotopia where dominant societal conventions can be challenged by
players and viewers.

In part, this occurs because the sneaker-clad Tadai functions as both a character and as a stand-in for the director and for the viewer. She is a participant in and
observer of public power relationships and of her own reaction to them. Tadai is
at once oblivious and weary of the inevitable attention that she receives. Even in
the campsite to which she is brought by a hustling maternal 'beggar', her would-be
exploiter saves her from a potential molester from whom she had attempted to flee.
As an adolescent, Tadai straddles two worlds. She is simultaneously a potential sexual victim and an innocent observer of the male-dominated Iranian society. Tadai's
removal of her solid-coloured head scarf in favour of the multicoloured one her 'beggar' benefactor gives her, signals this liminal status.

Because the headscarf attractively frames her, we are aware that Tadai's youthful form and beautiful face might be viewed as a passive object for voyeuristic
consumption. Nevertheless, we cannot assume that Laura Mulvey's (1975) classic reinterpretation of the Lacanian gaze can be simply applied to Iranian cinema.
While the close-ups of Tadai's face clearly command our attention, her youthful
innocence challenges our scopophilic desire. Tadai's childlike questioning and rebellion – her look back – disempower those who would subject her adolescent body
to an all-powerful consuming gaze. These differing looks suggest that conflicting
gazes are operating here. Along with the male gaze, the feminine 'matrixial gaze'
is also present in this liminal borderspace along the water. Bracha Ettinger writes
that 'with the matrixial gaze ... I am transformed by *it* only insofar as *it* is also transformed by me ... The metamorphosis through which borderlines between subject
and objects ... become thresholds is a process of bringing into being-together, or a
becoming-women-with' (2006: 86–7). But is Tadai transformed by our gaze back?
Or by her rebellion? Her face tells us nothing. She simply walks away. Though Tadai
has asserted her independence at the end of the film, we still do not know what the
conclusion to her story will be.

In contrast to Sadr Ameli's depiction of the public square as protective of adolescent girls, the women in Panahi's *The Circle* cannot safely walk the streets alone. Even the anonymity provided by the *hijab* cannot guarantee their safety. This occurs, in part, because Panahi's film focuses on women who have escaped or been recently released from prison. These individuals are isolated, 'marked' women who furtively move through a public square framed by the panoptical male/camera eye. The lone *chador*-clad figures are shadowy non-specific persons who cling to the walls that enclose them. As the title of the film suggests, their lives are circumscribed by a patriarchal system that seeks to curtail their independence and individuality (see Teo 2001). The camera circles round the grown women and does not linger long in the settings in which their stories take place. Panahi does, however, pause on each of their faces. We see the terrified and knowing eyes of a grandmother who witnesses the prison birth of a granddaughter, the desperate expression of an abortion-seeking young woman (whose lover had been executed), and the swollen face of a frightened eighteen-year-old who wishes but is terrified to return to her village. Because the director jumps from character to character, the viewer can only conjecture as to the reason behind the emotional trauma incised in the figures' canyon-like facial furrows and fear-stricken eyes.

The faces of these young and old women, especially that of the downcast mother who has abandoned her daughter, are similar to the denuded landscapes onto which the passing of time is clearly etched and impossible to alter. The mother has made the harrowing decision to abandon her daughter for economic reasons. Her face, which is framed by a dark headscarf and night-time shadows, emerges from the veiled gloom to directly confront the viewer. We see the furrowed circles beneath the mournful liquid eyes. As with any portrait of the elderly Georgia O'Keefe (who abandoned home and husband to pursue her art in New Mexico), we are presented with a knowledgeable woman who has made the one difficult choice available to her. The director does not suggest, however, that this is the correct choice. Has the woman broken the circle that imprisons her and her daughter? Or has she consigned her orphaned daughter to the same fate? We cannot know. These young girls – whether abandoned or aborted – are silenced. Their faces, identities and futures are unclear. For Panahi, *The Circle* is the inevitable conclusion to the more idealistic but equally enigmatic *The White Balloon* and *The Mirror*. Panahi states, 'in the life of adults, like in *The Circle*, the characters come out of idealism and they're more realistic – they are the same children but now they have grown up and they see the world with realistic eyes' (quoted in Teo 2001).

For the director, children tell a very different story from the one an adult might narrate. This may be the reason for the opposing narrative approaches in *The Circle* and in *The Mirror*. Panahi concludes that 'through the eyes of children, it's a much nicer world that they see, because children are in a world where they are not really aware of the difficulties of adults. They're trying to achieve their ideals' (ibid.). But this is not entirely accurate. Halfway through *The Mirror*, the young protagonist Mina rips off her headscarf and declares that she is tired of making a movie. She is striking out at a world that seeks to confine her literally and cinematically. Unlike the furtive, older women of *The Circle*, Mina apparently breaks free of the circle and expresses her independence. But we cannot know if she is ultimately successful.

We see some of Mina's independence in one female character in *The Circle*. In contrast to the other women in the film, this young teenage prostitute consciously projects a sexualised femininity. She wears lipstick, a colourful headscarf, and defiantly smokes a cigarette in a police van that is taking her to prison. Yet hers is a quiet defiance. Her beautifully framed face is an impassive, aesthetically compelling mask. Unlike the tortured visage of the abandoning mother which emerges from the 'velvet darkness like a Rembrandt portrait' (Pallasmaa 2005: 57), Panahi's young prostitute confronts the camera directly. Yet we cannot 'read' her face. Her portrait is an impenetrable and 'poetic conception of [an Iranian] neorealism' (Chaudhuri and Finn 2006: 389) that refuses narrative resolution.

In other words, the young prostitute refuses to give up her secrets. Her face is a cosmetically decorated mask that both covers and highlights the girl's sensuality. Thomas Elsaesser states that the face is 'not just a surface to be read', but should also be regarded as 'a pure phenomenal presence'; he argues that 'faces take revenge by looking at us' and that 'they make us more naked than naked bodies looking at us' (2009). Elsaesser's analysis is especially appropriate for Iranian filmmaking and, in particular, for understanding the powerful yet impassive face of the young prostitute in *The Circle*. While the portrait-like close-up would suggest the heroic in a Western movie (see Codell 2006: 361), in Panahi's film we see a naked face that combines the real and the cinematic (see Chaudhuri and Finn 2006: 390). On it, the director metaphorically inscribes the cinematic history of the Iranian woman – a story whose ending has yet to be written.

The lack of a narrative resolution is also central to the plot in Marziyeh Meshkini's *The Day I Became a Woman*. Though the film is about three specific moments in the unrelated lives of a girl, a young bride and an older woman, the film is also an allegorical rendering of a woman's life cycle in Iran. These interrelated tales of childhood, youth and old age take place on the paradisiacal Iranian island of Kish. The island represents a heterotopic place where the magical and real coexist in Felliniesque fashion. On the one hand, the stories appear unrelated and seem to take place concurrently. On the other hand, they are part of a single allegorical narrative. As Hamid Dabashi notes,

> this bodily breakdown of one person into three narrative instances, cast into three different people, gives Meshkini's film the parabolic realism that simply portrays the evident reality of the stories told and yet implies the surreal mutation of that reality into a realm beyond the mundane matter-of-factness of things that have and could very well have happened. (2007: 373)

In other words, the director does not allow us to easily categorise the film and distance ourselves from it. Dabashi suggests that Meshkini turns her films into 'fables' that make us uncomfortable because of their 'facticity' (2007: 375). Although she presents us with particular facts surrounding her characters' lives, these facts reveal very little about the protagonists' emotions or about any likely outcomes for their stories.

Unlike the female characters from Panahi's and Sadr Ameli's films who inhabit Tehran's gritty urbanscape, Meshkini's occupy a non-urban liminal space that is largely free of men. She centres the film's narratives near the uninhabited beach rather than a more conventional setting. The beach represents a place which would not be a centre of Iranian female community or of single women showcasing their independence. The filmmaker and videographer Shirin Neshat argues that 'if you were to see a Moslem woman by the sea, or by the mountain, or by the forest, it would seem odd. Something appears to be strange, as if they don't belong there. I examined the issue by asking: "What if you remove these women from that expected urban environment and place them in the context of nature, a landscape that has absolutely no evidence of civilization?"' (in Neshat and Ebrahimian 2002: 45). The young girl of the first tale (Hava) and the bicycle-riding young bride of the second (Ahoo) occupy just such a space. In these imagined spaces by the sea, they can challenge the dominant cultural and patriarchal forces that inscribe their lives.

In the first narrative we meet Hava, a girl who is about to celebrate her ninth birthday and will soon have to forgo the simple headscarf she is accustomed to wearing in favour of the adult *hijab*. She will also have to give up her male playmates. In the story's opening, we see Hava pleading with her grandmother to give her one more hour of playtime with the boy who had called earlier for her. Because her actual birth hour has not yet arrived, the grandmother agrees if she promises to return when the shadow cast by the sun on a stick has disappeared. After she has attained her freedom, Hava learns that her friend must stay at home to finish his homework. As an inducement to talk to her, Hava promises her friend that she will buy some candy for him. When she returns, they take turns sucking on a lollipop that she passes through the barred window to him. The director closes in on Hava's face as she smacks her lips on this last shared treat. Clearly, we are meant to interpret her lips rounding the lollipop as an erotic gesture. While many Iranian films 'channel' adult love and sexuality through the innocent relationships of children, in this case Meshkini is implying much more than this sexual innuendo (see Mir-Hosseini 2001: 28). Hava's innocent yet erotic act also represents one of her last pure gestures of female independence and choice.

In what might be another last gesture of freedom, Hava trades her head kerchief for a toy fish. She gives her scarf to boys playing on the beach who wish to use it as a sail for their homemade raft. Like Hava, it would seem that these boys also long to escape the adult strictures soon to be placed upon them. In a short time, they too will not be able to freely converse with her or with any unescorted young females. The director uses the innocent 'veil' to foreshadow how it will be used by the grown-up boys and girls to 'organize the field of vision' (Naficy 2000: 50). Though the wearing of the *hijab* affects both boys and girls, clearly it has a special significance for women. During the Revolution, the *hijab* represented a nationalist symbol. Its wearers signalled their rejection of imperialist Western power and conventions (see Sadeghi 2008). Though the *hijab* is still a nationalist Islamic symbol, it also represents the failure of the Revolution to live up to its promises to women.[1] In the film's final scene, in which Hava acquiesces to her mother's request that she wear the traditional covering, the young girl's fate seems to be sealed by this tarnished, former symbol of hope. In the next story, however, the 'veil' becomes an ambiguous marker of gender and of freedom.

The second narrative in *The Day I Became a Woman* concerns Ahoo, a young woman who is participating in a bicycle race along a coastal road on the island. Most of the story is told through visual gestures and ancillary sounds rather than dialogue. As Ahoo furiously rides, her husband approaches her on horseback and begs her to stop the race. When she refuses, he threatens to divorce her. She whispers her assent. Because his threat does not elicit the response he wishes, Ahoo's husband rides away into the desert accompanied by the sound of a horse's hooves and folkloric chanting. He returns with an Imam who also begs Ahoo to change her mind. When she refuses again, the tribal elders and then her father try to stop her. Her breathing gets heavier and the chant becomes a lament.

Meshkini places the camera squarely in front of Ahoo's face. We see the character respond to the threats and pleadings of her pursuers with nuanced facial gestures and focused expression. Though Ahoo rides along a path that parallels sea and sand – a metaphorical space that suggests transformation and change – we never learn where she is going nor why she wishes to elude her pursuers. We can only guess what is behind her penetrating gaze. Ahoo's powerful forward stare not only signifies the character's struggle to complete the race, but also symbolises her struggle to assert her individuality and independence. Ahoo's silence, except for her barely audible responses, suggests that her battle between defiance and compliance is a difficult one.

This conflict is also evidenced by Ahoo's ongoing efforts to adjust her headscarf. Whether or not to cover her hair is, however, beside the point. Ahoo is also battling the competing forces of tradition and modernity. For the moment, she appears to be absent-mindedly playing with this choice. As Dabashi notes, 'the fate of Iranian women is still very much found on the borderline where their own creative imagination and their material conditions collide and implode' (2007: 388). Indeed, the *hijab* is a visible symbol of the ambiguous role of gender in Iran.

Though modest dress is clearly a part of Ahoo's identity, the young woman is hardly able to keep her head covering in place. Nevertheless, she manages to do so while she simultaneously confronts her turban-clad, horse-riding male pursuers. In these scenes, Meshkini questions the usefulness of the mythic, revolutionary images of 'warrior brother' and 'veiled sister' that had inspired young people during the Islamic Revolution (see Moore 2005: 8). She implies that Iran's utopian revolution has failed and that its 'male warriors' have turned into horse-riding enforcers of repressive, medieval codes.

In the end, Ahoo's brothers stop her on the road and succeed in pulling her off her bicycle. Like many neorealist film directors, Meshkini uses a long shot to alert us to the debate that occurs between Ahoo and her brothers. Because we see Ahoo over the shoulder of the last female rider, we are distanced from the discussion she has with her brothers. Thus, we have no idea as to what its resolution might be.

In the third and final segment about the elderly woman Houra, two young women from the bicycle race discuss Ahoo's fate. One believes that Ahoo continued to compete while the other does not. Meshkini leaves it up to us to supply the answer. In this regard, the director underscores Kiarostami's belief that filmmakers 'are never able to reconstruct truth [and] that it is the audience who should seek the reality' of a conclusion (quoted in Moore 2005: 3).

Kiarostami's sentiment is particularly evident in the third and final segment of the film. In it, we are introduced to the elderly Houra who travels to the free-trade island of Kish to purchase those goods that she had been denied all her life. When she arrives at the airport, young boys waiting with trolleys offer to help the wheelchair-bound Houra with her purchases. They accompany her to an upscale, duty-free shopping mall where she buys tables, chairs, a refrigerator and other goods. All of them go to the beach, where Houra arranges her purchases as though she is furnishing a home or a stage set. Initially the boys and Houra act as though they are 'playing' house. The characters' play soon turns into one between the director and the viewer (are we looking at a film set or an imaginary house?). As if by magic, the raft that the boys construct in Hava's story reappears as part of a floating flotilla in the final segment. Hava and her mother also reappear and watch the raft that contains Houra and her belongings sail off to a ship that waits in the distance. Whether or not this is the beginning of a new-found freedom or her final journey is unclear.

During this final narrative, Meshkini dissolves the boundaries between the real and the virtual. In doing so, she exposes the artificiality of the cinematic narrative. More importantly, she creates an actual imaginary space in which Hava and all viewers can 'see' how choices made for us impact future events. Hava's fate and that of all young girls, the director suggests, are not sealed. Thus, Meshkini breaks not only the power of cinema as a creator of myth but also that of the Islamic Revolution (see Sullivan 2008). With *The Day I Became a Woman*, she redefines the theatre as an imaginary but actual heterotopic space in which a genuine discussion about gender may occur. Such a discussion, in which girls like Hava participate, can facilitate a change in cultural norms. As Kiarostami concludes, 'cinema and all the arts ought to be able to destroy the mind of their audience in order to reject the old values and make it susceptible to new values' (in Moore 2005: 4). This is clearly evident – to both the viewer and the bicycle-riding Ahoo – in *The Day I Became a Woman*.

Meshkini and other Iranian New Wave directors do not follow Hollywood plot conventions nor do they give us a Bergman-like portrait of the characters' inner turmoil. They allow inner emotions to register on their characters' faces but provide no background story as to why. Though the *mise-en-scène* figures strongly in these directors' films (as in an Antonioni film), the Iranian cinematic landscapes and settings do not mirror their characters' emotions. Rather, Iranian New Wave filmmakers weave their characters' stories into a visual artform that encapsulates Persian cultural conventions. Their narratives are closer to the art of the classic poet Hafez than they are to those of the West; as Ziba Mir-Hosseini notes, Iranian cinema is an 'art of ambiguity' (2001: 27). The directors invite us to enter the magical protected spaces where a variety of narrative endings might occur. Young girls and women, in the films discussed above, function as screens onto which these possibilities are written.

At the conclusion of *The Girl in the Sneakers*, an elderly night-time park resident turns on the colourful lights that illuminate the lovers' long anticipated but anti-climactic meeting. Here in this heterotopic but dreamlike space, Tadai claims her independence and her freedom. Yet her fate remains unknown. In contrast, in the surreal, claustrophobic spaces of Panahi's *The Circle*, former female prisoners live out the nightmarish dreams from which there is no apparent escape. Although we expect to see the abandoned child of the imprisoned woman join the mother in the prison cell to which she is confined at the end of the narrative, we cannot be certain of this conclusion. In *The Day I Became a Woman*, Meshkini also leaves us with no certitude or narrative resolution. We can only surmise what the fate of nine-year-old Hava might be.

Thus, unlike earlier Iranian films in which children are metaphorically utilised as innocent commentators on public cultural life, in these films no final judgement or resolution is offered about the difficult choices young women face. Although young Iranian adolescents and girls are hardly agents of their own destinies in contemporary New Wave Iranian cinema, these Iranian directors suggest the possibility that girls and young women have some control over their choices and thus their lives. At the very least, their fate is not sealed.

In other words, the narrative – the story – is to be continued.

Acknowledgement

Although this is a different essay, some of the ideas and comments in this chapter have appeared in 'Telling the Girl's Side of the Story: Heterotopic Spaces of Femininity in Iranian Film', in a special edition titled *Images of Childhood in the Middle East*, edited by Christiane Gruber and Pamela Karimi, of *Comparative Studies of South Asia, Africa and the Middle East*, 2, 2012, 375–91.

Note

1   Norma Claire Moruzzi writes of her surprise regarding Iranian women's empathetic reception to the 'heavy-handed sensationalism and passivity of *Two Women*' (1998: 94). In other words, they donned the *hijab* as a revolutionary symbol and then were surprised by a government that forgot their revolutionary fervour and contribution to the Islamic state. She states that 'collectively, they felt betrayed by a national shift that had cut them off from the future they had expected and stranded them in a landscape of changed gender relations that proscribed the conditions of their individual fulfillment. It wasn't just that times were tough, politically and economically. It was the feeling that they had personally paid the price for a national experiment in gender relations, and the experiment hadn't worked' (2001: 97).

Bibliography

Chaudhuri, S. and H. Finn (2006) 'The Open Image: Poetic Realism and the New Iranian Cinema,' in J. F. Codell (ed.) *Genre, Gender, Race and World Cinema*. Malden, MA and Oxford: Blackwell, 388–407.

Codell, J. F. (2006) 'Introduction' to Part IV 'World Cinema: Joining Local and Global,' in J. F. Codell (ed.) *Genre, Gender, Race and World Cinema*, Malden MA and Oxford: Blackwell, 359–68.

Dabashi, H. (2007) *Masters and Masterpieces of Iranian Cinema*. Washington DC: Mage.

Elsaesser, T. (2009) 'Bergman in the Museum?', unpublished lecture from 'Image and Movement: Film Studies and Art History' Symposium, Clark Art Institute, Williamstown, MA, March 13–14.

Ettinger, B. (2006) *The Matrixial Borderspace*. Minneapolis: University of Minnesota Press.

Foucault, M. (1997 [1985/6]) 'Of Other Spaces: Utopias and Heterotopias', in N. Leach (ed.) *Rethinking Architecture: A Cultural Theory*. London and New York: Routledge, 350–6.

Horton, A. (2003) 'Reel Landscapes: Cinematic Environments Documented and Created', in I. Robertson and P. Richards (eds) *Studying Cultural Landscapes*. London: Hodder Arnold, 71–92.

Mir-Hosseini, Z. (2001) 'Iranian Cinema: Art, Society and the State,' *Middle East Report*, 219, 509–30.

Moore, L. (2005) 'Women in a Widening Frame: Cultural Projection, Spectatorship and Iranian Cinema', *Camera Obscura*, 20, 2, 1–34.

Moruzzi, N. C. (2001) 'Women in Iran: Notes on Film and From the Field', *Feminist Studies*, 27, 1, 89–100.

Mulvey, L. (1975) 'Visual Pleasure and Narrative Cinema', *Screen*, 16, 3, 6–18.

Naficy, H. (1995) 'Iranian Cinema under the Islamic Republic', *American Anthropologist*, 97, 3, 548–58.

_____ (2000) 'Parallel Worlds: Shirin Neshat's Video Works', in G. Matt and J. Peyton-Jones (eds.) *Shirin Neshat: Exhibition Catalogue*. Vienna: Kunsthalle, 47.

Neshat, S. and B. Ebrahimian (2002) 'Passage to Iran'. *PAJ: A Journal of Performance and Art*, 21, 3, 44–55.

Pallasmaa, J. (2005) *The Eyes of the Skin: Architecture and the Senses*. Chichester: Wiley-Academy.

Sadeghi, F. (2008) 'Fundamentalism, Gender, and the Discourses of Veiling (*Hijab*) in Contemporary Iran', in M. Semati (ed.) *Media, Culture and Society in Iran: Living with Globalization and the Islamic State*. London: Routledge, 207–22.

Sadr, H. R. (2002) 'Children in Contemporary Iranian Cinema: When We Were Children,' in R. Tapper (ed.) *The New Iranian Cinema: Politics, Representation and Identity*. New York: I. B. Tauris, 227–37.

Sullivan, Z. T. (2008) 'Iranian Cinema and the Critique of Absolutism,' in M. Semati (ed.) *Media, Culture and Society in Iran: Living with Globalization and the Islamic State*. New York: Routledge, 193–204.

Teo, S. (2001) 'The Case of Jafar Panahi', *Senses of Cinema*, 15, 1. Available: http://archive.sensesofcinema.com/contents/01/15/panahi_interview.html (accessed on 19 December 2009).

Cinematic Images of Women at a Time of National(ist) Crisis: The Case of Three Yugoslav Films

Dijana Jelača

In one famous medieval Serbian epic poem, *The Building of the Bridge on the Bojana*, a story is told of a woman buried alive in the foundation of a bridge in order to keep it from collapsing. Similar stories of sacrificing the female body for the greater good of building a patriarchal culture have been a *leitmotif* in many regional cultural texts since. This chapter explores questions of national identity and territoriality in relation to the female body in three Yugoslav films made in the decade before the country's violent break-up. The three films, *Petrijin venac* (*Petria's Wreath*, Srdjan Karanovic, 1981), *Ljepota poroka* (*The Beauty of Sin*, Zivko Nikolic, 1986) and *Virdžina* (*Virgina*, Srdjan Karanovic, 1991), expose the subversive potential of challenging myths of nationhood and purity. All three have rural women as their main protagonists – women whose stories curiously align with the plight of the Balkan territory they inhabit. What is revealed through this chapter's contextual reading of the films is their own implicitly feminist critique of masculinist violence, even before that violence completely overtook the territory of former Yugoslavia. In *Petria's Wreath*, this critique is deployed through the narrative of one woman's personal emancipation; in *The Beauty of Sin* through sexual liberation; in *Virgina*, through destabilising the fixed, heteronormative gender/sex binary along a performative axis.

All three films are narratives about a troubled rural land in which the struggle to retain tradition proves to be futile in the face of coming changes. They offer a critical look at tradition and identify in it a source of inequality and centuries-long suffering for women, who are seen as oppressed by patriarchy and struggling to break free from its confines. *Petria's Wreath*, *The Beauty of Sin* and *Virgina* rely on depictions of ancient customs as a way of offering a critique of the stubborn masculinist insistence on cultural authenticity which needs to be preserved at the expense of those in the weaker, less powerful, positions in society. In that respect, all three films can be read as overtly feminist texts which expose the mechanisms by which traditional customs become tools of control and reiteration of power imbalances and societal inequity.[1] However, because the films are complex and multi-layered texts, this feminist aspect in all three is further complicated by the often murky relationships between such dualities as East/West, male/female, traditional/modern and so on, which they por-tray in ways that defy easy definition. The stories depicted in these three films are, additionally, treated in this chapter as inexplicably tied to the tumultuous times of their making, and through that, as addressing and being influenced by the uncer-tainty that was increasingly marking the reality of the country – the uncertainty which eventually turned into a fulfillment of its most devastating threats: violence, bloodshed and war.

The motif of custom has been a frequent fixture in the cinema of the former Yugoslavia, especially in films which sought to overtly reiterate the rural/urban binary, which was usually accompanied by a narrative of progress and modernity as being explicitly tied to the urban environment, and tradition and 'backwardness' as tied to rural areas. This potentially problematic set-up was used in film for various purposes – from the problematising of stubborn insistence on traditional customs in some works of Yugoslav 'Black Wave' filmmakers, to uncritical celebration of the village as a site of authenticity in its faithfulness to customs (in films such as *Zona Zamfirova* [Zdravko Sotra, 2002]), to satirical views of rural superstitions (*Predstava Hamleta u selu Mrduša Donja* [Krsto Papic, 1974]; *Iskušavanje đavola* [Zivko Nikolic, 1989]) and so on. The connecting thread in virtually all Yugoslav films set in rural areas is their insistence on recognising the particularities and specificities of rural Balkan territories as a site of many problematic and potentially contradictory ten-dencies. These tendencies are tied to the perceived intrinsically liminal position of the Balkans as being located between two opposing ideological forces – the 'moder-nity' of the West and the 'Orientalism' of the East. A number of influential scholars in recent years have shown that even when one is critical of such problematic binary divisions, their effectiveness in the narratives being created through various forms of cultural production (here film) cannot be neglected or completely dismissed (see Bijelić and Savić 2002). This is precisely why I bring up the East/West, rural/urban binaries here as an influential factor in the storytelling of the films in question.

Storytelling as intervention: critique of tradition, patriarchy and nationalism

The three films analysed here are complex texts whose stories operate on several levels of signification. While they utilise ancient customs located in rural parts of the former Yugoslavia as a driving force for the storytelling, these customs are not used uncritically, or as a static device for plot progression. On the contrary, the very symbols of traditional society are used to represent the oppression of the films' hero-ines, and in this way, these customs are inexplicably tied to the patriarchal order and maintaining of the power imbalance between the sexes. Since in all three films the heroines' lives turn out to be closely tied to the fate of the (rural, Balkan) territory they inhabit, the symbolism of the customs illustrates the films' critique of national-ist ideals about femininity, motherhood and the position of women in society. As a result of this, and through a very complicated set of associations, *Petria's Wreath*, *The Beauty of Sin* and *Virgina* are then read as anti-nationalist feminist texts. This aspect proves to be even more important when the context of the films' making is taken into consideration – further subversion is added to the already subversive underly-ing idea of anti-patriarchy when one knows that this meaning was being created at a time when nationalist sentiments in the former Yugoslavia were rising and would in a few years result in bloodshed and war.[2] In fact, I would argue that the context of the films is bound to their meaning in such a way that all three serve as examples of cinematic storytelling being driven by the upheavals in society, which in turn get exposed on screen through a metaphoric displacement to different times and seem-ingly different contexts.[3]

Srđan Karanović's *Petria's Wreath* and *Virgina* belong to his so-called ethnologi-cal films. Nevena Daković claims that 'in these films, it is popular tradition, manners and customs that determine the framework, and it is their dynamics that create the necessary conflicts in the plot' (2006: 163). In *Petria's Wreath*, the story takes place over a span of three decades, starting with the years leading up to World War II. It is a story of a woman called Petria as depicted through her relationship with the different men that come into her life. Petria, who is the narrator, starts her tale with her first marriage, to Dobrivoje, a man who was good to her in the beginning, but too much under the influence of his mother to commit himself to his wife completely. This exaggerated dependence on his mother proves to be the obstacle Petria cannot overcome in her efforts to make their relationship work. Her firstborn son dies after the mother-in-law fails to assist with the birth, and her second child, a daughter by the name of Milana, dies from a grave illness at a very young age during World War II. The death of Petria's second child marks the end of her first marriage – Dobrivoje concludes that she must be 'flawed' in some way, since her children cannot live, and tells her she has to leave. After leaving Dobrivoje, Petria gets a job in a local bar, whose owner is Ljubiša, the second man in her life. This phase marks Petria's eman-cipation through being able to support herself and gaining experience in dealing with men by working at a bar where they are often drunk and out of control. With Ljubiša, Petria is able to discover her sexual side as well, something that had been missing in her marriage to Dobrivoje.

However, because of the political changes that the country is going through after World War II, Ljubiša's bar is forcibly closed by the authorities, who are turning against private businesses in favour of state-owned establishments. Ljubiša leaves the town and Petria marries her second husband, Misa, whom she meets while working at the bar. Misa is a miner in the local mine, which is also the cornerstone of the entire local economy. After Misa suffers an accident at work, he ends up permanently disabled. His physical state is not helped by his increasing drinking problem. After several years of difficult marriage caused by Misa's stubbornness and refusal to stop drinking, he dies, and Petria is a widow. His death coincides with the closing of the mine, a symbolic death of the rural community. In the end, Petria is surrounded by photographs of the people who came and went through her life, and is occasionally visited by the ghosts of her daughter and Misa.

The film is set in rural Serbia, in Okno, a poor *palanka* (province, small town), inhabited predominantly by working-class people and peasants. In his seminal work *Philosophy of the Palanka* (1969), Radomir Konstantinović located this type of Serbian province as being in limbo between rural and urban, unable to identify with either. Nevertheless, he claims that the *palanka*'s attitude is one of extreme self-sufficiency and righteousness, often perceiving itself as the only authentic site of national identity.[4] This liminal status of the *palanka* echoes the notion of the Balkans itself as being caught in between that ideological binary of the West and its Other, the East. The Balkans is conceived of as being on the crossroads between the two, unable to fully become either.[5] Taking this analysis of the *palanka* into consideration, *Petria's Wreath* can be viewed as a metaphor for the Balkans itself, in a time of the tempestuous changes of World War II and its aftermath. When this motif of tumultuous social change and uncertainty is translated into the time of the film's making (the 1980s), what is revealed is a poignant critique of nationalism and its myths of authenticity, normativity and belonging. In this world of normative *palanka*, Petria makes her way through life in stages that always coincide with the abrupt and often violent changes in society. Therefore, Petria's fate is closely tied to the fate of the land she inhabits, creating a metaphoric woman/land relationship familiar from feminist studies.[6] This metaphor at the same time reveals both the woman and the land as objects of patriarchal control.

Petria starts off as a naïve young woman who is very dependent on others – her husband and her mother-in-law in particular. When they refuse to help her, things go awry because Petria is unable to take control of her life. The most tumultuous times of Petria's first marriage coincide with World War II. As her daughter dies in her arms, the war fades away as well. Later in the film, we see Petria being less of a victim of circumstance and taking control at exactly such times when her situation gets more difficult. Petria's life as a waitress at Ljubiša's bar is set against the backdrop of political changes in the newly formed post-war socialist Yugoslavia. In accordance with the new recognition of the important role played by women in the war, the socialist republic of Yugoslavia called for greater emancipation of women, and provided them with opportunities to work hand in hand with men. As an illustration of the new state attitude towards women, Petria goes through emancipation as well. She stops wearing her traditional rural clothes, removes the scarf from her head, and gets a new hairstyle. Petria gains psychological independence as well – formally through becoming financially independent, and symbolically by learning how to look people in the eye. This is arguably the greatest lesson Ljubiša teaches her. He does so with disarming simplicity of argumentation. 'You should be your own man' is all he offers as explanation. Petria does not take long to master the art of waitressing in what is a potentially hostile environment for a woman. The only customers we ever see in the *kafana* (traditional bar) are men, more often than not drunk. Petria's growing independence and confidence coincide with the growing independence of the newly formed federal state of Yugoslavia, which is another example of the parallels that are perpetually being drawn between the two. Nevertheless, while the premise of the film rests on the patriarchal woman/land dyad, at the same time it works against the patriarchal order that creates the dyad, by making Petria's story one of emancipation and the search for her own agency and power.

By the time she is married for the second time (to one of the bar's regulars), Petria is the driving force and the strength that guides the relationship, which is further illustrated by her husband's increasingly failing mental and physical state. As Petria gets stronger, the patriarchal figure in her life gets weaker, and similarly, her destiny is less tied to the circumstances of the land she inhabits. Petria's failure to fulfill one of society's ideals for a woman – to become a mother – is initially treated as the source of her doom. However, as she gains more agency in life, the lack of a child becomes a less defining element in her life. In the end, we see Petria, who addresses the camera directly (another sign of her agency), as a wise old woman whose difficulties in life have amounted to strength and defiance of patriarchy, whose expectations she has symbolically 'failed' on her way to self-reliance. Failing the expectations of a patriarchal order is the film's way of easing the tension created by the anxieties about the future of the country whose complicated political present is metaphorically depicted in its story.

Self-reliance is an element similarly missing in the life of the heroine of Živko Nikolić's *The Beauty of Sin*. The beginning of the film narrative is set in a distant half-deserted village in the Montenegrin mountains, a place where ancient rituals are still being performed while the rest of the country presumably engages in various levels of modernisation, as illustrated by the trend of nudist tourism at the seaside. When compared with the *palanka* of *Petria's Wreath*, the rural world of *The Beauty of Sin* shows a deeper conflation of womanhood, tradition and territory – the metaphorical lines between the three are more firm in this rural space than they were in the rural/ urban liminal position of *palanka*. By setting the story in such a distant and isolated 'backward' place, and by bringing out the importance of myths of common history and heredity in the lives of its characters to a greater extent, *The Beauty of Sin* reiterates the claim that deeply traditional upbringing and surroundings contribute to strict identitarian notions stereotypically centred in and around rural worlds. While Petria succeeded to an extent in transgressing the confines of the *palanka* through her growing independence and agency, this will prove to be impossible in the rural land of *The Beauty of Sin*, whose main characters' possible transgressions happen only when they visit the more urban areas of the Montenegrin seaside in search for jobs. In this way, *The Beauty of Sin* again reiterates the potentially problematic dyad of urban/rural, further aligning it with the West/East division, since the modernity of the urban areas is depicted through a distinctly Western point of reference, thus by implication making the rural areas stand in as metaphors for Balkan tradition and patriarchy.

In the rural world of *The Beauty of Sin*, women are punished by a deadly hammer blow to the head if they are unfaithful to their husbands. As the film opens, we see the husband of an unnamed couple performing this ancient ritual of revenge on his wife, presumably because of her infidelity. This scene immediately situates the rural land within the strict patriarchal traditional framework in which customs confirm the power imbalance between the sexes. After this violent introduction, the movie turns to Jaglika, the main protagonist of the story, and her wedding to Luka. Jaglika and Luka's first wedding night illustrates the kind of sexual practice customary in this rural world, in which the wife's eyes are covered with a black cloth while the husband penetrates her. She is not allowed to watch or see during the intercourse. After their wedding night, the film cuts to a few years later, when the couple already have a small daughter and are deciding to take up the offer of their best man Djordje to work for him at his seaside resort. They leave their daughter with Jaglika's father and go to the city. Djordje, who goes by George in the city, is able to find work for Jaglika at the local nudist resort for Western tourists. Luka is reluctant to let Jaglika work there in the beginning, but gives in after George convinces him they desperately need help at the resort. Jaglika is at first traumatised by having to be a maid to naked foreigners, and the strict resort manager does not help Jaglika adjust. As Luka is pushed into various adventures of urban life, all of which emphasise his naïve ignorance and 'Otherness' with respect to a modern lifestyle, he is constantly being ridiculed by the local population. George tries to get him to work for a gay textile industry manager, who develops a crush on Luka, leading Luka to attack the man physically in fear of his affectionate touching.

Through these experiences, Luka begins to lose his illusions about urban life. At the same time, Jaglika becomes increasingly infatuated with a Western couple she works for, due to their lack of inhibition and the clear physical affection they show each other. As her own inhibitions slowly disappear, Jaglika becomes freer in her interactions with the couple, culminating in a naked swim she takes with the two of them, a scene that marks the unlocking of her sexuality and discovery of her body. However, the following day Jaglika discovers that the couple had left the resort without saying goodbye. Disappointed, she asks Luka to take her back to their village, which he readily accepts, fed up with city life himself. On their way home, Jaglika admits she has 'sinned', which leaves Luka with no choice but to perform the ancient ritual of lethal punishment. As Jaglika says goodbye to her child, she and Luka leave the house to get things over with. Jaglika kneels to receive the blow from the hammer in Luka's hands, but he unexpectedly drops it and returns to the house. From the house, a gun shot is heard, indicating Luka had taken his own life instead. The film ends with a close-up of Jaglika's face, and the tragic expression in her eyes.

The story of Jaglika's struggle between sexual liberation and the expectations of her own conservative environment parallels a similar struggle happening on a larger societal scale, which again, as in the case of *Petria's Wreath*, makes the social and political context of the film's making relevant to the interpretation of the story. At the time, Yugoslavia was a society torn between tradition that reiterated patriarchal order, and the ever increasing modernisation. A tension existed between the official socialist politics of the state, which claimed equal rights for both sexes, and its denial in practice. The looming threat of violence for a woman who becomes too independent and sexually liberated (as illustrated through the custom of the hammer blow to the head) metaphorically addresses the looming threat of violence to the land of Yugoslavia, only several years before that threat materialised in the worst possible way. This masculinist violence in the film is then closely tied to the national identity which sees its affirmation in such exercises of power that (re)create the us/them binary opposition. At the time when Yugoslavia was seeing a rise in nationalist sentiments, the film's alignment of masculinist violence with nationalism and patriarchy proves to be a poignant critique of the times whose worst parts were yet to come.

Sexual practices prove to be a site in which these power relations get exposed and potentially subverted the most. As Jaglika's oppression is illustrated in the beginning through not being allowed to see during intercourse with her husband, so is her liberation later illustrated through the emergence of what I treat as queer desire in the larger sense of the word (queer as anti-normative and disruptive).[7] Through her passionate embraces and dancing on the beach naked with the Western couple, Jaglika challenges the patriarchal order of her own culture at the level at which it is most subversive to do so, since this patriarchal order rests on the traditional confined heteronormativity whose main, and possibly even only, purpose is a reproductive one. Because queer desire does not rest on a reproductive premise, Jaglika's acts are highly disruptive of the oppressive order she has been brought up in. Yet it is not only for a woman that this heteronormative order proves confining. Her husband Luka, who is ridiculed throughout most of the narrative because of his stubborn insistence on tradition, becomes in the dramatic twist at the end a tragic figure who, in his final act, finds a way to deny the tradition he was so desperately clinging to. Through his refusal to punish his wife for her actions by enacting the custom that would reiterate the patriarchal order, and through taking his own life instead, Luka denies the most powerful premise that this order rests on – the masculinist policing and disciplining of female desire. Luka's suicide is the film's gesture towards a possible, albeit utopian, resolution to the threat of masculinist violence. This again extends further to the context of the film's making, where such threats of violence are closely tied to nationalist sentiments of intolerance towards 'Others'. If the film is read this way, it is possible to see its claim as leaving no other way out of the cycle of violence than self-sacrifice and the assisted suicide of patriarchal order.

Similar hints at the necessity of the demise of patriarchy if perpetuation of violence is to be avoided is offered in Karanović's *Virgina*. The film was made in the year of Yugoslavia's break-up and is considered by many the last Yugoslav film. As in the case of *Petria's Wreath* and *The Beauty of Sin*, it is centered on the difficult life experience of a rural female character. This time, however, the conflict is pushed further into the mythical heritage of the region, taking on an ancient custom which was practiced in some rural areas of former Yugoslavia, as well as Albania, in which families without male children raised one daughter as a boy.[8] The film presents the story of a family with only female children – as the film opens, another daughter is born, prompting the father to react in anger and almost kill the baby, who is saved only by her mother's desperate screams. The father, Timotije, then decides that this daughter will be brought up as a *virgina*, and that the rest of the village will be told that they got a son. The story moves forward to a few years later, where we see the *virgina*, Stevan, entering puberty. The problems in her relationship with her father become more apparent since she starts rebelling against being treated as a boy. Instead of helping her father in the field, Stevan would rather play with her sisters' dolls. She also develops a crush on her male friend Mijat, who is unsuspecting of her actual sex. When Stevan's mother dies after giving birth to another baby girl, Stevan decides it is time to leave. She tells Mijat about her real sex, and after an initial shock, a plan is made for them to leave together and go to 'America'. They are helped out by the village wise man, Paun, who, in a very telling scene towards the end, is revealed to the viewer as a *virgina* as well. Stevan's father decides he would rather kill Stevan than see his 'son' go, but is killed instead by Paun. In the end, we see Paun, Stevan (carrying her newborn baby sister) and Mijat slowly leaving the rural land and making their way towards a boat that will take them to 'America', which they call the promised land.

Virgina is a film that struggles with an inner paradox. On the one hand, it offers itself as a progressive feminist text which forcibly argues against the oppression of women under patriarchy, while at the same time being a conservative text which treats gender roles as inherent and stable.[9] For instance, Stevan simply cannot help but play with her sisters' dolls because it is something that comes naturally to girls. This naturalising of femininity is somewhat resolved by the fact that Stevan does perform the role of a son quite well when she wants to, and by the fact that Paun is seen as a revered village wise man by the entire community, and not a person imprisoned in a gender performance not of his choosing. Therefore, regardless of the film's potentially conservative naturalising of femininity and masculinity, the story is nevertheless a subversive narrative about the crisis of masculinity, and with it, the crisis of traditional ways which are marked by the history of violence. Kevin Moss (2004) uses Marjorie Garber's work on cross-dressing to claim that the appearance of *virgina* as a transvestite figure in the last Yugoslav film functions to indicate a category crisis elsewhere. Considering that the film was made in the year that marked the demise of Yugoslavia, it can be read as an attempt at an intervention against the claims of national pride in tradition. These claims quickly lead to a rationalisation of an impending war as something inherently tied to the traditional ways of the Balkans. *Virgina*, similarly to *The Beauty of Sin*, offers a way out of such a cycle through the death of the main patriarchal figure in the film, and with it, argues that in order for further violence to be avoided, patriarchy must be put to rest. This in turn further couples patriarchy with nationalism, since the film is a subtly masked critique of the looming violence which was at the time threatening to destroy Yugoslavia.

In both *Virgina* and *The Beauty of Sin* modernisation is tied to the West, and with this, the West is coded as a space where women are not oppressed. This potentially problematic reiteration of stereotypical binary divisions between the backward East and the progressive West are somewhat eased by the films' occasional ironic distancing towards such a scenario. In *The Beauty of Sin* this distancing is most visible in the Western couple's lack of full understanding of Jaglika's position, and their careless treatment of her as someone who is there to merely help the couple have fun. The most meaningful and subversive actions for Jaglika are for the Western couple simply careless fun that is forgotten soon after. In *Virgina*, the modernity of the West resides behind the many mountains that Stevan must travel through at the end, and while we see her walking off, an endless landscape view of the rural land is offered as a reminder that the world Stevan is seeking is impossible for the film to even imagine, let alone have Stevan inhabit it. That world is then seen as only an illusion that is needed in order for one to set off on a different path from the one demarcated by tradition, and not a world that occupies any actual physical space.

In the three films discussed here, the one device that proves to be the most effective tool for criticising masculinist attachments to myths of national identity is the possibility of modernisation and change/transgression. This hope is embodied in stories of rural women on their way to claiming greater agency in denying traditional oppression. In order to create such a position for the rural women, all three films initially rely on a stereotype (national, gendered) of the women's default lack of agency. Agency then has to be claimed only through violent disruption and divorce both literal (from men), and figurative (from tradition). Modernisation is seen as a tool for gaining greater female agency through freedom of choice (*Petria's Wreath*), discovering alternative, or queer, desires as ways to oppose oppressive male-Oriented heteronormativity (*The Beauty of Sin*), or a promise of a life more comfortable and prosperous, in the myth of a distant promised land (*Virgina*). What all three films have in common is the claim that in order for this modernisation to arrive, masculinity needs to be sacrificed and ultimately abolished. In all three films, the main male characters die in the end, as symbols of patriarchal power over oppressed women coming to an end.

The analysis of the films today cannot be divorced from the awareness of the bloody conflicts that came after they were made. With this in mind, one is able to

potentially interpret certain aspects differently from how we would had the conflicts not taken place. In that respect, one has to admit to a bias of a sort – one can
see the films' critique of gendered nationhood and territory through the prism of
subsequent more literal utilisations of these very narratives (women as sites where
masculine power is battled over) to perpetrate violence on a much larger scale. What
the films' stories offer as a looming threat was realised in concrete terms in what followed in real life. And that becomes a point at which the analysis of these films can
be both enriched through utilising this knowledge, but also impoverished through
the inability to view the films' cautiously optimistic endings as something other than
wishful thinking.

In the process of depicting various stereotypical binaries – East and West, masculine as violent and feminine as passively innocent – there exists the possibility that
the films irrevocably reiterate them nevertheless. However, the simple fact that Petria,
Jaglika and Stevan subsequently find ways to disrupt the patriarchal order destabilises
the image of feminine-as-passive and argues that this stereotypical perception was in
place only while the films were engaged in depicting (and critiquing) the patriarchal
habitus that the women were born into. Once the women are on the path of transgressing its figurative and physical borders, the passive/feminine equation collapses,
temporarily disrupting the patriarchy that created it in the first place.

Notes

1 My claim that the films are overtly feminist challenges Dina Iordanova's (1996) observation that
   women's issues depicted in films such as *Virgina* are not utilised for feminist purposes, but rather for
   depicting 'other issues, such as oppression in interpersonal relations, social injustice, and political
   hardship' (Iordanova 1996: 25). Iordanova claims that this is partially due to the fact that the filmmakers are typically male. I would counter that regardless of the filmmakers intentions to create
   feminist films or not (which can only be speculated about), the fact that these films criticise patriarchy and oppression of women in such a system cannot not be read as a feminist claim.

2 For a more detailed discussion of this context, see Jelača (2007).

3 In her work on *Virgina* and the context of its making, Nevena Daković (1996) argues that the growing
   crisis of Yugoslav society created a need for films to produce strong female characters, as an antithesis to the typical male hero prevalent in Yugoslav film up until that point.

4 Everything outside of the *palanka* is perceived as the anti-world. That way both extremes – urban
   'decadence' and rural 'backwardness' – are something the *palanka* sees as being very foreign and far
   from itself. In this respect the *palanka* acts as what Konstantinović calls the 'theater of normativity'
   (1969: 16), setting the standards for normal and abnormal, familiar and foreign.

5 See Bakić-Hayden (1995) and also Maria Todorova's seminal book *Imagining the Balkans* (1997).

6 Here I lean on the work of Annette Kolodny, among others, who in her book *The Lay of the Land*
   (1975) proposes the possibility of reading certain cultural texts as implying a metaphor of land as
   a female body that nurtures people. Kolodny deploys this metaphor in looking at early American
   history and the way the land was won and tamed by powerful men, who, nevertheless, regained
   respect for the offerings the land produced in return. The land and female body thus became equally
   mythologised, often used to reference each other, especially in works of literature.

7   Nikola Mijović (2006) points out that 'Jaglika's swim with the pair is a gratification of desire for free-dom rather than for sexual fullfilment. The couple awaken love in her, but this love is never defined in clear gendered or sexual terms. She is drawn not to the man, or the woman, but to a promise of liberation of feelings and needs elaborately repressed until that moment' (2006: 234–5).

8   That daughter would then be called a *virgina*, and would be required to live her life as a man who would inherit the property and stay on it until death. The film offers several reasons for the enact-ment of this custom. One is a purely religious superstition which carries the belief that families without male children are doomed and bound for extinction. Another reason, somewhat connected to this religious belief, is a sense of shame the family without sons endures in the eyes of other fami-lies in their surroundings. The third, practical reason is an attempt to keep one child with the parents after their daughters marry and leave. In rural areas in which this custom is believed to have taken place, families rely on agriculture for survival, and that reliance requires young healthy bodies which can endure the difficulties of hard labour.

9   Kevin Moss (2004) claims that despite *Virgina*'s focus on gender performativity, the film 'ends up reaffirming traditional gender roles' (Moss 2004: 91), precisely because feminine traits are treated as naturalised and inseparable from persons of female sex.

Bibliography

Bakić-Hayden, M. (1995) 'Nesting Orientalism: The Case of Former Yugoslavia', *Slavic Review*, 54, 4, 917–31.

Bijelić, D. I. and O. Savić, O. (2002) *Balkan as Metaphor: Between Globalization and Fragmentation*. Cambridge: MIT Press.

Daković, N. (1996) 'Mother, Myth and Cinema: Recent Yugoslav Cinema', *Film Criticism*, 21, 2, 40–9.

_____ (2006) 'Petrijin Venac', in D. Iordanova (ed.) *The Cinema of the Balkans*. London: Wallflower Press, 160-69.

Iordanova, D. (1996) 'Women in New Balkan Cinema: Surviving on the Margins', *Film Criticism*, 21, 2, 24–40.

Jelača, D. (2007) 'The Cinematic Construction of Authentic Balkan-ness: Women's Bodies and Metaphors of Territory', unpublished MA thesis, New York University.

Kolodny, A. (1975), *The Lay of the Land: Metaphor as Experience and History in American Life and Letters*. Chapel Hill, NC: University of North Carolina Press.

Konstantinović, R. (1969) *Filosofija palanke*. Belgrade: Otkrovenje.

Mijović, N. (2006) 'Ljepota poroka', in D. Iordanova (ed.) *The Cinema of the Balkans*. London: Wallflower Press, 228–35.

Moss, K. (2004) 'From Sworn Virgins to Transvestite Prostitutes: Performing Gender and Sexuality in Two Films from Yugoslavia', in A. Stulhofer and T. Sandfort (eds) *Sexuality and Gender in Postcommunist Eastern Europe and Russia*. New York: Routledge, 79–94.

Todorova, M. (1997) *Imagining the Balkans*. New York: Oxford University Press.

History as Science Fiction:
Women of Action in Hong Kong Cinema

Saša Vojković

According to Clifford Geertz, even though common sense seems to be about the mere matter-of-fact apprehension of reality, or down-to-earth colloquial judgements, we have to consider the fact that the diversity of artistic expressions stems from the variety of conceptions we have about the ways things are (Geertz 1983). In Geertz's view, vernacular characterisations of what happens are connected to vernacular imaginings of what can. He brings forward the notion of 'legal sensibility', implying that stories and imaginings are contingent on a law; this law is rejoined to the other cultural formations of human life such as morals, art, technology, science, religion, division of labour and history. Traditional Chinese society was male dominated and men were regarded as superior to women. Confucian teaching codified this hierarchy.[2] Although the feminine element is so essential in the philosophical sense (particularly in Taoist thought, for it is interwoven with the masculine element), such a balance of forces cannot be found and confirmed in the actual position of women in everyday life in traditionally patriarchal Chinese society.

This chapter argues that the fact that women in Hong Kong films are depicted as skilled fighters is related to the specificities of the martial arts genre incorporated into the process of cinematic storytelling, but it is the specific vision of the film, a vision that exceeds the level of the fictional world, that determines what kind of female subject is conceivable and which actions she can perform. The intelligent women fighters, women who are knowing subjects, the types of female characters that can be found in Beijing opera, martial arts novels or the Chinese traditional stories of the fantastic and the supernatural, are dependent on the norms that circulate within Chinese cultural heritage.[1]

Cultural embeddedness of narrative

One prototype that has served as a model for many Chinese girls and women who wished to abandon a strictly feminine role and gain access to the political sphere is Hua Mulan (Fa Mulan in Cantonese), the heroine of the Five Dynasties (420–588). A legendary figure, she has remained famous (and even absorbed by Hollywood in the Disney film *Mulan* (1998)) because of an anonymous poet who sang her praise in the famous 'Song of Mulan'.

Maxine Hong Kingston is one of the writers who stress the importance of telling stories about becoming woman-warrior. In her fictional biography, Kingston invents a story of how she herself became a woman-warrior, but first she tells stories of women-warriors recounted by her mother. She tells of Fa Mulan, the girl who took her father's place in a battle, and of the woman who invented white crane boxing:

> It was a woman who invented white crane boxing only two hundred years ago. She was already an expert pole fighter, daughter of a teacher trained at the Shaolin temple, where there lived an order of fighting monks. She was combing her hair one morning when a white crane alighted outside her window. She teased it with her pole, which it pushed aside with a soft brush of its wing. Amazed, she dashed outside and tried to knock the crane off its perch. It snapped her pole in two. Recognising the presence of a great power, she asked the spirit of the white crane if it would teach her to fight. It answered with a cry that white crane boxers imitate today. Later the bird returned as an old man and he guided her boxing for many years. Thus she gave the world a new martial art. (1977: 19)

In this socio-cultural imaginary, a woman can give the world a martial art, which conversely implies that through a martial art she can confirm her female identity.

This tradition of women-warriors has made its way into Hong Kong film. In *The Temple of the Red Lotus* (Jiang hu qi xia/Tsan hong tsu, Chui Chang Wang/Hung Hsu Tseng, 1965, for example), all the female members of the family are trained in martial arts, including Lianzhu/Lian Chu (Chin Ping), the central female character in the film. On Lianzhu's wedding night, her mother enters the newlyweds' bedchamber and whispers something mysterious to her. The young husband (Jimmy Wang Yu) is unpleasantly surprised when he learns that the mother has reminded the daughter of her daily kung fu lesson with her father.

In this film the grandmother (Lam Jing) is depicted as the highest authority. When the young couple want to leave Jin Castle, a family rule is applied – they have to fight their way out. Since the men are not in the castle, Lianzhu and her husband Wu have to fight a series of women: Lianzhu's sister-in-law, aunt, mother and grandmother. The young couple overcome each barrier not by outshining the martial arts expertise of their opponents but through pleading and crying. The grandmother, however, is not as merciful, and since Lianzhu has greater knowledge of kung fu than her husband Wu, she engages in a duel while Wu waits on the other side of the river. Ultimately, the grandmother too spares their lives, and soon Linazhu and Wu are on their way.

There is one female authority, however, who is on an even higher level; this is the Red Lady Sword (Ivy Ling Po), the best fighter of all. She acts as Lianzhu's and Wu's guardian angel, coming to their rescue on several occasions. Her superior position is indicated quite literally in the film; her point of vision and action are 'from above'; that is, she appears on the rooftops or hills. The Red Lady watches over those who need help, and through her effective interventions she controls the outcome of events.

The women in *The Temple of the Red Lotus* can be linked to the women-warriors in the traditional legend of the Yang family, with its several generations of women generals, with the grandmother as the grand matriarch at the top of the pyramid. According to the legend, the Yang women took part in battles in order to avenge their husbands and fathers, the male warriors of the family, or to serve the country in place of the male members, who had all lost their lives in battles. The legend has inspired several artistic creations, from novels to films to operas.

Drama historian Adolphe C. Scott describes the Beijing opera matriarchs (*laodan*) as 'halting in step but firm in spirit, forceful in expression and emotional in their grief, they are constantly concerned with the honor of family life and the unity of the clan' (1983: 125). Within this cultural imaginary, it is not unusual to encounter female characters in the resistance. Martial arts novels such as those of Jin Yong/Louis Cha also celebrate women rebels, famous examples being the One-Armed Princess from his novel *The Deer and the Cauldron* (1969–72) or the female rebels from his *Fox Volant of the Snowy Mountain* (1959).[3]

Those representations were also inspired by historical accounts of women rebels. Women rebels were members of secret sects and groups that had their own blood oaths, religious rituals and brotherhoods. Once recruited into these ranks, women were given a prestige and a function in a society that largely denied those things to them. According to some accounts, women who joined Triad lodges in advance of their husbands could claim precedence within the household over their own spouses. In Chinese high society and particularly in non-Han, non-Confucian families, a certain freedom was accorded to women – ambiguous, but nonetheless effective. Thus, the daughters of Taoist 'Boxers' received a military education like their brothers, and took part in political struggles as rebels or 'bandits' fighting against feudal law. Female brigades of the Taiping were instructed in the art of war (see Spence 1990). It is thus logical that the appearance of women fighters does not require special narrative justification and explanation.

Evidently, narrative representation is not only determined by the process of cinematic storytelling/narration, but also by a certain mode of cultural expression that informs the film's fabula. The actions these women are able to perform have to do with the connection between the narrative and the rules and norms that regulate what kind of female character is imaginable and conceivable. Speaking generally of Hong Kong films that feature fabulas populated with female heroes, it is possible to argue that these films work contrary to the laws of common sense that govern the social imagination of Western traditions. The viewing pleasure derives from the exhilarating action scenes and the superhuman skills of the characters but at the same time the sense of empowerment emanates from the fictional worlds/fabulae predicated on specific conventions and practices. In spite of female subordination in daily life, the stories of women-warriors remained alive, and remarkably, women play heroic roles in Hong Kong cinema to an extent that is without parallel in European or Anglo-American action-adventure films.

A furhter inspiration behind such representation is the third dominant religion in China – Buddhism. Since the way towards transcendence under Buddhism is equally applicable to both men and women, it is not strange that this would emerge in films. For example, in *Wing Chun* (Yuen Woo Ping, 1992) Wing Chun's teacher of martial arts and the highest narratorial authority in the film is a Buddhist nun. There is an egalitarian principle at work in Buddhism, where both men and women can achieve spiritual fulfillment. Quite understandably, then, Wing Chun could find refuge in a Buddhist temple and learn kung fu from a Buddhist woman.

Wing Chun: the film's fabula as a mode of cultural expression

A narrative text is a text in which an agent relates – tells – a story in a particular medium such as film (see Bal 1997). To follow Mieke Bal's working definition of narrative, a story is a fabula that is presented in a certain manner, and a fabula is a series of logically and chronologically related events. The story determines a specific rhetoric that has direct implications on the epistemological value of the text; the way the events are ordered into a story, the way a fabula is framed or re-framed through the process of storytelling enables us to draw conclusions about the concerns that are embedded into the fictional world.[4]

As viewers, we are able to re-construct the fabula only at the very end, after it has been presented in some way as a story, and thus we tend to disregard the fact that fabulas of narrative texts are dependent on concerns derived from the outer world. Or, as Bal explains, fabulas make describable a segment of reality that is broader than that of the narrative text itself (ibid.). The fabula of Wing Chun confirms this: according to the legend, Yim Wing Chun learned the art of kung fu from a Buddhist nun by the name of Ng Mui who was famous for her skill at fighting on top of the 'plum blossom poles'.[5] Hers is a southern style of fighting founded on direct, close contact, a combination of straight and intercepting lines and deflecting arcs. The style was named 'Wing Chun' after Ng Mui's female pupil. As the legend goes, Wing Chun's beauty attracted the attention of a local bully. He tried to force Wing Chun to marry him and his persistent threats became a source of worry to her and her father. Ng Mui learned of this and took pity on Wing Chun. She agreed to teach Wing Chun some fighting techniques so that she could protect herself. Wing Chun followed Ng Mui to the mountains, where she trained night and day until she had mastered the techniques. In this place of exile, Wing Chun redefined herself, as did the heroine from *A Touch of Zen*/Hsia nu/Hap lui, for example, when she retreated to the Buddhist temple in King Hu's 1969 masterpiece. Hidden away in the mountains, she was taught swordplay skills by Buddhist monks. The fabulas of these films echo the structures of meaning on the extradiegetic level. An example from literature is Maxine Hong Kingston's novel *Woman Warrior: Memoirs of a Girlhood Among Ghosts* (1977), which tells of a young woman who goes away to learn kung fu, and then returns as a general, riding at the head of an army of men to defend her village from a monstrous horde. When Wing Chun returns to her village she challenges the bully to a fight and defeats him.

This myth of emancipation of the female Shaolin Temple student is a pre-text to Yuen Woo Ping's 1994 film *Wing Chun*. The events that occur in Yuen's film take place after that, continuing Wing Chun's story past the legend. This implies that the film deals with a possible narrative/fabula/history, or a succession of events that could have occurred after Wing Chun returned home from her training and established herself as an authority in the martial arts. The pre-text, that is, the legend, conditions the premise (of the filmic narrative) that in a seventeenth-century village in China the best fighter is a woman by the name of Wing Chun. Constantly engaged in kung fu training and, dressed in male attire, she seems to have sacrificed her feminine side to sustain her position as the kung fu expert and a protector of the people. She lives with her aunt, who runs a bean curd business. Although the past problem (of power and gender) is solved, a new, yet similar, pressure is put on her female identity. In the course of the film, the tale about the woman being pressured into marriage repeats itself, illustrating for us that history, the pre-text, is mirrored in the film's story.

The characters and stories that we can find in the traditions of Hong Kong cinema are bound up with cultural and social framings, options and constraints. The emergence of powerful female characters is strongly connected to the stories that occurred 'a long, long time ago in a universe far, far away', but this is not the case of a generic clash between fairy tale and science fiction that infers a temporal disjunction and a past that is yet to come.[6] If we recall some of the most famous action heroines in the Hollywood films – characters such as Princess Leia from the *Star Wars* series (1977–2005) or Ellen Ripley from the *Alien* series (1979–97) – we notice that the first and the most important difference between the Hong Kong and the Hollywood heroines is that the latter come from the future.[7] The reason for this is because no narrative justification could be found to situate them in the past (or the present).[8]

Discussions on the reinvention of femininity through the action genre as it is manifested especially in contemporary Hollywood have occasionally been geared toward the female warriors of Hong Kong cinema who appeared on the big screens many decades earlier than their Hollywood counterparts (see Tasker 1993). One of the reasons for this, as has been pointed out, is that the diverse traditions of Hong Kong cinema permit different sorts of characters, and not just the main protagonists, to be fighters. In Yuen Woo Ping's film *Drunken Master* (Zui quan/Jui kuen, 1978) for example, there need not be a special narrative justification for a middle-aged mother to engage in a martial arts combat with the young Wong Fei Hung who has threatened her daughter's chastity. In terms of Hong Kong cinema, this is an act of common sense. In these narratives the action is set in the past but the women seem to be emancipated in ways unimaginable in Western traditions. Here, almost literally, history comes to figure as science fiction.[9]

In Western traditions the reinvention of femininity and masculinity through the action genre involved cases such as men being turned into spectacle as well as women becoming both masculinised and musculinised (see Jeffords 1989 and 1996). In contrast to the Hollywood examples, the women warriors in Hong Kong action films cannot be described as masculinised, for their bodies are not muscled and man-like even when they have a masculine appearance. Even though Wing Chun's aunt tells her she has lost everything except her fists, Wing Chun (Michelle Yeoh) does not really display the masculine features of characters such as Sarah Connor in *Terminator 2* or Ripley in *Alien Resurrection*. Her 'masculinisation' can rather be attributed to the Chinese cultural imaginary.

I am referring in the first place to the 'body of Tao', the Taoist priority given to the human body over social and cultural systems. We can trace this tradition in Beijing opera, which had such a profound influence on the martial arts and swordplay genre of Hong Kong cinema, including the kung fu comedy. Traditionally, the 'masculinisa-tion' of female fighters in Hong Kong cinema is not perceived as a problem, and it does not bring the character's femininity into question. Their masculinity does not presuppose the loss of femininity, for their character entails duality, two in one, as is typically the case in Beijing opera. This type of female character is called *wudan*, and it designates a cross-dressing woman of action who maintains her feminine appeal (see Scott 1983). It is useful to recall that the two fundamental phases of action in Taoism, yin and yang, serve to designate feminine and masculine. The first of the commandments of the adepts who received Tao teaching was to practice non-action and gentleness, or rather, to keep their femininity and never take the initiative. In *The Taoist Body*, Kristofer Schipper explains that the Taoist doctrine inspired by Lao Tzu's teachings – to know the masculine and yet maintain the feminine – 'is to become the valley of the world' (1993: 128). The physiological practices of nourish-ing the Vital Principle require that one first realise the female element, which also includes the adoption of a female posture. Interestingly, until the very end of the film, Wing Chun is dressed as a man. On the one hand, the film draws on the tradi-tion of female cross-dressing, but in this kung fu comedy, cross-dressing also evokes contemporary play with gender, in particular the idea of gender as performance. This is especially evident in scenes where Wing Chun is confused with a man; this can be perceived as subversive confusion, and we could say that in such instances cross-dressing provokes, in Judith Butler's sense, gender trouble (1990). For her, gender trouble has positive connotations, as does the parodying of gender through cross-dressing. Even though cross-dressing is a cultural stereotype and Wing Chun dressed in male attire can fool everyone, including her childhood sweetheart, we know that she is of the female sex. Therefore, Wing Chun's tender interaction with another woman can inevitably be perceived in today's context as 'queer'. Her 'queer-ness' points to the unstable structure of gender, and it has a deterritorialising effect. These strategies were pushed to phenomenal extremes in films directed or produced by Tsui Hark starring Brigitte Lin, for example, *Peking Opera Blues/Do ma daan* (Tsui Hark, 1986), *Swordsman II/Xiao ao jiang hu zhi: Dong Fang Bu Bai* (Siu Tong Ching, 1992) and *The East is Red/Dung Fong Bat Baai: Fung wan joi hei* (Siu Tung Ching, Raymond Lee, 1992). One can argue that the cultural heritage, or rather, the tradi-tion of cross-dressing that was imported into film from Chinese opera, is one reason behind Lin acquiring the status of a filmic gender-bending persona.

Apart from the influence of Taoism, kung fu comedy as a genre draws on the tradi-tion of street acrobatics, the northern-style martial scenes featured in Beijing opera, and even the scene with the middle-aged mother, Miss Ho, in *Drunken Master* con-firms these connections.[10] It goes a step further however, because the theatricality and the camp aspect of this scene, thanks to Jackie Chan's performance, enhance the comical aspect of the film and mock the tradition. Within the Western imaginary, it is unthinkable that an older woman could be a skilled kung fu fighter. In mainstream Hollywood films, female fighters are appearing more frequently, but they are gener-ally young and attractive women.[11] The fact that in Yuen's films middle-aged or older women (*Drunken Master; Dance of the Drunk Mantis/Nan bei zui quan/Laam bak chui kuen* [1979]) and even a fat woman (*Drunken Tai-Chi/Xiao tai chi/Siu taai gik*, 1984) can be expert fighters capable of defeating arrogant and abusive men is depen-dent on the connection between narrative and rules and norms that regulate what is imaginable and conceivable. Undoubtedly, this is connected to the representation of both men and women in cinema. The notion that some forms of activity are more appropriate for men and some others for women has its roots in the common-sense understanding of acceptable male and female behaviour, the categories of which are best expressed in images, stories and in general fictions.

As mentioned earlier, the law that determines what is possible in the first place concerns the level of the fabula. The way a female subject is expressed in a filmic text is closely related to the way the story is told, but it is first of all dependent on some form of understanding of the world such as the following: that the hero needs to be goal oriented, that happiness entails a union of a heterosexual couple (as is most often the case in classical Hollywood cinema), or, and this is relevant for Hong Kong cinema, that a woman can be a martial arts expert, that she can signify action and even single-handedly save the (fictional) world. Contrary to all expectations, the fat woman in *Drunken Tai-Chi* turns out to be a skilled kung fu fighter who teaches the imprudent man a lesson.

Wing Chun, a 'flat' or a 'dense' character?

In a filmic narrative such as *Wing Chun*, represented subjects can principally be observed in terms of their function as diegetic agents, i.e. characters. The character who has the capacity and the power to see, whose vision we share, has the advantage over other characters, and thus accordingly functions as the subject of vision. The character who has the capacity to act and to directly affect the course of events can be termed the subject of action; in *Wing Chun* the subject of action is most strikingly expressed through the main female character. Hence, by tracing the relationship between subject positions, we can establish the subjects of action, vision and narration; this implies that a particular scene, part of a scene, sequence, or even single shot can be understood as a unit of narrative discourse depending on the intersubjective engagement in question.

Considering that Wing Chun's main function in this narrative is to propel action, she can also be understood as a frame of reference, a slot to be filled. The fact that she is elaborated as a 'flat' rather than a 'psychologically rounded' character may give the impression that this film is banal, too obvious, and overtly simplistic. In terms of cinematic storytelling, the construction of Wing Chun's character-image is basically restricted to a series of tableaux where she repeatedly overpowers her male opponents. According to David Bordwell, by American standards many Hong Kong films (of all genres) 'look broadly played, perhaps seeming closer to silent film conventions than to those post-Method Hollywood' (2000: 88). Bordwell suggests that this is part of a distinct aesthetic in which expressive amplification is central to the performance of actor and ensemble.

When it comes to the traditional notions of cinematic art, style in principle refers to the systematic or inventive use of cinematic devices as these are related to the process of narration, and therefore, 'broadness' presumes in fact a certain simplicity of expression (for the discussion on style see, for example, Bordwell 1985). It has been pointed out that by the standards of festival cinema the Hong Kong approach to narrative seems obstinately naïve. Film scholars suggest, however, that in place of overarching coherence, we should look for a tension between 'spectacle' and 'narrative' (see Bordwell 2000: 178).

In *Wing Chun* the women are principally on the side of good, whereas the men (with the exception of Pok To) are bad (and potential oppressors), weak or ridiculous. Wing Chun can thus primarily be defined in terms of her position within the fabula because on the level of the story her principal aims as an actor are not developed further so as to display complexity and psychological depth. I am referring to the notion of 'actor' in the narratological sense, as operating on the level of the fabula, and hence, before it is developed into a character through the storytelling process.

Discussing Wing Chun's 'flatness' within the narratological framework then, I would add that her status as a character overlaps with her position as an actor.

According to Algirdas Julien Greimas (1987), an actor is a structural position, while a character is a complex semantic unit. Mieke Bal adds that the character is the actor provided with distinctive characteristics, which together create the effect of a character. On the basis of semantic content, that is, of different principles that work together, the image of the character is constructed.

> The actors have an intention: they aspire toward an aim. That aspiration is the achievement of something agreeable or favorable, or the evasion of something disagreeable or unfavorable. [...] An actant is a class of actors that shares a certain characteristic quality. That shared characteristic is related to the teleology of the fabula as a whole. An actant is therefore a class of actors whose members have an identical relation to the aspect of telos which constitutes the principle of the fabula. (1997: 197)

Here, we also have to consider the fact that kung fu comedy as a genre makes much less of an appeal to authenticity, reminding us also that it draws its origins from Beijing opera. A. C. Scott observed that the Chinese 'have always sought their enjoyment in theater in the sensory immediacy of the actor's presentation' (1983: 160).[12] Moreover, *Wing Chun* plays with certain types, such as those of the comic actors, the *chou*, but more pertinently, Wing Chun's character-image echoes the female type skilled in fighting and riding and accustomed to forceful action. This type of character provides ample opportunities for spectacular displays of acrobatics and different combat forms but it retains at the same time its feminine appeal.[13] The point is that Wing Chun's simplicity and 'flatness' are additionally supported by the concrete expectations based on extratextual information inherent in this cultural stereotype. While it draws its origins from tradition however, one of the main intentions of kung fu comedy is to simultaneously subvert tradition and mock the principles of the martial arts genre. 'Gender trouble' is an example of such subversion. This is acceptable precisely because there is less appeal to authenticity.

Taking into account Wing Chun's function in the fabula, I would argue that her 'flatness', transparency and simplicity secure her 'density' and stability as a female heroine; paradoxically perhaps, her ability to act as the protector on the side of good and execute a series of effective physical performances which cause that 'flatness', generates at the same time a sense of empowerment. The sense of empowerment conditions and ultimately confirms her image as a female warrior. Moreover, she is depicted as the 'puppeteer', the one who controls the event; in a specific scene she is engaged in combat without leaving her chair. This type of female fighter draws its roots from the past and from other media; in the martial arts novel *The Deer and the Cauldron*, one of the most authoritative and superior female characters, the one-armed White Nun, just like Wing Chun, is capable of fighting fiercely while seated.

In these narratives action is set in the past but the female characters seem to be emancipated in ways unimaginable in Western traditions – almost literally, history comes to figure as science fiction.

Notes

1   Speaking of legendary Beijing opera stereotypes where a female character is made to be both a pretty heroine and a military hero, the most famous one is certainly Hua Mulan (Fa Mulan in Cantonese pronunciation). In the *Legends of China* series presented at the Hong Kong Cultural Centre there was a magnificent opera, *The Ladies of the Great Yang Family*, based on a heroic story of twelve women warriors of the Song Dynasty, all of whom are skilled in martial arts, and the head of the family is the grandmother. For examples of women warriors in martial arts novels, see for example Jin Yong's (Louis Cha) *Deer and the Cauldron* (1997) and *Fox Volant of the Snowy Mountain* (1996). See also *Classical Chinese Tales of the Supernatural and the Fantastic* edited by Karl Kao (1985), in particular the story 'Li Chi, the Serpent Slayer'.

2   Women were expected to follow the strict code of the three 'obediences' – at home obey your father, after marriage obey your husband, after your husband's death obey your son.

3   Indicative are these passages from Luis Cha's *Fox Volant of the Snowy Mountain*: 'The lady went by the name of Sign Tian. Though she was young, she had already made a name in the Martial Brotherhood of the border region. As her beauty was matched by sharp intelligence and quick wit, the elder members of the Liaodong Martial Brotherhood had given her the title of Glistening Sable. The sable can make great speed on snowy ground, and is sharp and intelligent' (1996: 10); 'At length, Fox asked Orchid, not without surprise in his voice, "I understand that your father is the Invincible Under the Sky. Why did he not transmit to you his esoteric martial feats? I have heard that both genders in your house have equal entitlement to the Miao's Swordplay, as the esoteric techniques of your family are passed on to all male and female descendants alike"' (1996: 229).

4   Needless to say, the separation of the fabula from the story or the text is only theoretical because the functioning of the narrative involves the simultaneous interaction of all three layers.

5   The Buddhist nun is referred to as Wu May in the Mandarin version and Ng Mui in the Cantonese version.

6   I am referring to Princess Leia from *Star Wars*. Generic clash (and a temporal paradox) comes from the reference to the past, event that happened a long, long time ago juxtaposed with futuristic space vehicles.

7   We have to add that these fantasy narratives with exaggerated physical types are often derived from comic books, within imaginary locations.

8   George Lucas's statement regarding his decision to set the *Star Wars* story in outer space is indicative of this: 'I researched kids' movies and how they work and how myths work; and I looked very carefully at the elements of films within that fairy tale genre which made them successful. […] I found that myth always takes place over the hill, in some exotic far-off land. For the Greeks it was Ulysses going off into the unknown, for Victorian England it was India or North Africa or treasure islands. For America it was out West. There had to be strange savages and bizarre things in an exotic land. Now the last of that mythology died out in the mid-1950s, with the last of the men who knew the old West. The last place left 'over the hill' is space' (quoted in Pyle and Miles 1979: 80). It was out there in a galaxy far, far away, that scary monsters, androids and princesses could be in charge.

9   This assertion is inspired by De Certeau's concept of history in his *The Writings of History* (1975).

10 Also from stage adaptations of episodes from the story of Monkey King.

11 A possible exception is Demi Moore in the sequel of *Charlie's Angels, Full Throttle* (McG, 2003), although she plays an attractive professional in the film, rather than the mother of what is practically a grown up.

12 Also, many filmmakers came from Beijing opera academies, including Yuen Woo Ping.

13 As noted, the loss of Wing Chun's feminine self in Yuen's film is also a certain disruption of this character-type.

Bibliography

Bal, M. (1997) *Narratology: Introduction to the Theory of Narrative*. Toronto: University of Toronto Press.

Bordwell, D. (1985) *Narration in the Fiction Film*. Madison: University of Wisconsin Press.

____ (2000) *Planet Hong Kong: Popular Cinema and the Art of Entertainment*. Cambridge, MA: Harvard University Press.

Butler, J. (1990) *Gender Trouble: Feminism and the Subversion of Identity*. New York: Routledge.

De Certeau, M. (1975) *The Writings of History*. New York: Columbia University Press.

Geertz, C. (1983) *Local Knowledge: Further Essays in Interpretive Anthropology*. New York: Basic Books.

Greimas, A. J. (1987) 'Actants, Actors, and Figures', in *On Meaning: Selected Writings in Semiotic Theory*. Trans. P. J. Perron and F. H. Collins. Minneapolis: University of Minnesota Press, 106–20.

Hong Kingston, M. (1977) *The Woman Warrior: Memoirs of a Girlhood Among Ghosts*. London: Picador.

Jeffords, S. (1989) *Remasculinization of America: Gender and Vietnam*. Bloomington: Indiana University Press.

____ (1996) *Hard Bodies: Hollywood Masculinity in the Reagan Era*. New Brunswick, NJ: Rutgers University Press.

Pyle, M. and L. Miles (1979) *The Movie Brats: How the Film Generation Took Over Hollywood*. New York: Holt, Reinbart and Winston.

Schipper, K. (1993) *The Taoist Body*. Berkley: University of California Press.

Scott, A. C. (1983) 'The Performance of Classical Theater', in C. Mackerras (ed.) *Chinese Theatre: From Its Origins to the Present Day*. Honolulu: University of Hawaii Press, 118–44.

Spence, J. D. (1990) *The Search For Modern China*. New York: W. W. Norton.

Tasker, Y. (1993) *Spectacular Bodies: Gender, Genre and the Action Cinema*. London and New York: Routledge.

Storytelling and Religio-Cultural Encounters

Clouds of Unknowing: Buddhism and Bhutanese Cinema

Shohini Chaudhuri and Sue Clayton

The international co-production *Travellers and Magicians* (Khyentse Norbu, 2003) has been described as 'the first film to be shot entirely within the kingdom of Bhutan' (Marshall 2003: 18), despite the fact that the country has had a flourishing digital video (DV) feature film industry since the turn of the twenty-first century. These DV films have captured the local market but have rarely been seen abroad. Situated in the Himalayas, between India and China-occupied Tibet, Bhutan has been relatively isolated culturally, due to conscious policy and geographical inaccessibility. There were no roads or electricity until the 1960s and, since then, heavy tourist taxes have restricted the flow of foreign visitors. With the lifting of the ban on television in 1999, the government, under the fourth king, Jigme Singye Wangchuck (who ruled 1972–2006), moved towards entering the global stage and opening up the media but, wary of the potentially disastrous consequences of swift change, it sought to preserve 'unique' Bhutanese values, thought to inhere in the culture's indebtedness to oral tradition and Buddhist beliefs.[1] In this chapter, we consider oral tradition and Buddhism and how they have impacted upon storytelling within the material context of filmmaking in Bhutan. We show how cinematic storytelling functions as a kind of 'secondary orality' (Ong 2006: 3), by exploring the depiction of time, place, and multiple realities in *Travellers and Magicians* and three local DV films. Finally, co-author Sue Clayton, herself a screenwriter and director, describes how working in dialogue with Bhutanese writers provides further insights into storytelling structures.

Historical context

Despite rising levels of literacy, the legacy of oral tradition is still key to film culture in Bhutan, where film is now the main form of mass entertainment and where numerous local languages and dialects are spoken but only one – the official national language, Dzongkha – has a written form.[2] The first Bhutanese film, *Gasa Lamai Singye* (Ugyen Wangdi, 1989), was made on VHS in 1989. However, it was the introduction of broadcast television together with public access to the internet in 1999, combined with the availability of cheaper digital technology, that really fuelled the film industry. As there are no film schools in Bhutan and no state funding for film, the industry benefited from technical training offered through the national TV station, the Bhutan Broadcasting Corporation (BBS). Most films are made in Dzongkha; however, some screenwriters initially write their scripts in English and then commission translation into Dzongkha.

Built in 1969, the Lugar theatre in the capital, Thimphu, historically screened films from Bhutan's neighbour and almost sole trading partner, India. Today's filmmakers speak of only ever having seen Bollywood films for their whole childhood, with Bollywood providing their main cinematic model with song and dance sequences considered integral to box-office success. Over the last decade, the Lugar has increasingly shown Bhutanese films. The majority of the audience is drawn from the lower classes and monks. Films are also toured around cinema halls and fields in the provinces. The producer acts as exhibitor, arranging bookings and organising projection equipment and publicity. He or she will personally carry and supply the film to safeguard against piracy – one of the biggest problems facing the industry, despite the introduction of copyright laws in 2001. Therefore, although old Bhutanese films are aired on BBS and Thimphu's now-numerous cable operators, they are not released for sale or rental on DVD (local video rental shops stock mainly Bollywood and Hollywood films). This mode of production, distribution and consumption complements the oral performative and seasonal character of cinema in Bhutan.

Buddhism and the oral tradition form a rich repertoire of stories which filmmakers are now increasingly attempting to mine. Kunzang Choden, author of *Folktales of Bhutan*, remarks: 'For a largely illiterate society, the oral tradition, mainly storytelling, was a powerful means to share and inculcate the society's values' (email communication to Shohini Chaudhuri, 16 July 2007). Since language in oral cultures exists only as an ephemeral utterance, not externalised in writing, the story, or oral narrative in general, became the forum for transmitting wisdom and belief. In his book *Orality and Literacy* (2006), Walter Ong identifies certain formulaic elements in oral storytelling – the exploits of heroes, monstrous villains and mnemonic verbal patterns – which organise knowledge in a way that is helpful for oral memorisation. These appear to be present in Bhutanese folktales, which are populated by ghosts, spirits and demons and – despite the country's isolation and claims to 'uniqueness'

– bear many resemblances to other orally-told stories from India, Tibet and Nepal. Like fairy tales, which also derive from oral tradition, they tend to have an indefinite time-frame, beginning with the formula '*Dangbo..o..o Dingbo..o..o..*' ('long, long ago'). Unlike Aristotelian unities, the conception of time in the folktales is fluid, and subordinated to space, as in many other oral narratives: place, especially Bhutan's mountainous landscape, plays a central role, its geographical features and locality evoked in detail. The concept of time as repetitive and cyclical, implicit in storytelling structures, can be linked to cosmic cycles of day and night, seasonal change and the Buddhist conception of time as a karmic cycle of births and deaths.

The form of Buddhism practised in Bhutan belongs to the Tantric branch of the Mahayana tradition that arrived in Bhutan from Tibet. Syncretically woven into it are elements of the animistic Tibetan Bon religion, which features 'guardian spirits and demons, controlled by rituals and the ecstatic techniques of shamans' (Moore 1977: 197). The guardian spirits of mountains, lakes and other localities were absorbed into Bhutanese Buddhism as protector deities and are worshipped by the local population. As Bernard Faure has argued, one cannot reduce Buddhism to a philosophy or set of teachings; it cannot be freed from mythology and ritual: 'Buddhism itself is double, hybrid, bastardized', both rationalistic and also 'local, pagan, quasi-shamanistic thought' (2004: x). Dasho Karma Gaylay, arts advisor to the fourth king, has claimed that 'Buddhism in Bhutan is not a religion but a way of life' (interview with Shohini Chaudhuri, 26 December 2006). Buddhist belief takes on material forms in stories, traditional arts and crafts (classified as 'the Thirteen Arts' since the seventeenth century), religious rituals and visual artefacts, the circumambulation of religious buildings, the taste and smell of food offerings, and people's behaviour towards each other, towards nature and all living beings. Such artefacts and rituals are signs didactically pointing a way to spiritual experience, a sacred presence or absolute reality beyond the empirical world.

Mahayana Buddhists, in common with most other branches of Buddhism, believe that human beings are repeatedly re-born to gain progressive wisdom until they finally reach Enlightenment. The Enlightened Ones, usually monks who are given the appellation *tulku*, are fully aware of their previous incarnations, and though they have nothing further to learn, are thought to choose to continue with successive re-births to help the less enlightened reach a similar goal – hence the meaning of Mahayana ('Greater Vehicle'). Mahayana Buddhism prides itself on being large enough to carry all humanity to Enlightenment: a religion for everyone. This evokes parallels with cinema, a medium of mass appeal, capable of being mobilised for the dissemination of religious stories and symbols.

The notion of repeated reincarnation, which each time enhances knowledge, significantly informs the cyclical worldview expressed in Bhutanese narrative. Murals in Buddhist temples and *dzongs* (fortresses) represent scenes from the life of Buddha sequentially (rather in the manner of a film storyboard), but not as a linear narrative: instead, the narrative is episodic, cyclical, spatialised (time is handled in terms of spatial movement) and allegorised. This traditional form of visual storytelling shares many characteristics of oral narrative which, especially in lengthy formats, has an aggregative quality, an 'episodic looseness' rather than a single, unified narrative thread, which enables the storyteller to improvise and adapt the material for different occasions (Paniker 2003: 7). The teachings of the Buddha were, of course, orally transmitted. They consist of didactic and formulaic features that are the hallmarks of oral culture: the Three Jewels (*buddha*, *dharma* and *sangha*); the Four Noble Truths and similar lists (see Faure 2004: 90). The Buddha's parables epitomise the principles of oral didacticism, using stories to illustrate his teaching. Thus, ordinary people may glimpse the truth through these tales, rather than through abstract arguments which only the Enlightened can apprehend. The authors found similarities here with the multi-levelled organisation of symbolism in English Medieval religious texts, hence the title of this chapter. In works such as *Pearl* (fourteenth century) and *The Cloud of Unknowing* (circa 1370), the central symbol can be interpreted at many levels from the literal to the occult and obscure, creating different levels of reader address. In Buddhism, 'the truth' is comprehended in a similarly differential way, but from different levels of knowledge on the karmic cycle.

Relying on popular, well-known stories, oral narrative and its film adaptation have the quality of ritual, repeating familiar content but varying it from one performance to another. That element of '(re)-interpretation' is crucial as, despite the desire to preserve stories, they are unlikely to 'speak to a new audience without creative "reanimation"' (Hutcheon 2006: 8). Transposing a given work may involve transcoding motifs from one medium or one set of conventions to another. In *A Theory of Adaptation*, Linda Hutcheon discusses this transposition in terms of shifts between the main modes of audience engagement, showing, telling and interacting: 'Telling a story, in words, either orally or on paper, is never the same as showing it visually and aurally in any of the performance media available' (2006: 23). However, oral narrative works by means of gestural, aural and visual elements, which are bound up with memory associations, therefore it arguably blurs the boundaries between Hutcheon's categories of showing or telling. Moreover, although it is not participatory in exactly the same way as ritual, filmgoing for Bhutanese audiences is highly interactive – they are extremely talkative before and during film screenings, overtly react to the appearance of the hero onscreen, and burst out with applause and laughter at comic moments. It is also customary for them to attend repeat viewings of the same film. Spectators are not passive, but *join in* the experience, thus the reception of films in Bhutan (and, indeed, in many other Asian cultures) suggests a mode of interacting with stories rather than simply being told or shown them. Ong describes the phenomenon of 'secondary orality' fostered by electronic media such as television, dependent on the developments of literacy and print, yet creating a form of communication with certain oral characteristics; he does not name film, video or the internet, but it is clear that these are also encompassed within secondary oral culture (2006: 11). Below, we look more closely at how cinema has succeeded in

Bhutan as a 'secondary oral medium' for local audiences, exploring four Bhutanese films – the first by Buddhist monk, religious teacher, and Oscar-nominated cult director Khyentse Norbu and then three films made in the local vernacular – and one film project in development.

Enlightenment at 24 frames per second: *Travellers and Magicians*

A former assistant to Bernardo Bertolucci on *Little Buddha* (1993), Khyentse Norbu's first feature film was *The Cup* (1999). His second feature, *Travellers and Magicians*, is similarly made for an international market and enjoyed a high-profile release. It is a conscious attempt at a Buddhist storytelling methodology, using the allegorical form of a parable. This is inserted within a contemporary story about a young man, Dondup who – dreaming of emigrating to America – hitchhikes to the capital Thimphu from his home in central Bhutan to obtain a visa. Narrated by a monk whom he encounters along the way, the inset parable tells the tale of Tashi, another restless young man, who drinks a magic potion that leads him to a faraway place where, with tragic consequences, he falls in love with Deki, the young wife of an old woodsman, then wakes up back at home. Although the film was critically acclaimed internationally, reviewers have tended to read the film at a surface level, without accounting for the parabolic narrative. Lee Marshall, reviewer for *Screen International*, assumes the film's 'rather trite message' is 'the grass is not always greener' (2003: 18). However, this disregards the relationship between the inner and outer structures of the text in Asian storytelling in which, K. Ayyappa Paniker has argued, 'surface simplicity is often a clever device to interiorise a deeper and more complex end' (2003: 5). It is common for a story to have a framing device; however, the real significance is not to be found on the surface but inside the kernel of the story.

Norbu claims that the film is adapted from a Buddhist fable about two brothers, one an aspiring magician (Zeitgeist Films 2004). However, its underlying theme – desire as the root of suffering – is common to many Buddhist parables. According to the Buddha's Four Noble Truths, the world, governed by the cycle of birth and death (*samsara*), is full of suffering. What causes suffering is desire, in which the self craves at the expense of others, or an ignorant attachment to things of this world which are ultimately illusory and impermanent. The Buddhist conception refers to desire as an existential condition. In his inset tale, the monk portrays desire in its most intense, self-consuming form – erotic desire – which thus serves as an *emblem* of the more abstract idea. Tashi covets another man's wife and conspires to murder him in order to satisfy his desire. Finally, he beholds Deki's drowned image in the water, a symbol of loss and the impermanence of worldly things.

The story has a further level of meaning, however. By embedding this parable about desire and suffering within the story of Dondup negotiating the conflicting demands of tradition and modernity, Norbu makes its teaching relevant and immediate to Bhutan's present-day dilemmas, as the country ends its cultural isolation and undergoes modernisation, weighing up the relative merit of values – such as accumulative consumption – being imported from outside. Moreover, it is a monk who tells the inset tale; thus, the film upholds the importance of Buddhism as a value system in modern Bhutanese culture and in its storytelling heritage and conscience. The self-reflexive role of the storyteller within the film refers to oral tradition, the interactive character of which finds a cinematic parallel in the form of the road journey, with its assorted cast of characters (an apple-seller, a drunkard, a papermaker and his daughter) who mediate and alter the flow of the story.

The telling of the story creates a sense of multiple times and spaces in the narrative, a coexistence of different fictional worlds, which segue into each other: Dondup on his journey and the monk's inset tale with its 'reality' and 'dream' components. However, even the 'reality' of the monk's tale has otherworldly qualities, as shown by its folktale character and the role of the magic school, which Tashi reluctantly attends and from which his smarter brother learns the magic potion. Indeed the tale's diegetic 'reality' suggests a liminal realm between multiple possible worlds, 'where transformation, metamorphosis, dissolution are common, where magic is a branch of naturalism, or pragmatism' (Zamora and Faris 1995: 6). As in magic realism, it is a hybrid space in which the ordinary and fantastic coexist, in which 'one world … lie[s] hidden within another' (Wilson 1995: 225). Rawdon Wilson describes the 'boundary-slipping between worlds' in magic realism in terms of 'an occulted and latent dimension of the surface world' which erupts into it (1995: 210, 225). This notion of another, adjacent world which spills over into this world is not alien to Bhutanese Buddhism where, due to the prevalence of superstition, myth, legend, beliefs in deities residing in the phenomenal world and memories of past lives, reality is imbued with the fantastical. Indeed, the boundary between reality and fantasy is more flexible than in the West which has long repressed the mythological in favour of its post-Enlightenment logic and rationalism.

While we tend to discount the truth-value of alternative realities, including those witnessed in dreams, the conventional distinctions between waking life and dreams and between reality and illusion are often questioned in Buddhist thought. Visions of past lives, legends, myths and dreams all have value as part of reality. In Buddhist cosmology, everything is an illusion/dream from the ultimate perspective (thus lending itself to analogies with cinema). That is, the reality we know is a projection of another more complex reality that only the Enlightened can comprehend. Our own, subjective perspective is limited, only able to 'read' the signs at different levels: nature, parable, dream, ritual and tantric practice. Hence, the distinction between 'reality' and 'dream' itself is illusory and artificial: together with the illusory quality of external phenomena, one must accept the wisdom of the dream. Therefore, when Tashi wakes up in the parable, it does not signify relief that reality has superseded ('Thankfully, it was only a dream' or, 'There's no place like home') but a spiritual lesson learned about the corrosive nature of desire.

At a Bhutanese cinema near you: Popular local films

Bhutanese films that have been popular among local audiences also use cyclical devices and the multilayered approach to reality that we have associated above with Buddhist storytelling. One of these films is *Six Boys* (Karma Tshering, 2003) which is based on a real incident, the disappearance of six boys on the mountains after their visit to Tango monastery in 1996. But it also deals with a superstition: the boys threw stones into Dhomenday Lake and its deity reportedly rose up in retribution, causing them to lose their way. The film opens in the present day, with a young couple lighting butter lamps as offerings in the monastery. When they retire to a balcony overlooking the mountains, the man – Sonam, one of the real six lost boys, who plays himself in the film – asks his girlfriend what she prayed for and this becomes the occasion for the storytelling. The story is, therefore, embedded within ritual practice (the lighting of lamps and uttering of prayers for Sonam's deceased brother), with Sonam's voiceover guiding viewers through the flashbacks to the events of the disappearance. He begins his narration by telling us that we should pray for 'the benefit of all sentient beings', embodying the Buddhist ideal of selfless desire and accumulation of merit/salvation for others, not just for oneself.

The notion of compassion in Buddhism is not limited to the human race but includes nature and all its species. Kinship extends to all sentient beings, so one is encouraged to act towards entities in the natural world as if they were one's own relations. This is linked to karmic belief in the interdependence of all things. The notion of karma grants that everything that happens to you results from your past actions and everything that you do now affects what will befall you in future. Similarly, in ecological thinking, 'everything is connected to everything else' (Glotfelty and Fromm 1996: xix). As Faure observes, 'Buddhism has managed to produce a system of ecological thought in advance of its time', that is, an ethics of responsibility (2004: xiii). In Bhutan, environmental issues are linked to Buddhist teaching, lifestyle and animistic perspective in which the natural world is held to be inspirited with intelligent, autonomous and sacred 'life'. Together with material factors such as low population density and a historical lack of modern technology, these ethical systems have enabled the Bhutanese to live sustainably.

Six Boys lends itself to interpretation as an ecological fable. Like many of the other superstitions that Buddhism assimilated from Bon animism, it embodies deeper truths in a form more accessible to the mass of people. Throwing stones into the lake is an act of irresponsibility – an analogy for karmic retribution, in which actions rebound to the doer. This is vividly rendered in the film, when the boys arrive at the lake. Their stone throwing is depicted as an act of disturbance which destroys the equilibrium. To a soundtrack with an ominous drumbeat, the camera lingers in slow-motion medium close-up on the lake as it spurts and bubbles. We cut to a long shot of forests and mountains in the distance, as mist begins to roll downhill, then a close-up from the water's surface – the unusual angle hinting that this is the lake's point-of-view – followed by an overhead close-up, showing the lake seething with activity, like an awoken monster. Finally, we are shown the boys' point-of-view, as they realise that the lake is moving. According to the superstition, when a lake moves, one must run uphill to avoid being chased by it. Instead, the boys flee downhill and the chasing, vaporising lake is shown in long shot, using atmospheric special effects. The landscape suddenly becomes charged with mysterious malevolence and filled with obstacles: roaming lost for twelve days, the boys suffer the ordeals of leeches, hunger, and illness, and two of the boys die, including Sonam's brother Tshering.

The importance of place is evident in the sentient characterisation of the landscape. Nature is not the silent, inert backdrop against which the tale of the boys unfolds. Nor is it to be mastered by superior powers: the army's searches are fruitless and there is a total lack of landscape survey shots, often used to indicate visual mastery in Western cinema. Rather, nature is a dynamic participant in the drama.

The most expensive local Bhutanese film to date and the most successful, in terms of revenues, is *Chorten Kora* (Gyem Dorji, 2005).[3] A *chorten* is a term for a *stupa*, a religious construction frequently found at the roadside, or on the way to significant places. *Kora* means circumambulation, a popular ritual of walking around a sacred building or site. In the legend of the three thousand-year-old Chorten Kora in East Bhutan, the people of Karmaling Valley consult a *lama* on how to pacify a demon and are advised to build a *stupa*, offering him a virgin sacrifice. The film combines the appeal of this well-known traditional story with the novelties of computer animation – used for the first time in Bhutanese film to depict the demon and the building of the *stupa*. Parallel to the community in East Bhutan, it shows the princess Chorten Zam, who has been singled out for sacrifice, learn her destiny from dreams in which a *dakini* (female spirit) appears to her with a spiritual message. The princess's acceptance of her sacrifice is one of the means by which the film alters the legend, itself transmitted through oral tradition, in which there is no such thing as the original, just multiple versions, none of them 'definitive'. According to the legend, the Bhutanese abducted virgin(s) from Tawang (in the Indian province of Arunachal Pradesh) and *forcibly* sacrificed them; many of the changes made in the film accommodate the legend to Buddhist values, which shun ritual sacrifice (the practice of which belongs to the Bon religion). The filmmakers also rework the legend by creating a love story with four song sequences to add poignancy to the princess's situation, showing her falling in love. The use of dream as a method of revelation, another addition to the legend, is consistent with the Buddhist tradition of dream prophecy. The *dakini* appears to the princess not once, but twice, hailing her the second time just as the princess is about to sleep with her fiancé. The *dakini* makes the full revelation to exhort her to keep her purity and offer herself for eternal meditation, promising her escape from the cycle of rebirth. The visual conventions for depicting *dakinis* are taken from folktales and festivals showing processions of deities. The film ends with the princess being entombed in the *stupa* and her fiancé encircling it in devotion and, finally, a flash forward to the present day, in which pilgrims come from Tawang and all over Bhutan to celebrate the festival of Chorten Kora.

Golden Cup: The Legacy (Tshering Wangyel, 2006) is based on Rinzin Rinzin's short story, *The Talisman of Good Fortune* (2002), itself an adaptation of folk beliefs and superstitions which the writer heard in his own village. The heroine of the story is Lhamo, whose family is afflicted by a curse passed down the generations in the form of an ancient golden cup. When they come of age, women of the household inherit the curse and become poison-givers, killing anybody who eats from their hands. The only person who is immune is the village shaman; he alone knows the magic spell that neutralises the poison. Hearing of the curse, Lhamo's lover Tshering abandons her, even though she is pregnant with their child, and he marries another woman, leaving the sorrowful Lhamo longing for revenge. Superstitions about poison givers still prevail in modern-day Bhutan, not just in remote rural areas. Unlike *Chorten Kora* where the adaptation of legend, however knowingly, serves to confirm its patriarchal bias – the necessity of virgin sacrifice – *Golden Cup*, and the short story upon which it is based, revises the patriarchal ideology of its source through sympathy with the female poison givers. Yet, despite their similar outlook, the short story and film tell the tale very differently: the latter resorts to a more linear structure to make the story more accessible to its audience.

Belying its folktale appearance, the short story deploys a complex flashback structure, shuttling between past and present, starting with Lhamo's seasoned cruelty as a poison giver, then narrating the cause – Tshering's betrayal and the family's curse. The film, on the other hand, foregrounds the narrative of romance and betrayal, going back and forth in time only after establishing Lhamo's misfortune. *Golden Cup* ostensibly favours a linear causal chain and more resolute closure but its transposition of the short story needs to be considered in terms of the orality/literacy shift, this time from a narrative written by manipulating text on a computer to the secondary oral medium of film. The film incorporates oral storytelling within its flashback structure – with different characters narrating the origins of the curse and other events shown out of chronological order. The multiple flashbacks are anchored within the present of the storytelling situation, hence, the storytelling function of the dissolve, used to signal the start and end of each flashback – the cinematic equivalent of the oral performer's rhetorical flourish as he/she makes impromptu moves from one narrative segment to another.

The superstition of a curse handed down through the generations and resulting from an ancestor's actions has a deeper significance in terms of the retributive chain of karma – inescapable fate. Successive generations inherit the qualities of previous generations, which is underlined by casting the same actors. The notion of the transgenerational curse illustrates the complex causality of karma – the idea that 'you die from a bullet that you shot at yourself in an earlier life' (Faure 2004: 89–90). The film's full title, *Golden Cup: The Legacy* points up this notion of debts resulting from evil-bringing acts in the past.

Jumolhari: the Western hero meets Dharma and Karma

Jumolhari is a feature film project in development, to be directed by co-author Sue Clayton and scripted by Clayton with Bhutanese and other international writers. Initially, Clayton was approached by Bhutanese film actress Lhaki Dolma and producers Dorji Wangchuk and Pema Rinzin to develop a feature film which would reflect on how Bhutanese people have had to re-appraise their traditional values and way of life as the influences of Western tourism, global media and consumer choice are felt. It was agreed the film would also explore the motives and desires behind this burgeoning outside interest in Bhutan – the appeal to Westerners of its Shangri-La tag, its Tibetan-style culture and religion and its utopian ideals such as its GNH (Gross National Happiness) programme (see Clayton 2007). Thus the project from the beginning involved self-reflexive analysis on both sides of the cultural divide: what did each party fear and desire from the other; what did we have to learn from each other; and in what storytelling tradition could this interface be explored cinematically?

Initially scripting work involved Clayton and her Bhutanese partners plotting out stories of both Bhutanese and Western characters, and the screenplay was to develop further a number of these: a European woman in Bhutan who is attracted to Buddhism through her friendship with a *gomchen* or trainee monk; the *gomchen* himself who is tempted to leave Bhutan but is committed to his religious life at home; an old Bhutanese woman who prepares for her death but is fearless because she expects to be reincarnated; a Bhutanese actress who is tired of the Bollywood-style singing and dancing routines she must regularly perform; and an American expat who, having finished consulting on a satellite station in the remote West of Bhutan, plans to climb one of Bhutan's most famous peaks, Jumolhari – which is off limits to foreigners. The interconnectedness of the stories would, it was hoped, help build a broad thematic mosaic of issues around belief, tradition, modernity and identity, sparking off collisions of meaning and address, in the same register as films such as *Traffic* (Steven Soderbergh, 2000), *Crash* (Paul Haggis, 2004) and *Babel* (Alejandro González Iñárritu, 2006). The address was thus to be thematic, and with themes not dissimilar to *Travellers and Magicians*, but intended to be told in a realist style. However, despite these intentions, and the fact that Bhutan does indeed produce some modern realist dramas (such as *Muti Thrishing* [Pelden Dorji and Tshering Gyeltshen, 2005]), each story began in the telling to acquire unique narrative features to do with the Bhutanese worldview and the influence of its oral history and mythology. For instance, in the story of Ellis the American IT consultant, the mountain Jumolhari, which he seeks to climb, had for the Bhutanese co-writers a range of symbolic functions which began to inflect the narrative content and form. Jumolhari, a peak of over 7,300 metres, forms part of Bhutan's border with China and, since China's invasion of Tibet (1950), Bhutan has deeply feared a similar fate – a fear exacerbated by the recent surge of Chinese military activity and rail- and road-building close to the border. In this way, Jumolhari represents aspects of the country's political identity and its precarious safety – its dangerous altitude its only defence. Also, mountain-climbing by foreigners is forbidden by the Bhutanese government on environmental grounds; a ruling underpinned by a belief, particularly among tribal groups such as the Layas, that mountains are home to deities and that bad luck will occur if the deities are provoked. Thus, Jumolhari figures as a complex symbol of Bhutan itself as it attempts to maintain its independence and protect its myths and mysteries.

American expat Ellis's job at the satellite station prefigures his agency as one who will disrupt the natural equilibrium. Powerful by virtue of his nationality and his professional status, he hires a bright but rather awed young trekking guide to take him on a permitted trek near Jumolhari's base. Ellis smuggles climbing gear with him then, when at the base of Jumolhari, announces that he intends to make the climb and faces down the guide. He then goes on to climb the mountain, but becomes disorientated and lost, and a blizzard descends. The story thus far follows a classical Western three-act structure: the first act explores Ellis's conflicted character and why he is driven to make the climb; the so-called 'inciting incident' is his decision to trick the guide and thus commit to an irreversible course of action; and the second act is the trek itself, with its narrative reverses or 'rising and falling action' (warnings from the local Layas that the mountain and the weather is in an angry state, then glimpses of the tempting mountain peak which spur him on with his secret plan). In classical terms this would be expected to lead to a late Act Two crisis on the mountain, a cataclysmic event which would force the hero to choose one path or another, both fraught with tragic implications – the so-called 'dreadful alternative' which, according to the *diktats* of screenwriting, would result either in a tragic, cathartic ending or a Hollywood-style 'lifeline' to lift the hero out of his dilemma and its physical and moral consequences. This typical trajectory preserves the notion of the hero-subject as being in control of his actions and in control of the point of view of the camera and, therefore, our identification as audience in the narrative structure.

What was interesting to Clayton was that the Bhutanese writers did not see Ellis's mountain journey in that way. As this chapter has suggested earlier, in the Bhutanese Buddhist cosmology, human subjects and the world they inhabit are considered simply as a dream projection: *samsara*. The greater reality is elsewhere, which contradicts the notion of the self-willing, self-knowing hero-subject driving the story. This went alongside the Bhutanese writers' view that other perspectives could infringe on Ellis's story, possibly in a way that fractures its unities of time and space. In Western cinema we are familiar with the idea of cutting between points of view, but the fundamental grammar remains a kind of see-saw between establishing shots and the protagonist's point-of-view: this simple grammar functions to guarantee the credibility of the film's diegetic space rather than disrupt it, the wide shots confirming the unities of time and place in which the hero acts, and the point-of-view shots locking us into the protagonist's perspective – we see the world, we see the hero seeing that same world, the characters in that world return the hero's look and thus corroborate his place in it. But what if they do not see the hero? Or do not return his look? Or if he cannot see them? And more crucially, in this context, who would these other entities be, how would they arrive or appear in the story? The Bhutanese co-writers were very clear that the mountain itself would be populated by characters who may or may not be visible to Ellis.

As we have discussed in relation to *Six Boys*, Bhutan's animist belief-system dictates that certainly the mountain itself, like the lake in that film, would be a crucial entity, and one in this case with a clear causal motive to enter the story: the mountain deity Jumo is angered by Ellis having disturbed the mountain by coming there deceitfully. In addition, Clayton was astonished by the extraordinary number of further possibilities assumed by the Bhutanese writers as to who or what would necessarily confront Ellis – as ghosts, karmic messengers or fellow protagonists on the mountain top. The list ran as follows: Jumo the goddess; Jumo in human form, so Ellis may see her; Tashi, his guide, who comes to rescue him; the ghost of Tashi who dies rescuing him; the Italians who last climbed Jumolhari (these were the last mountaineers to make an ascent in the 1960s and several of them died, so prompting the climbing ban); the climbers' ghosts; Chinese soldiers drinking tea (there are mountain tea houses on the Chinese border from where the Bhutanese believe they can see clearly into Bhutanese territory); and finally, perhaps most extraordinarily, Ellis's own ghost (having died on the mountain, he confronts himself). Within this range of potential narratives, there was little attention to chronology and little distinction between the living and the dead: the mountain top seemed instead to represent a portal through which characters and story material could freely and atemporally flow, evoking both the cyclicality of Buddhist time and the hybrid spaces of magic realism.

The question of whether or not Ellis would be aware of such activity, or it of him, raised further interesting issues around Mahayana Buddhist beliefs, wherein all human beings are seen as being on a longer, more complex journey than that of the simple action hero and, as well as living by the Four Noble Truths, must be alert to wisdom and teachings that they may receive from monks and *lamas*, and from guardian spirits and deities who will communicate to them in dream form. By Western standards, Ellis is a charismatic adventurer who, like all action-heroes, breaks rules to achieve his personal goal. However, to the Bhutanese, far from being a princely Aristotelian hero, he is particularly unevolved in the cycle of rebirths towards wisdom. He fails to heed the ban on climbing and successive warnings from the guide and Laya tribesmen. He jeopardises the life of his guide, whom he does not realise will feel obliged to follow him onto the stormy mountain. Crucially, he does not believe in guardian spirits or mountain deities, therefore he cannot see them – or at least cannot see them for what they are.

This was the point at which the story became formally complex in a way which both parties of writers on the project found fascinating and challenging. The straightforward classical linear story arc was retained (as something that would help promote the film's international saleability) but enveloped by a structure which encapsulated the dialogue between East and West about two different notions of dreaming. Another portal was thus created – this time a simple Bhutanese hospital ward, from which Ellis remembers his adventure and rescue through a foggy haze of drugs. The hospital ward, like the mountain, is peopled with characters who all have their own stories, many of them from the original first-draft narratives. An illness, named Qi (not a physical ailment but spiritual failure), from which Ellis is said to suffer was playfully invented. Ellis was also given a partial deafness, to emphasise that he may have survived his mountain catastrophe but has failed to learn its lesson – for our thematic purposes far more important. In this dream state, in recalling his mountain adventure, Ellis does indeed remember seeing the strange characters: the ghost of his guide and the Italian climbers. He does not read these dreams as significant, but puts them down to altitude sickness and exhaustion. This is credible to the Western audience, for whom dreams are simply a product of the individual's psyche. However, in Buddhist tradition, dreams are regarded as important communications from alternative realities: moreover, 'people say they have seen a dream, not they have *had* a dream' (Young 1999: 13), implying that it is the dreamer who is interpolated by the dream and not vice versa. Thus, at one level, Ellis, the typical Western hero, proceeds through his adventure story; at another, he is observed and judged by entities who are wiser than him and may see him differently.

But as Ellis's 'spiritual illness' progresses, those dreams revisit him and gradually their significance becomes clear. Crucially, he unravels the mystery of Jumo, the goddess of Jumolhari, and her message to him. While, as discussed earlier, Bhutanese and other Asian cinemas often represent deities onscreen, the writers – mindful of their international audience – drew instead on one of the earlier stories, that of Lhawang, the actress who plays Bollywood-style roles. Earlier in the story before he goes on his trek, Ellis sees a poster for a Bhutanese Bollywood-style film, showing Lhawang in exotic dress, performing the role of a deity. Later, in the hospital ward, he dreams/remembers that after being trapped in the blizzard on the mountain for many days, he stumbles down another route and sees in the distance a dancing swirling figure dressed in goddess-like costume. As Ellis approaches, he sees that it is Lhawang performing on a remote location shoot. While he rests at the 'Bollywood camp' awaiting the rescue helicopter, there are further clues (which the audience may see but to which Ellis is still oblivious) that the role Lhawang is playing is that of Jumo, the mountain goddess. As Ellis progresses in his delirium in the hospital ward, we, like Ellis, begin to question whether this episode could have been 'real' or not (especially as there is a temporal clue to its unreality – he could not have seen the poster of the finished film first and the film shoot later). The true climax of the film is not Ellis's rescue from the mountain, but his bravery, in the face of increasingly troubled hallucinations, to face surgery in the decrepit local Bhutanese hospital, during which he does in a blinding revelation actually 'see' and believe in

Jumo, acknowledge the wisdom she offers him and gain a degree of absolution. This exchange is made more palatable to the international audience by the fact that Jumo is played by the Lhawang actress – and is interesting to the actress/writer concerned, because it satisfies an ambition to do more than 'dance around trees', as she has ironically described the Bollywood style of film she seeks to transcend. To Clayton, the appeal of this narrative resolution lies in its ability to address both Bhutanese and international audiences, playing against each other not only the traditions of the conflicted Western hero and the dancing heroine, but also Western and Bhutanese notions of dreaming. For Ellis, the dreams and visions begin as disruptions in his psyche: a conventional Freudian understanding of dreams. Indeed, it is possible to read the whole film as 'only a dream' in a way which is perfectly within the canons of Western cinema. But the clues are also there, through expositional dialogue, symbolic locations and visual tropes (such as guardian animals which symbolically appear, often in unreal circumstances), to read the story at a number of more profound levels where it comments on cause and effect (karma), and on the value of wisdom and humility as greater virtues than physical bravery.

Conclusion

In this chapter, we have looked at how Buddhism and orality have been translated into film in Bhutan. We have argued that cinema operates as a secondary oral medium, through the various rituals of production, distribution and consumption and, most significantly, at the level of story construction. Although Bhutan has a remarkably strong oral legacy, cinema and electronic media have undeniably changed its traditional narrative culture, re-mediating it and, in the process, creating new storytelling forms. The encounter with Bhutan's orality and animist and Buddhist belief systems equally challenges and potentially transforms classically-established cinema conventions of story structure and point of view. These belief systems pose complex notions of agency and causality that disrupt ideas of coherent time and space (Aristotelian unities) and the self-knowing hero whose desires drive the narrative. With their reverse perspective on dream and reality, Bhutanese films subtly decentre individual human subjectivity as the controlling force of narrative cinema. They permit a differential model of interpretation, pointing to a complex reality glimpsed at many different levels – ritual, superstition, parable – and gleaned through the progressive wisdom of lifetimes: a totally different kind of hero's journey.

Acknowledgements

For their inspiring contributions, many thanks to *Jumolhari* co-writers Lhaki Dolma, Dorji Wangchuk and Pema Rinzin. Shohini Chaudhuri was fortunate to interview

Karma Gaylay (arts advisor to the fourth king), Lungten Gyatso (Head of Institute of Language and Cultural Studies, University of Bhutan), Wangchuk (producer, *Chorten Kora*), Rinzin Rinzin (writer, 'Talisman of Good Fortune') and Tshering Penjore (screenwriter, *Golden Cup*). We are also grateful to Kunzang Choden, Karma Tshering (director, *Six Boys*), and Tshering Gyeltshen. Finally, a special thanks to Thukten Yeshi for reading an early draft. Another version of this chapter has been published in *Journal of Screenwriting*, 3, 2 (2012), 197–214.

Notes

1   For further detail on Bhutan's culture and modernising processes of the last decade, see Clayton 2007.
2   Written Dzongkha was developed in 1971. Estimates of the number of spoken languages in Bhutan tend to range between 13 and 24.
3   *Chorten Kora*'s production cost 5.6 million ngultrum (approximately £65,700).

Bibliography

Clayton, S. (2007) 'Film-making in Bhutan: the View from Shangri-La', *New Cinemas*, 5, 1, 75–89.
Faure, B. (2004) *Double Exposure: Cutting Across Buddhist and Western Discourse*. Trans. J. Lloyd. Stanford: Stanford University Press.
Glotfelty, C. and H. Fromm (eds) (1996) *The Ecocriticism Reader: Landmarks in Literary Ecology*. Athens: University of Georgia Press.
Hutcheon, L. (2006) *A Theory of Adaptation*. New York: Routledge.
Kunzang Choden (2002) *Folktales of Bhutan*. Bangkok: White Lotus.
Marshall, L. (2003) '*Travellers and Magicians*', *Screen International*, 1426, 18.
Moore, A. C. (1977) *Iconography of Religions: An Introduction*. London: SCM Press.
Ong, W. (2006) *Orality and Literacy: The Technologizing of the Word*. Abingdon: Routledge.
Paniker, K. A. (2003) *Indian Narratology*. New Delhi: Indira Gandhi National Centre for the Arts.
Pommaret, F. (2001) 'Bhutan: A Kingdom of the Himalayas' in Department of Culture, India and the National Commission for Cultural Affairs, Bhutan, *The Living Religious and Cultural Traditions of Bhutan*. National Museum: Janpath, New Delhi, 1–17.
Rinzin R. (2002) *The Talisman of Good Fortune and other Stories from Rural Bhutan*. Thimphu: Helvetas.
Wilson, R. (1995) 'The Metamorphoses of Fictional Space: Magical Realism', in L. P. Zamora and W. B. Faris (eds) *Magical Realism: Theory, History, Community*. Durham: Duke University Press, 209–33.
Young, S. (1999) *Dreaming in the Lotus: Buddhist Dream Narrative, Imagery and Practice*. Boston: Wisdom Publications.
Zamora, L. P. and W. B. Faris (eds) (1995) *Magical Realism: Theory, History, Community*. Durham: Duke University Press.
Zeitgeist Films (2004) *Travellers and Magicians US Press-Kit*. Available: www.travellersandmagicians.com/TandM_PRESS_KIT_US.pdf (accessed on 7 May 2008).

Claiming Space, Time and History in
The Journals of Knud Rasmussen

Darrell Varga

The twin forces structuring the visual representation of Northern peoples have been the romantic and the administrative. The romantic impulse begins with *Nanook of the North* (Robert Flaherty, 1922) which Flaherty presented, famously, as entertainment rather than exposition. As a consequence, the film corresponds with the then-emergent narrative and genre conventions for dramatic stories, and also gave rise to a plethora of marketing products which contribute to the image of the North in popular consciousness, from clothing to ice cream. At the same time, the film claims an indexical value and remains highly influential in documentary practice in spite of the fall from fashion of its humanist impulse. In this way, *Nanook of the North* encompasses the second administrative structuring force arriving with the extensive use of photography and film on the part of the state apparatus in the exercise of sovereignty in the Canadian Arctic. In his history of film and photography in the Canadian North, Peter Geller provides this comment from an Inuit political activist: 'The Inuit are probably the most photographed race of people on earth. The first time I saw a white man, he had a camera and it seems that whenever government officials or tourists came North, they always had cameras and they projected what we considered to be the wrong images of the Inuit – the Hollywood image or the stereotype image.'[1] The presence of a camera is no guarantee of truth and, indeed, can provide more insight to those who are behind the lens than in front. The film I will discuss in this chapter is as much about forces that are hidden as it is about the surface of this world. Both the romantic and the administrative forms of representation are interesting for what they do not show, and both are informed by a common sense assumption that the subject of the gaze is somehow detached from the forces of modernity. However, the very presence of image-making in the North is a decisive measure of the thrust of modernity in the everyday life of the Inuit. The moving image provides visual evidence of culture and the everyday as well as an implicit theory of its own presence and structure.

It is this context which gives shape and meaning to Inuit filmmaking activity in the North. When *Atanarjuat: The Fast Runner* (Zacharias Kunuk, 2001) became a celebrated international hit, winning the Camera d'Or at the Cannes Film Festival in 2001, the popular perception was that this film came out of nowhere since this long history of administrative and romantic representation is largely provided through an external point of view. It is the first Inuktitut-language Inuit-produced feature film, but it is made by producers with an extensive history of grassroots production and in the context of the immense tradition of storytelling in Inuit culture. *Atanarjuat* conveys a vital traditional story through a mastery of cinema – it is a beautiful and highly-compelling action-adventure love story.[2] The energy and style of the film contradicts the narrow-minded assumption that Aboriginal media, as offshoot of anthropology, is simply a utilitarian recording.[3] If their first feature film demonstrates a mastery of narrative cinema deployed to tell a traditional story, the next film by these artists turns away from mainstream conventions, bringing cinema into the realm of traditional oral culture, rather than the other way around. *The Journals of Knud Rasmussen* (Zacharias Kunuk and Norman Cohn, 2006) is about the loss of traditional Inuit culture upon contact with Christian missionaries. While the story of *Atanarjuat* was evoked through dynamic movement, *The Journals...* requires stillness and quiet observation in order to really see culture and difference rather than filter this world through stereotyped conventions of representation and ways of seeing produced through a European perspective.

The film begins with a visit to the remote camp of Avva, the last great Igloolik shaman, by Danish explorer Knud Rasmussen during his fifth Thule expedition (1921–24) accompanied by two other outsiders, the traders Peter Freuchen (played by leading Danish actor Kim Bodnia) and Therkel Mathiassen (played by Danish stage and TV actor Jakob Cedergren). Rasmussen records the story of life and culture as told by Avva and his wife Orulu, a story of the interconnection of everyday life with the rhythms of the landscape, of the lived relation between material reality, spirit life, animals and the complex practices and taboos governing these relationships. While *Atanarjuat* is set in the distant past, though retold in a manner that makes the lesson vital for a contemporary audience, *The Journals...* is set in 1922, the year of the release of *Nanook of the North*, but told in a manner that demands we accommodate the pace and tone of traditional storytelling. Traditional life is not the territory of ancient legend; rather it is within the lived memory of a few of the community's elders and it is told in the wake of the massive cultural displacement brought on by Christianity and the accompanying loss and struggle faced by present-day Inuit. In other words, *The Journals...* is a story of the present, but told in a manner that requires attention to the rhythm and perspective of the past, and thus attention to a way of seeing that is particular to time and place – forcing our attention to the moment of discord and displacement. If the thrust of this story is at odds with expectations formed through the conditioning of mainstream cinema, we are also left unprepared by the experience of having seen the more conventionally structured *Atanarjuat*. In the case of both films, we are thrust into a world we do not understand and have to generate understanding through the experience of seeing rather than through didactic explanation or the attachment of preconceived expectations formed through the experience of mainstream Western cinema.

That which we see is not simply explained within the conventions of narrative; instead, we have to make up our own mind through a process of seeing and learning how to see. Likewise, lengthy sections of the film remain untranslated, we are not to be given a straightforward relationship between language and action since so much action is rooted in untranslatable cultural practices. The point of this experience is not simply to celebrate cultural pluralism as another marketable commodity within the capitalist cultural sphere. Instead, we can turn to this vital Inuit cinema asking how we have come to understand Third Cinema, not as simple nationalist expression but as a model for critical engagement with the terms of social organisation under capitalism. We are invited, following Fredric Jameson, to see in terms other than exchange value, where 'the production of aesthetic or narrative form is to be seen as an ideological act in its own right, with the function of inventing imaginary or formal "solutions" to unresolvable social contradictions' (2002: 79). The film is made first of all for an Inuit audience and whatever progressive consciousness encouraged by the film shall emerge first of all within that audience.

The film begins with Avva's family posing for a picture in a brief scene ten years earlier than the period of the story and narrated by the voice of Avva's daughter Usarak, known as Apak at the time, whom we see as a young girl (not yet adorned with facial tattoos) and whom we now hear as an old woman recalling her long-ago first encounter with white men. This is the story of survivors working to reconstitute a culture that has been shattered. While the location is not explained, we see that it is a wooden building with some sparse furnishing and is likely a building associated with trade. In an extended static shot, Nuqallaq (played by Natar Ungalaq, who played the title role in *Atanarjuat*) is seen arranging the group for the photograph. We do not see the photographer. The static form of *The Journals...* is mirrored in the act of photography – time is frozen, but in the events that follow, the time-bound world is usurped by the spatial dimensions of empire. Later, we see Apak happily playing an accordion (an instrument introduced into the Arctic by nineteenth century whalers) and an image of syllabic Inuktitut writing (introduced to the Inuit by a Wesleyan missionary in the mid-nineteenth century). The image of writing is shown in the scene as a playful amusement but within the thematic thrust of the film as a whole, it is the Trojan Horse of colonialism; as ethnographer Bernard Saladin d'Anglure describes: 'Syllabic writing acted as a Trojan horse. Surreptitiously, it let in an invisible cohort of Christian values and concepts, hidden amid the little esoteric characters. [...] As Inuit began to read the Bible in their own tongue, they were struck by its unyielding constancy and authority – in stark contrast to the variable, adaptable forms of the shaman's teachings and messages' (2002: 225). As counterpoint to the appearance of text, we see the elder Evaluarjuk, Avva's brother, draw for Rasmussen a map detailing the coastline and their present location in relation to Igloolik. This brief image conveys the remarkable knowledge of the environment and spatial awareness existing within Inuit culture at a time before the use of printed maps and drawings. Throughout, the film navigates between tradition and the new, between suggestions of cultural devastation as well as adaptation and continuity. At the end of this brief scene, we see two men making a wax recording of a traditional song – the fluid experience of voice being engraved in the hard material of mechanical reproduction. Apak tells us that at the time she was travelling with her lover Nuqallaq who was, even then, working for the whites.

While it is tempting to gloss over this opaque sequence and begin discussing the film's main narrative of the encroachment of Christianity, this introduction provides important tools for understanding what is to follow. The first is the recognition that we will have to work to understand the various relationships – between characters, but also with respect to cause and effect. We also learn something of the history of contact rather than assume that it begins as *tabula rasa* with Rasmussen. As the scene is dominated by the photographic moment it can be understood as referential to the process of making *The Journals...* as well as reflection on the impossibility of claiming to represent in absolute terms a pre-contact era from the contemporary context. In this way, it provides a theory of its own coming-into-being. If this suggests a limit to realism, it also signals the dialectical relation between past and present through which the conventions of realist representation are deconstructed. We are provided with a collective portrait – the photograph – rather than an individual narrative trajectory, and the taking of the photograph is a frozen moment in time, serving as an artefact for future understanding (for which there are always more questions than answers) and suggesting that the pre-Christian era is free from linear time. Co-director Norman Cohn describes the concept of time in the film as a turn away from paradise:

> We made a film about the Inuit who lived in a timeless universe. They were totally independent, totally self-reliant and mostly joyful. But when you meet time, time takes you with it. [...] It's about a walk out of Paradise – Paradise was when there was no time and you celebrated life in balance with your world. [...] When you walk out of Paradise, you're into time, modernity. (Quoted in Anderson 2006)

Finally, we are invited to pay attention to the intertextual references between *Atanarjuat* and the present film.

Our experience of *Atanarjuat* may provide some comfort through familiarity with this world, but that is a false hope. Both films open by thrusting the viewer into an unfamiliar environment, but the previous film's reliance on narrative conventions provides a degree of accessibility that is absent in the *The Journals....* However, there exists an important relation between the two films through a continuity of subject matter and the ensemble collective of performers. For the filmmakers, the process of production as cultural and economic endeavour within their home community of Igloolik is as important as the finished film itself.[4] The concept of national cinema has been problematised in contemporary film studies for its tendency to elide difference for the sake of a homogenous national narrative, a problem especially endemic to film studies in Canada.[5] However, if this mode of enquiry has continuing value, it is in the context of Aboriginal practices understood as the expression of community through which the demand to rethink the concept of nationhood is articulated. This articulation of a communal experience and identity is present in the community of performers at work in these films.

The place of nationhood in cinema has become an increasingly difficult question as media flow more freely across borders and where financial support for independent cinema is increasingly linked with global media marketability. In fact, part of the important contribution of these filmmakers to Canadian cinema is the challenge they have made to the financing orthodoxy which has, until the changes brought in to accommodate *Atanarjuat*, ghettoised Aboriginal filmmakers in a separate and limited funding envelope from the nation's primary film investor, Telefilm Canada, and ineligible to compete for funds from the more generous Feature Film Fund. At the time of writing, the filmmakers are conducting a similar campaign to seek increased support for the marketing of *The Journals....* The filmmaker's community of Igloolik was the last Arctic settlement to accept broadcast television (in 1983) out of long-standing concern over the influence of mainstream media, but the present use of film and video in the community is dedicated to using media as a means of redrawing the link between tradition and the present, a link severed with the introduction of Christianity and modernisation. Many of the performers in both films are drawn from the community and their appearance across various productions emphasises the communal process of production and shared collective identity. This process also reflects the traditional belief in the continuity between past and present, preserved through the practice of naming children after deceased family members, thus enacting a literal continuity of the dead in the body of the living through the performative act. An actor playing a role in these films is both representing a character as well as presenting him or her self, if not the literal self of the present then the self across time. With this in mind, the film process, if not the final product, is a means of maintaining traditional life, a tradition always adept at adopting new tools.

However, the tradition is transformed in the context of Christianity so that the actor Natar Ungalaq (Nuqallaq), highly recognisable from the title role in *Atanarjuat*, a figure embodying the strength and resilience of tradition here is working for the whites – though he is by no means seen as defeated; rather, he is a figure of transition, motivated by material necessity rather than belief. There is also the suggestion that he is guilty of murdering a white man: the details of this incident are left unexplained but this fact hangs over the community as a portent of violence in encounters with whites still to come – namely the violence of assimilation. Nuqallaq may also be a convert to Christianity as a means of affording some cover from the revenge to be sought for his crime. This incident is mirrored by the story of another murder within the Inuit community. Again, the cultural differences are not explained in didactic narrative; rather, as viewers we have to give ourselves over to the spatial and temporal relations made evident within traditional culture and come to our own conclusions about action and morality, and how traditional practices situated in the world of time are at odds with, and cannot be explained by, the spatial practices of white colonisation. While I have earlier referred to the Inuit encounter with white society as a *coming into time* because time in Western thought is associated with history; here, I am making use of Harold Innis's (1995) essential distinction between time-bound and space-bound societies. To be time-bound refers to living within traditional practices and beliefs extending through time via storytelling. Space-bound societies are, according to Innis, print-based, and this means of knowledge communication significantly transforms the way that knowledge is understood and used in relation to everyday life. To be space-bound is also a colonial practice of conquering territory.

Apak's first husband was murdered and the crime was settled by taking another husband into the community. This is how Apak came to be unhappily married to Taparte, a Netsilik Inuit for whom she has no affection (she continues to have sex with her dead husband by using her shamanic powers). We observe Apak and Nuqallaq gazing at each other, suggesting desire between the two that is deflected by the needs of the community. This expression of desire is not delivered explicitly in narrative but is something implied as we begin to learn about the world of the film through observation. It is the conflict between communal needs and individual desires that is precisely the theme of *Atanarjuat*. In that movie, Atanarjuat's brother Aamarjuaq is brutally murdered but in the present film the same actor, Pakak Innukshuk, embodies a living continuity with the past through the role of Avva, the last great shaman. Naqallaq was to be his son-in-law until he went to work for the whites. His wife, Orulu, is played by Neeve Irngaut Uttak, who also plays the wife of Pakak Innukshuk's character in *Atanarjuat*. Atanarjuat's rival Uqi (played by Peter Henry Arnatsiaq) is named Natar in *The Journals...*, the real name of his fictional rival, and volunteers to lead the Danish explorers to Igloolik, thus leading Avva's family to the unrelenting influence of Christianity.

Following the intriguing pre-credit sequence, we see Avva's daughter Apak have sex with her dead husband. Within the subsequent narrative these recurring sex scenes are lamented by Avva as a waste of her power and distraction from the crisis facing his community. What they do, however, is demonstrate the lived reality of shamanism. The sex is real in these scenes, even as they are cast apart from the main narrative through oblique angles and soft focus black and white. The camera appears to be equipped with a macro lens, causing an extremely shallow depth-of-field with brief flashes of sharp focus as the body, recorded against an over-exposed white background, moves in close to the lens. She is both apart from and a part of physical reality – a distinction that does not apply within Inuit cosmology. Many of the shots in these sex scenes are of Apak's face moving in close toward the camera lens. In effect, we are provided with the point of view of the dead man but have to work to accommodate the perspective and conceptual tools with which the living and the dead can co-exist. The story as a whole likewise does not unfold in a strict linear trajectory since that which we hear, in for instance Avva's descriptions of Inuit beliefs, is often accompanied by images of the various characters interacting in the present. The images serve not to simply illustrate; instead, they provide a co-existence of temporal experiences. The sex scenes demonstrate the complex erotic charge of traditional belief against the tendency, framed by anthropology, to see Aboriginal culture strictly in instrumental terms. As Jerry White points out, this filmmaking functions against the standard problems of ethnography, being romanticisation and objectification: 'Kunuk's work, and especially his early work, is constituted as an attempt to make an ethnographic practice relevant for the community that it documents' (2007: 351).

An important role of the shaman is to mediate between the realms of the living and of the dead, as well as between the world of humans and of animals. In the body of the shaman, the entire community is structured through the fluidity of these domains. Avva's sex scenes are interrupted by the appearance of another shaman who questions why she is having sex with the dead, and this appearance disrupts pleasure but also casts doubt on the system of belief that makes these relationships possible. The interruption is also a warning of the trouble that is to come. The sound of this shaman's laugh, made after he interrupts Apak, recalls the voice of the shaman Tungajuaq (Abraham Ulayuruluk) in the opening scene of *Atanarjuat*, a laugh which punctuates his warning to be careful of what one wishes for. The warning follows his victory in battle with another shaman, and subsequent awarding of power to Uki's clan – marking the start of the conflict and rivalry which shall tear apart the community. The work of the shaman does not function in a fantasy spiritual place in the heavens but is, like the spirits, within the world even while they can transcend physical limits. In *The Journals...* Abraham Ulayuruluk is Evaluarjuk, a shaman and older brother of Avva. Here, they stand as final holdouts against the onslaught of Christianity. In the earlier film, Atanarjuat's father (Samuellie Ammaq) is passed over in the awarding of power and is subsequently mistreated (his family is not provided with adequate shares of the hunt). In *The Journals...* Ammaq is cast in the role of Umik, leading his clan with a strict adherence to Christian doctrine whereby shamanism is declared Satanic.

In a reverse echo of his character in *Atanarjuat*, Umik exercises strict control over the community meat supply. Hunters are obliged to deliver meat to Umik, and he then distributes it, but only following prayer sessions. In this way, the particular cruelty of Christianity is entrenched as a new apparatus of power through control over both discourse and body. While the turn away from tradition frees the community from the many taboos and restrictions structuring everyday life, the past is given up for a whole host of new restrictions with the control over meat being the literal control over life and death. It is to this bitter end that Avva's clan is travelling as they journey to Igloolik. That journey visually punctuates Avva's story of his coming-into-being as shaman. While Christianity is associated with death, Avva describes being born dead, due to a shaman's curse upon his mother, but then comes into life in order to fulfill the role of mediator between living and dead. As he explains to Rasmussen, 'We don't fear death, but we fear suffering. [...] All our customs come from life and turn toward life.' Likewise, as viewers we are not given expository introductions to the characters and incidents but are instead immersed in relationships which are in turn integral to the environment rather than an outcome of Cartesian duality.

The fear of suffering is given as reason for the complexity and specificity of the taboos structuring life. When misfortune is encountered, it is understood as a consequence of the breaking of taboos. In this way, the cohesion of the community is maintained through the integration of individuals with the whole. For instance, the eating of certain animal parts such as the heart and the lung is forbidden for shamans. It is this meat that Amik provides at the film's conclusion. We see Apak consume this, and the look of quiet resignation on her face echoes the devastation of the church on Inuit culture. She had just separated herself from her father's resistance to Christianity out of fear of suffering hunger and after having admitted breaking a taboo related to childbirth – she had improperly disposed of a stillborn child, another marker of death for the community. Yet what we learn of shamanistic practices cannot simply be associated with fear and death. When Avva relates his process of becoming a shaman, he describes being overcome with good feelings and spontaneously singing 'Joy Joy Joy'. As he speaks, we see one of his spirit helpers quietly listening in the background. It is not until the devastating end of the film, when Avva calls forth his spirit helpers in order to cast them away, that we learn the identity of this figure – a figure of life turned toward death. Life and spirituality is held dear by maintaining a separation from Christianity. When Avva is asked by Rasmussen why his camp is so far removed from Igloolik, the women laughingly perform a mock hymn, singing 'Jesus, Jesus'. The scenes of drumming, games and singing are embodied expressions of communal joy, punctuated by Orulu's narration of her own life as having been marked by great happiness as well as hardship. These moments of pleasure are in stark contrast with the scene of arrival in Igloolik and the droning refrain of Christian song performed by Umik's clan – expressions of duty, obligation and resignation – the performance of culture stripped free of joy. At the same time, we come to understand that people have turned to Christianity in response to physical suffering – following a period of famine – and so they must be understood not simply as having been easily manipulated but as having had to make complex choices in the face of extremely difficult material conditions. Even with the overwhelming sadness of the final scene, the spirit helpers, while wailing in grief, turn away as they know that the people have made their choices and an external view cannot simply be imposed.

This is a film about seeing the spirits, and about the loss of sight that accompanies cultural and spiritual change, but it is also providing us with a lesson in how to see. The concept of story as a vehicle of history and tradition collides with prevailing notions of cinematic pleasure. These conventions presume a universal humanism of narrative, but it is erroneous to assume that these terms can be overlaid onto Inuit culture. While *Atanarjuat*, by and large, functions within mainstream narrative by drawing us into the story through identification with characters and a cause-and-effect story structure of mounting action toward climax and resolution, *The Journals...* demands work on the part of the viewer; we are provided with viewing positions both inside and outside the conceptual frame. Avva is, however, a great storyteller and his narrative invites audience involvement and the long takes help produce a great sense of intimacy mirrored by extended wide shots of people moving through the landscape. The landscape shots themselves often make indistinct the separation of the ground and the sky, with figures seemingly floating in between. But at the same time, we have to work to understand the relation between various characters and the important interrelation between both *The Journals...* and *Atanarjuat*, and the concepts of space and time underpinning all these relationships (a difference that negates the presumption of universal humanism) together push us outside the flow of narrative. While we learn important details about shamanism and Inuit culture, the brutal success of Christianity in the North limits the extent of knowledge and the films are themselves part of a continuing process of recovery. Cinematic conventions invite us to watch these films informed – if we are not watching as Northerners – by the baggage of how the North has been imagined from outside: as mythic empty space rather than as lived place. Inuit viewers watch history, but without the distinction between story and information and without having to assume that what we are given is a complete picture; the film is an invocation to watch, listen and learn. Peter Geller points out that our understanding is limited by the points of reference: 'The North became an ordered environment, often defined in reference to a marker of southern "civilization"': the RCMP [police] detachment, the mission station, the HBC [Hudson Bay Company] post' (2004: 165). These physical spaces are just becoming entrenched at the time of the film and, other than a brief glimpse of the interior of a trading post at the film's opening, we do not see them, yet their presence overwhelms existing culture and comes to shape conceptual understanding. The film functions at the ground level of material change and social upheaval rather than providing an all-encompassing view from above.

This ground of culture is in the process of transformation and the narrative emerges through many layers of translation. In the first instance, it is composed of story fragments revealed to Knud Rasmussen. Rasmussen himself is an interesting figure of transition and translation, as he was the son of a Danish missionary and

Inuit mother raised among the Greenland Inuit and fluent in Inuktitut. It is his story that has become well known and it is in part through his journals and archival materials that the filmmakers have come to know the Inuit experience of encounter. All of this is further translated by the idiom of cinema with its convention of a forward-moving narrative applied to a story that gestures back and forth through time. It is a story that is intensely personal for Inuit reflecting on the place of culture in the face of the brutal thrust of modernisation, and it is a story produced through the complex machinations of international co-production (Canadian/Danish) marketed both within the North but also across the world. It emerges in a space of negotiation between auteur-driven assumptions of Canadian cinema and the commercial thrust of contemporary film financing. Finally, the film has iconic value as an artefact of Canadian culture, evoking notions of multicultural tolerance and diversity, while standing at odds with the prevailing concept of national culture and providing sharp criticism of that culture. Indeed, as Zoë Druick (2007) has pointed out, the use of film in Canada has historically been directed at the mobilisation of consensus around a government-sanctioned image of the nation, that is to say, for the purposes of citizenship training. The task of these filmmakers is to displace training with education, to transcend the broad ideological function of the nation through the rupturing of a narrative trajectory bound to Western philosophical notions of space and time. This narrative is a process integrated with the rhythms of place and with a concept of time encompassing past and present as a unified entity rather than discrete moments in time or lines on a map.

Notes

1   The comment is from John Amogoalik, former president of the Inuit Tapirisat of Canada, a national political advocacy organisation, as presented in the 1981 documentary film *Magic in the Sky*; cited in Geller 2004: 14.

2   For a close analysis of *Atanarjuat: The Fast Runner*, see my article in J. White (ed.) (2006).

3   Jerry White makes this point regarding earlier Inuit filmmaking in his article 'Asivaqtiin: The Hunters' in *The Cinema of Canada* (2006: 106).

4   For an overview of the production company Igloolik Isuma Productions, visit www.isuma.ca

5   For an excellent overview of the limits of national cinema studies, see Higson 1989.

Bibliography

Anderson, J. (2006) 'Ideal of North' (film review), *Eye Weekly*, 15, 52. Available: http://www.eyeweekly.com/eye/issue/issue_09.28.06/film/lead.php (accessed on 28 September 2006).

d'Anglure, B. S. (2002) 'An Ethnographic Commentary: The Legend of Atanarjuat, Inuit and Shamanism', in P. A. Angilirq, et. al., *Atanarjuat: The Fast Runner* (screenplay). Toronto: Coach House Books.

Druick, Z. (2007) *Projecting Canada: Government Policy and Documentary Film at the National Film Board*. Montreal: McGill-Queen's University Press.

Geller, P. (2004) *Northern Exposures: Photographing and Filming the Canadian North, 1920–45*. Vancouver: University of British Columbia Press.

Higson, A. (1989) 'The Concept of National Cinema', *Screen*, 30, 4, 36-46.

Innis, H. A. (1995) *Bias of Communication*. Toronto: University of Toronto Press.

Jameson, F. (2002) *The Political Unconscious: Narrative as a Socially Symbolic Act*. Ithaca, NY: Cornell University Press.

Varga, D. (2006) '*Atanarjuat: The Fast Runner*', in White, J. (ed.) *The Cinema of Canada*. London: Wallflower Press, 224-233.

White, J. (2006) 'Asivaqtiin: The Hunters', in White, J. (ed.) *The Cinema of Canada*, London: Wallflower Press, 101-10.

____ (2007) 'Zach Kunuk and Inuit Filmmaking', in G. Melnyk (ed.) *Great Canadian Film Directors*. Edmonton: University of Alberta Press, 347–62.

Qissa and Popular Hindi Cinema

Anjali Gera Roy

South Asian film scholars' examination of the Indian epic, narrative, visual and the-
atrical traditions underpinning the cinematic text has elevated Hindi cinema from a
'bad copy' of Euro-American cinema to an alternative cinematic genre with a distinctive visual and narrative grammar derived from a diversity of ancient and modern
sources.[1] In addition to locating its narrative origins in Indian epics and myths, those
scholars have also formulated an indigenous aesthetic for Indian cinema predicated
on Hindu religious practices.[2] As a consequence, Hindu religious imagery employed
to describe the subject, effects, gaze and spectatorship of the Hindi film has become
naturalised in the analyses of Hindi cinema over the years. While these studies
engage in great depth with the ancient legacies of the epics, the *Mahabharata* and
Ramayana, and with more recent ones like Parsi theatre and calendar art, which
reveal a strong intermediality, their privileging of the Hindi film's Hindu Sanskritic
sources produces a homogenous discourse of indigeneity.[3] Their emphasis on
Sanskrit narrative and aesthetic traditions in the theorisation of Indian cinema is
increasingly being interrogated for its globalising sweep.[4] While acknowledging the
contribution of the dominant Hindu Sanskritic narrative tradition to the shaping of
popular Hindi cinema, this chapter aims to explore the alternative narrative streams
that have governed storytelling in Hindi films, particularly the Perso-Arabic legacy
of the *qissa* and *dastan* that has been erased or marginalised in the construction of
national cinema.[5] Through tracing the disruption of the dominant Hindu epic narratives by the Perso-Arabic *qissa* or *dastan*, it will show that it is the imbrication of
the Perso-Arabic heritage with the Hindu Sanskritic that constructs the syncretic

cinematic universe of the Hindi film. In place of the principle of *dharma* (law) that underpins the aesthetics of the Hindi film formulated by South Asian film scholars, the best known *daftar* or chapter of the 46-volume *Dastan-e-Amir Hamza* called the *Tilism-e-Hoshruba* or 'enchantment that steals away the senses' can provide an answer to the magic that Hindi cinema produces in its audience.[6]

In their book *Islamicate Cultures of Bombay Cinema* (2009), Ira Bhaskar and Richard Allen trace the Islamic connection 'to beginnings of cinema'. In an interview with Neelam Verjee, they pointed out that 'in early cinema, historicals (Sultanate and Mughal) were very popular, so too were oriental films or Arabian Nights fantasies' (Verjee 2009). Bhaskar and Allen relate the transformation of the range of expressive idioms to the coming of sound, which they believe led to the emergence of the Muslim social in the 1940s and its transformation into the dominant genre in the 1960s. Rachel Dwyer and Divia Patel (2002) speculate that the change in the Hindi film in the 1930s might have been due in part to the shift in cinema from being just a visual (silent) medium to an audio-visual medium with the addition of sound, in particular the creation of a musical cinema where songs and melodramatic dialogue soon established themselves as a major 'attraction'. But Dwyer is of the view that these changes were taken from the Parsi theatre, which 'drew on a rich repertoire of fantasy and historical romances from the Persian Shahnameh and Indo-Islamic romances as well as Shakespeare and Hindu mythologies' (2006: 102). Tracing a link between the decline of the Parsi theatre and the emergence of what she calls the 'Islamicate film' (2006: 7), she ascribes the Muslim invasion of the film industry to the migration of talent from the Parsi theatre to the Hindi film. In a similar vein, Iqbal Masud argues that

> the Muslim ethos in Indian cinema was not represented by 'Muslim' artists alone. A host of non-Muslims like Sohrab Modi, Guru Dutt or Shyam Benegal can well claim to be part of the 'Muslim' ethos of north India. There was, and is, certainly a 'Muslim' ethos of Bengal and South India which is equally important. (2005)

While the mythological framework of the silent film demanded a Hindu iconography, sound returned it to the speech community of Urdu and the repressed *qissa/ dastan* tradition.[7] The naturalisation of Urdu as the register of romance in Hindi cinema has been attributed to the cross-border migration of Urdu poets to Bombay after the partition of 1947 and their co-optation in the film industry as scriptwriters, lyricists and directors. But Dwyer locates the Urdu invasion of the Hindi film at the end of the regime of the silent film and the birth of the talkies, arguing that the coming of sound to Indian cinema meant that Hindi cinema needed stars with the right accents (2006: 101). As the first talkie *Alam Ara* (Ardhesher Irani, 1931) demonstrates, when the Hindi film began to speak, it spoke not in Hindi but in Urdu, which was not surprising in view of Urdu's dominance as the official language during the British Raj. However, it continued to speak in Urdu even after the propagation of a Sanskritised Hindi through the state-owned media such as the All India Radio (AIR) and Doordarshan and educational institutions. Due to the dominance of Urdu writers and poets in Bombay cinema, the Hindi film continues to serve as the syncretic space destroyed by the partitioning of the nation in which Hindi and Urdu, Hindu and Muslim are deeply implicated with one another. If one were to advance the history of Hindi cinema to Hiralal Sen's unreleased *Alibaba and Forty Thieves* or to begin with the history of sound films, the *qissa* and *dastan* tradition derived from the *1001 Nights*, the *Panchatantra* and the *Jataka* produces a syncretic history of a genre. Instead of looking at the Islamic influence on theme, genre or song and dance of Hindi films, it would be more appropriate to unpack an alternative aesthetic of the Hindi film that emerged from the other dominant Great Tradition on the Indian subcontinent, namely the Perso-Arabic.

Farina Mir (2006) has traced a fascinating genealogy of the *qissa* in Indian vernacular literatures to the Persian *qissa*. She points out that *qissa*, used in North Indian languages to mean story, is of Arabic origin and is derived from *qassa* or to tell a story, to narrate. Used in Islamic literature to refer to tales told by popular religious storytellers, its meaning expanded to allude to tales of no religious character by *qussas* and the term *qissa* came to mean story in general. Similarly, the Persian lineage of the term suggests biography, usually the biographies of religious figures or pseudo-biographies such as *Hamzanama*, which was disengaged from religion by the end of the second millennium to refer to stories in general and romance in particular.[8] Citing Amir Khusro's *Majnun Laila* composed in the masnavi form as evidence of the incorporation of *qissa* in the Persianate literary culture of the fourteenth century, she shows that these romances were incorporated over the centuries into Indian vernacular oral and textual traditions.[9] Frances Pritchett (1991) testifies to the presence of *qissa* in dakhani Urdu as early as the seventh century AD followed by those produced from 1780 at the Fort William College Kolkata. Unlike Mir, Pritchett confines herself to the genre of printed popular literature in Hindi and Urdu and is disheartened to discover that the flourishing *qissa* publishing business that she had documented in the 1970s was nearly extinct when she returned to India in the 1990s. Her definition of *qissa* as stories derived both from the *1001 Nights* and the *Kathasaritsagar* locates them in the syncretic cultural space revealed by Mir. Although Pritchett is right about the oral narrative art of North India dying due to the seductive power of the Hindi film, her view of printed *qissa* as displacing the oral narrative tradition is not altogether true because they have been successfully incorporated as the narrative or lyrical component of the cinematic romance.

Mahmood Farooqui, who has been trying to revive the traditional art of *dastangoi*,[10] confirmed that 'these stories have influenced the earliest writers of Hindi cinema. The masses are therefore familiar with the plots and characters of these *dastans*' (Farooqui 2006b). He reiterated this point in another interview when he said: 'Its modern day equivalent would be Tolkien's *Lord of the Rings*, or even Hindi cinema' (Farooqui 2006a).

Sudhir Kakar and John M. Ross in *Tales of Love, Sex and Danger* (1986) isolate two dominant elements in Hindi cinema as the Radha-Krishna, the divine lovers in human form in Hindu mythology, and Laila and Majnun, the passionate but doomed lovers in Arabic and Persian folklore and literature. According to Kakar and Ross, the Radha-Krishna tradition is an evocation and elaboration of here-and-now passion, an attempt to catch the exciting fleeting moment of the senses, not tragic but tender and ultimately cheerful. On the other hand, love is the 'essential desire of God; earthly love is but a preparation for the heavenly acme; the challenge to rights of older and powerful men to dispose of and control female sexuality; the utter devotion of the women lovers to the man unto death; loving in secrecy and concealment, yet without shame or guilt' in the Majnun Laila tradition (quoted in Masud 2005).

The *qissa* of Laila and Majnun forms a *leitmotif* in a large number of Hindi films either directly, through dialogue or through song and dance. Of the two filmed versions of the *qissa*, the 1976 version made by H. S. Rawail was a resounding success turning Ranjita Kaur Jhajjar who starred opposite the reigning romantic hero Rishi Kapoor into a celebrity overnight, a success that the teenage actress was not able to match in the films that followed. However, the *qissa* competes with or dominates Hindu romance tales in a large number of cinematic plots in addition to providing a template for heterosexual love in Hindi cinema.

The legend about the unfulfilled love of Majnun for his dark beloved that has inspired poets for centuries forms a dominant trope in the Hindi film not only in Muslim socials or historicals. If Sarat Chandra's classic novel has provided the template of the hero of the Hindi film since its translation into the Bengali *Devdas* (Pramathesh Chandra Barua, 1935), the *qissa* of Laila and Majnun has framed the romance tale articulated in Urdu, particularly in the song and dance sequences. If the Bengali popular writer provides one model of the hero, the Persian-Arabic *qissa* of *Majnun Laila* provides the other. In addition to two versions of the romance in 1953 and 1976, the underpinnings of the legend of Laila and Majnun are visible in song lyrics, visual imagery, characterisation and thematic conflict. In fact, Sarat Chandra's tragic novel of doomed love and the tragic hero that Ashis Nandy (2001) views as defining the Hindi film appears to have emerged from the Perso-Arabic tradition rather than from the *bhakti* lineage of *Gitagovinda*. From *Devdas* (1935) to *Veer Zaara* (Yash Chopra, 2004), the tale of tragic love in the Hindi film follows a Perso-Arabic trajectory.

The tales of unrequited love, echoing the yearnings of the poet lover Majnun, have provided the most memorable romances on the Hindi screen. Films based on a popular Bengali novel about a young aristocrat driven insane by his love for his childhood companion Paro mirrored Majnun's travails. Masud agrees that 'the first dominant note of the Muslim ethos was struck not in any specific Muslim film or by a Muslim director but in the film *Devdas* directed by P. C. Barua (Bengali 1935) based on a novel by Sarat Chandra Chatterji'; 'both elements are fused in Devdas. The Radha-Krishna element dominates the first half; the Laila-Majnun element the second' (2005). Like

Laila, Paro is married to another man when Devdas's *zamindar* (landowner) father rejects her as a suitable mate due to her low caste and Devdas, who had consented to his father's decision as a *dharmic* obligation to the family, leaves home but is plagued by Paro's memories, turns to alcohol and returns to die at her doorstep. Despite the reversal in the social status and the complication of the tale through the insertion of the dancing girl, Sarat Chandra's tale articulates the story of love driving lovers insane in a *dharmic* conflict between desire for the beloved and duty to the family. However, in the process of upholding Hindu social hierarchies, it glorifies relationships that challenge the existing social order by flouting all social laws.

Ashis Nandy's (2001) biographical reading of *Devdas* in relation to the life of its director Prathamesh Barua frames it against the impending demise of a feudal aristocratic Bengal shared by the character and the filmmaker. Nandy contrasts the magnanimous excess of the *zamindari* system with the gross instrumentality of capitalism that destroys the hero as well as the director. However, the text that *Devdas* returns to is the one that juxtaposes Devdas's consuming love for Paro against social rules and norms symbolised by his authoritarian father. Although both the novel and the film end tragically, warning against the dangers of obsessive love, they present love, however obsessive, as infinitely desirable. Irrespective of the unhappy consequences of love, the entire nation, we are told, wept after viewing P. C. Barua's *Devdas* in 1935. When K. L. Saigal, the hero of the Hindi version of the film (also directed by Barua) released a year later, died tragically at the age of 42, the coincidence of his reel life with real life made the nation weep once again. It continued to sob when Bimal Roy provided a new model of Devdas in Dilip Kumar's 1955 version and when Sanjay Leela Bhansali made Devdas enter the global imaginary in the image of Shah Rukh Khan in 2002. However, Devdas, the Bengali hero consumed by his love for Paro, is a Hindu avatar of Qais, who is driven mad by unrequited love and becomes *majnun* or possessed, in whom countless poets saw the symbol of their own state. The fact that the Devdas character in all the Hindi versions of the film was played by a Punjabi singer-actor and two Muslim actors may also have contributed to the unmistakable shades of *majnun* in the Bengali lover.

In contrast to Ashis Nandy, who singled out Prathamesh Barua and his hero Devdas as shaping the aesthetic of the Hindi film and the male lead, Kakar and Ross (1986) have proposed the notion of the 'Majnun hero' in the Hindi film. Over the years, Hindi cinema would produce numerous versions of Majnun reincarnated as Devdas or in any other form. The other cinematic romance that has paralleled Devdas's popularity in India is *Mughal-i-Azam* (K. Asif, 1960), and the legendary lover who competes for space in the Indian romantic imaginary is Prince Salim whose compulsive love for a slave girl Anarkali led to her incarceration by the Moghul emperor Akbar. Along with the 1953 film titled *Anarkali* (Nandlal Jaswantlal, 1953), *Mughal-i-Azam* has immortalised the tale of the Prince who was willing to die for the beautiful slave girl. The isomorphism of Islamic context of this legend with the Perso-Arabic *qissa* and the near-perfect fit of the Muslim actors with the legendary lovers produced an iconographic image through which Dilip Kumar, who played Salim in the film, came to represent the Majnun lover in addition to Devdas. The meeting of the Perso-Arabic Majnun with the Bengali Devdas in the body of the Muslim actor foregrounds the blurring of the two heroes and the Great Traditions in the cinematic regime of the Hindi film through the actor's performance of multiple identities. Dilip Kumar's biography that paralleled that of the characters he played imprinted him in the Indian imaginary as the Majnun image.[11] Like the Hindu *zamindar*'s son who leaves home for the sake of his beloved, the Muslim prince Salim who is ready to die to rescue a slave girl and the slave girl who sacrifices her life to protect the prince emerge from the same tradition. In an interesting play of *dharma* in its Islamic guise, the director of the film has the Emperor Akbar punish his own son and his beloved only to reverse his harsh judgement by sparing Anarkali's life at the end. The Majnun hero of the Hindi film, as Kakar and Ross (1986) memorably named him, is indelibly etched on the body of the Muslim actor and reappears in various incarnations, Hindu and Muslim, time and again in Hindi cinema. The actor Guru Dutt and the characters he played in *Pyaasa* (Guru Dutt, 1957) and *Kaagaz ke Phool* (Guru Dutt, 1959), of a poet smitten by his muse and his destruction by an apathetic social order, offer direct translations of the Majnun lover. Like Dilip Kumar, the actor/director's cinematic career and relationships mirroring those of his characters follow Majnun's doomed route to failure and eventual death brought about by frequent bouts of depression and alcoholism. The dark, brooding artist that Dutt played in both his films, driven by his passion for his muse, was in line with the anonymous poets, who, identifying with Majnun, took on his name and left the 'City of Reason' that destroyed their creativity. Majnun returned with a vengeance with the return of romance with Shah Rukh Khan, who began his career with playing the obsessive lover.

From *Baazigar* (Abbas Mastan, 1993) to *Rab Ne Bana Di Jodi* (Aditya Chopra, 2009), Shah Rukh Khan has introduced so many shades into the Majnun figure of the Hindi film that the actor has become one with the characters he plays on screen. If he put duty over love in *Dilwale Dulhania Le Jayenge* (Aditya Chopra, 1995) and *Pardes* (Subhash Ghai, 1997), unusual circumstances forced him to decide in favour of love in *Kabhi Khushi Kabhie Gham* (Karan Johar, 2001); in *Kuch Kuch Hota Hai* (Karan Johar, 1998), he played a bereaved husband unwilling to get into another relationship; in *Kal Ho Na Ho* (Karan Johar, 2003), he sacrificed his love for his beloved's happiness, in *Veer Zaara* (Yash Chopra, 2004) he remained in solitary confinement for 22 years to protect her honour, and in *Om Shanti Om* (Farah Khan, 2007) he died for her. By the time Shah Rukh Khan was cast in the new *Devdas*, the gap between Devdas and Majnun had closed completely. Irrespective of the lover he played, the dark, brooding Majnun was visible beneath his Bengali, Punjabi and other avatars.[12]

If Majnun provides a template for the hero of Hindi films, the object of his desire is clothed in the garb of Laila. The Laila heroine of the Hindi film serves as the antithesis of Radha. Unlike the fair Radha of Hindi love poetry, Laila, whose name means night, is dusky in complexion and the site of forbidden desire. Though the love poetry in the *bhakti* tradition is no less erotic than Sufi, the articulation of sensual desire in the Hindi film targeted at a family audience turns to the Muslim beloved whose racialised blackness serves as the perfect site for the voicing of repressed desires forbidden by the *dharmic* law. Although the sensual imagery of Sufi verse represents a spiritual longing in a manner similar to that of *bhakti* poetry, the Hindi film polarises Sufi and *bhakti* into languages of desire and worship respectively. The dark-skinned Laila in whose darkness the Sufi poet sought to dissolve himself, becomes an object of male desire in the Hindi film. Although the Laila in Hindi cinema is not necessarily dusky, she is made to serve as the object of the Hindu male's desire. The fetishisation of the Muslim female as Laila in the Hindi film is partially due to the historical positioning of the actress in Hindi cinema. Contradicting the discourse of veiling through which the female Muslim subject is projected as conservative in Indian society, her *purdahnasheen* (veiled) countenance intensifies her desirability in the Hindu male's imaginary whose gaze, averted in the Hindu female's presence, travels to explore intimate zones to enact forbidden fantasies. This play of forbidden desires is facilitated by the isolation of the Muslim *tawaif* or dancing girl from the *pak* or pure Muslim woman. In view of the absence of female performers in Hindu performative arts where cross-dressing enabled males to play female parts and the stigma attached to female entertainers, the top heroines of Hindi cinema until the 1960s like Noorjehan, Meena Kumari, Madhubala and Nargis had a courtesan past. They transported to their screen portrayals the sensuality and desire associated with the Muslim courtesan, an aura that was magnified by their unfulfilled romances offscreen. Their tragic past, unfulfilled relationships and untimely deaths produced a sensual mystique around the Muslim heroine of the Hindi films that translated into the Laila stereotype who serves as the object of the Hindu male's desire. Like Majnun, Laila is named directly only in the two adaptations of the *Majnun Laila* but is visible in all the images of male desire not necessarily Muslim. The heroines of the 1940s and 1950s like Suraiyya, Madhubala, Meena Kumari and Nargis produced the Laila stereotype in the male imaginary despite their Hindu names and the characters they played on-screen, largely through the overwriting of the cinematic romance with their personal autobiographies. Their relationships with their male co-stars were the stuff of the Perso-Arabic romance.[13] The dark-skinned Laila's gradual conflation with the dusky South Indian female lead replays the forbidden historical desire of the North Indian Hindu male, who is both the imagined subject and address of the Hindi film, for the Muslim or Dravidian female.[14] With the next generation of heroines, the dark-skinned beloved assumes the form of the South Indian heroine in real and reel life ironically through the mediation of the same actor. After Nargis, Raj Kapoor is alleged to have developed a fixation with his South Indian discoveries – Padmini, Vijayantimala and Hema Malini – inaugurating the romance between the light-skinned hero and the dusky heroine on and off screen. Vijayantimala, who played opposite both Dilip Kumar and Kapoor and whose name Radha in many of her films was evocative of the Hindu sub-plot, had shades of the Muslim Laila. The relationship between Hema Malini, who displaced Vijayantimala in Hindi cinema in the 1970s, with the married Dharmendra reiterated the theme of thwarted love. But the most celebrated romance on Hindi screens in the 1980s was that between Amitabh Bachchan and Rekha who became the object of the nation's desire along with that of the superstar of Indian cinema. Sridevi was the last of the South Indian heroines whose screen persona and real life took on the character of the dark Laila of Perso-Arabic poetry.

Like Majnun, the word Laila has become synonymous with the beloved irrespective of her ethnicity or religion. Apart from the number of praise songs composed in her honour by lyricists of Hindi films, the dialogues, composed by Urdu writers and poets, evoke the Laila stereotype more frequently than that of the Hindu Radha. The Indian male's adoration for Majnun's dark beloved is best summarised in the song from Feroz Khan's film *Qurbani* (1980):

Laila o Laila	I am the beauty
Aisi main laila	Whom everyone
Har koyi chahe mujhse	Wants to meet alone
Milna akela	Whoever I gaze at
Laila o Laila	Make him forget the world
Jisko bhi dekhoon	The one who turns everyone into a Majnun
duniya bhula doon	That's the woman I am
Majnu bana doon aisi main laila	

If the epic *Ramayana* offers a template for the idealised marital union through the figures of the duty-abiding Rama and his loyal wife Sita, Hindi cinema must turn to the lore surrounding the divine lover Krishna and his *gopis* to normalise young lovers cavorting on mountains and seas. But the portrayal of forbidden desire is facilitated through a turn to the fantasy of the desiring and desired Other, the Muslim, through the language of the Other whose florid flourish is preferred to the cadence of an arcane language. The romance plot in the Hindi film must choose between the two divine idioms Kakar and Ross (1986) isolated, the relationship between Krishna, the divine lover and his infinite *gopis*, and the Sufi merging of the self with that of the lover represented through the legend of Laila and Majnun. The tale of the lovers – Radha/Krishna or Laila/Majnun – is invariably embedded within the *Ramayana* myth and its flagrant violation of social norms disturbs the familial and social order that must be restored either through marriage or death.

If the Hindu *bhakti* tradition has formed one strand in formulating the idiom of romantic love in Hindi cinema, the Sufi concept of *Ashiqi* of which *Majnun Laila* is the prime example forms another. The conflict in the Hindi film is produced by the gap between the *dharmic* principle outlined by Vijay Mishra (2002) with that of *Ashiqi*. As the Hindu ethic of self-restraint in the observation of *dharma* is disturbed by the excessive desire of *Ashiqi*, the young lovers must ultimately submit to the higher authority of law. The *Majnun Laila qissa* is a story of obsessive love that must meet a tragic end because it challenges the *dharmic* law represented by the father. The Hindi film demonstrates a tension between the obsessive love expressed by young lovers and the call of duty that ends with either the death of the lovers or their submission to the law. Irrespective of the end that desire must meet, its seductive power not only over the actors but also the viewers cannot be denied. Even as the spectator is seduced by the power of the images and the melodies to 'live and die by love', reminders about the call of duty to a parent, family, society interrupt the pleasure of viewing. The disruption of the *dharmic* principle through the hyperbolic language of *Ashiqi* in the Hindi film shows the deep implication of the Islamic in the Hindu.

Notes

1   Ashish Rajadhyaksha, in his essay 'The Phalke Era' (1987), was the first to call attention to the Hindi film's continuity with Indian epics by viewing Dhundiram Govind Phalke's *Raja Harishchandra* (1913) as a visual translation of the epic narrative. In 'Hindi Cinema through the Ages', Saibal Chatterji (2003), arguing that Indian cinema's storytelling devices came from mythological ones, traces the stories to the epic tradition of the *Mahabharata* and *Ramayana* and the cinematic idiom to the ancient Sanskrit treatise *Natyashastra*. Sumita Chakravarty (1993), in her book *National Identity in Indian Popular Cinema 1947–1987*, foregrounds the centrality of the two epics in Hindi films' thematic conflicts and narrative conventions. Viewing Hindi cinema within the framework of national cinema, like Chakravarty, M. Madhava Prasad (1998) unpacks the co-option of the epic narratives in the ideological construction of the Hindi film. Vijay Mishra (2002) goes as far as to claim that all Hindi films were different versions of the epic tale of the *Mahabharata*.

2   Gita Kapur's (1987) notion of frontality in Indian visual arts has been applied by scholars including Kapur herself in the analysis of cinematic texts to propose a mystical aesthetic. Ashish Rajadhyaksha's (1987) borrowing of her concept of frontality in his analysis of the mythological and saint films in the Phalke era and the gaze of Hindi cinema was given a specifically Hindu slant through its formalisation in M. Madhava Prasad's concept of *darsana*, an aesthetic that has been uncritically accepted in studies that followed. Vijay Mishra, in *Bollywood Cinema: Temples of Desire* (2002), took the analogy further in his translation of Lacanian desire into Hindu religious practices by elucidating the *dharmic* principle, which he regards as the *grand syntagmatique* of Hindi cinema in relation to the *Mahabharata*. The iconography of the temple, gods and deification is reiterated by Ravi Vasudevan (2002) in his foregrounding of the Hindu address of the Hindi film and in S. V. Srinivas's (1996) examination of fan cultures in the South.

3   In focusing on Hindi cinema's role in the production of the nation and the national subject, film scholars such as Rajadhyaksha (1987), Madhava Prasad (1998), Chakravarty (1993) and Vasudevan (2002) have erased portions of both national and cinematic history. Mishra (2002), who engages with the Urdu sub-text of the cinematic romance, still articulates the production of the Indian diasporic imaginary in terms of his central thesis about the *dharmic* principle underpinning the Hindi film. In emphasising Hindu sources, these scholars run the risk of contradicting their own affirmation of the essential syncretism of the Hindi film. It is Prem Chowdhury's (2000) revisiting of the Empire cinema that throws new light on the Hindi film's production of the nation through her unpacking of resistance strategies forged by the Indian nationalist movement that converged on Hindu as well as Muslim myth and history. Even if it was co-opted in the propagation of the nationalist ideology before or after Independence, Hindi cinema's inherent syncreticism implicates the Islamic into the

Hindu and the Sanskritic into the Perso-Arabic so deeply that it would be erroneous to isolate meta-principles based on any specific aesthetic or sacral tradition.

4   For example, Philip Lutgendorf, in 'Is There an Indian Way of Filmmaking', questions 'grandiose claims' about the classical tradition and especially the two Sanskrit epics constituting 'the great code' of popular filmmaking made by film critics, which are reiterated by filmmakers (2006: 29). Rachel Dwyer offers by way of explanation that 'the mythological has been given prominence in India as its founding genre and because of Phalke's eminence (and the survival of so much of his output) but has always been perceived to be in decline and many other genres were popular during the silent period in Bombay including the stunt or action film, the historical, the Arabian Nights Oriental fantasy and the social' (2006: 14).

5   *Qissa* and *Dastan* that have a specific lineage in Persian tradition have been conflated in India to refer to story in general. Although they are distinguished in the original Persian, both *qissa* and *dastan* mean story in Hindi and Urdu.

6   Meenakshi Mukherjee, in her book *Realism and Reality* (1985) testifies to the popularity of the *qissa* tradition in other Indian vernacular languages. Mukherjee also points out that the Indian novel in the nineteenth century, in view of the absence of the notion of the romantic couple in Indian society, had to resort to historical, mythological or courtesan tales to depict tales of love. Mukherjee's argument about the Indian novel negotiating the centrality of romantic love in the Western novel in the absence of such possibilities in the lives of ordinary people in the nineteenth century by turning to historical and courtesan novels is applicable to Hindi cinema as well. The luxury of a romantic relationship was the prerogative of those who were not bound by the laws that regulated the behaviour of the common people. With arranged marriage or one approved by parents still serving as the ideal in the Hindi cinema, the romance that is dissonant with the duty to the family is deemed deviant unless it is sublimated by allusions to divine union. Therefore, early filmmakers resorted to depicting romantic love through socially acceptable romance figures such as princes, courtesans and gods in an idiom that would be acceptable to the viewers of Hindi cinema.

7   Vijay Mishra pointed out at a conference in 2006 that Urdu is used in Hindi cinema to signpost the trope of romance. Although Hindi equivalents of love such as *pyar* and *prem* exist in Hindi and are used frequently, romance in Hindi cinema slips into the register of Urdu for the expression of emotions that sound banal in Hindi. The Urdu terms *mohabbat* and *ishq* have been naturalised in the articulation of romantic desire over the prosaic *pyar* or sanskritised *prem* through centuries of the circulation of the *qissa* of the *Majnun Laila* through recitations, ghazals or Urdu poetry.

8   Focusing on one particular *qissa*, romance, Mir shows how the romance tradition was refined by the Persian poets Gurgani and Ansari and was perfected by Nezami by borrowing from both Persian and Arabic *qissa* leading to the evolution of a new poetic *masnavi* or epic poem in rhymed verse. Mir contends that Persian and Arabic romances travelled to South Asia with court poets, merchants, traders, Sufis and mendicants in the medieval period and were incorporated into the oral and literary traditions.

9   She shows that by the seventeenth century, *qissa* were circulating in Persian as well in Punjabi vernaculars (Panjabi *qissa* refers to epic-length verse romances) spawning a new genre that married the local with the extra local by deviating from the *masnavi* rhyme scheme while introducing local tales situated in the local landscape and local social relations. Mir concludes that *qissa* became central to Punjabi cultural life through the popularity they enjoyed both in literary circles and as oral texts by the end of the nineteenth century. Majnun Laila's India connection is established by a Rajasthani legend that has it that Laila and Majnun, originally from Sindh, sought refuge in the Rajasthani village of Sriganganagar before breathing their last breath and a two-day fair is held annually in June attended by lovers and newlyweds to commemorate the lovers.

10 'The tradition of *dastangoyee* goes back to medieval Iran, where *dastangoh* or narrators, inspired by the *Shahnama* (the story of kings composed in verse by the celebrated poet Firdausi), recited tales

around camp fires, in coffee houses or even palaces' (Farooqui 2006b).

11 His much publicised love for Madhubala who played Anarkali in the film and married the singer actor Kishore Kumar and her untimely death has dissolved the boundaries between the Majnun characters Dilip Kumar played on screen and the persona created for him by the media.

12 The Muslim actor's real life relationship with his Hindu wife Gauri entered into media lore as another tale of undying love sealing the identity of the actor with the characters.

13 The dark-skinned Suraiyya who the actor Dev Anand was smitten with was prevented from marrying him by her grandmother and died a spinster. Meena Kumari's tortured relationships with her exploitative directors and co-stars, her alcoholism and premature death turned her into a living legend. The *Majnun Laila* romance of Madhubala and Dilip Kumar was cut short by her marriage to the singer Kishore Kumar and early death. Nargis's relationship with Raj Kapoor and Sunil Dutt is the stuff of Bollywood romance. While her relationship with the already married Kapoor picked up the unfulfilled love angle of the *Majnun Laila qissa*, her miraculous rescue and marriage to her younger co-star in *Mother India* (Mehboob Khan, 1957) is straight out of *1001 Nights* with the tale ending unhappily with her death by cancer.

14 The reverse is the case in Pakistan where the assumption of Hindu names functions as a license to circumvent Islamic injunctions on propriety and modesty.

Bibliography

Bhaskar, I. and R. Allen (2009) *Islamicate Cultures of Bombay Cinema*. New Delhi: Tulika Books.

Chakravarty, S. (1993) *National Identity in Indian Popular Cinema: 1947–1987*. Austin: University of Texas Press.

Chatterji, S. (2003) 'Hindi Cinema through the Decades', *Encyclopaedia of Hindi Cinema*. New Delhi: Encyclopaedia Britannica, 3–23.

Chowdhry, P. (2000) *Colonial India and the Making of Empire Cinema: Image, Ideology and Identity*. Manchester: Manchester University Press.

Dwyer, R. (2006) *Filming the Gods: Religion and Indian Cinema*. London, New York and Delhi: Routledge.

Dwyer, R. and D. Patel (2002) *Cinema India: The Visual Culture of Hindi Film*. New Brunswick, NJ: Rutgers University Press.

Farooqui, M. (2006a) Interview with Shoma Chaudhury. *Tehelaka*, June 26. Available: http://dastangoi. blogspot.com/2006_06_01_archive.html (accessed on 17 December 2009).

____ (2006b) Interview with Pragya Tewari, June 28. Available: http://dastangoi.blogspot.com/2006/06/ mumbai-mirror-mahmood.html (accessed on 17 December 2009).

Kabeer, N. M. (2005) *Talking Songs: Javed Akhtar in Conversation with Nasreen Munni Kabeer and Sixty Selected Songs*. Delhi: Oxford University Press.

Kakar, S. and J. M. Ross (1986) *Tales of Love, Sex and Danger*. Delhi: Oxford University Press.

Kapur, G. (1987) 'Mythic Material in Indian Cinema', *Journal of Arts and Ideas*, 14–15, 79–107.

Lutgendorf, P. (2006). 'Is There an Indian Way of Filmmaking?', *International Journal of Hindu Studies*, 10, 3, 227–56.

Madhava Prasad, M. (1998) *The Ideology of the Hindi Film: A Historical Construction*. Delhi: Oxford University Press.

Masud, I. (2005) 'Muslim Ethos in Indian Cinema.' *Screen Weekly*. Available: http://www.screenindia.com/ old/fullstory.php?content_id=9980/ (accessed on 13 July 2009).

Mir, F. (2006) 'Genre and Devotion in Punjab's Popular Narratives: Rethinking Cultural and Religious Syncretism', *Comparative Studies in Society and History*, 48, 3, 727–58.

Mishra, V. (2002) *Bollywood Cinema: Temples of Desire*. New York: Routledge.

Mukherjee, M. (1985) *Realism and Reality*. Delhi: Oxford University Press.

Nandy, A. (2001) 'Invitation to an Antique Death: The Journey of Pramathesh Barua as the Origin of the Terribly Effeminate, Maudlin, Self-destructive Heroes of Indian Cinema', in R. Dwyer and C. Pinney (eds) *Pleasure and the Nation: The History, Politics and Consumption of Public Culture in India*. Oxford: Oxford University Press, 139–60.

Pritchett, F. W. (1991) *The Romance Tradition in Urdu: Adventures from the Dastan of Amir Hamzah*. New York: Columbia University Press.

Rajadhyaksha, A. (1987) 'The Phalke Era', *Journal of Arts and Ideas*, 14–15, 79–107.

Srinivas, S.V. (1996) 'Devotion and Defiance in Fan Activity', *Journal of Arts and Ideas*, 29, 67–83.

Vasudevan, R. (2002) *Making Meaning in Indian Cinema*. Delhi: Oxford University Press.

Verjee, N. (2009) 'Hindi Cinema's Islamic Connection'. LiveMint, May 12. Available: http://www.livemint.com/2009/05/12203627/Hindi-cinema8217s-Islamic-c.html (accessed on 17 December 2009).

Index